BBC

DOCTOR WHO

THE SEVENTH DOCTOR

Operation Volcano

WRITER
ANDREW CARTMEL

ARTIST
CHRISTOPHER JONES

COLORIST
MARCO LESKO

EXECUTIVE PRODUCER
BEN AARONOVITCH

THE 'COUNTER-MEASURES' CHARACTERS APPEAR COURTESY OF **BEN AARONOVITCH**.

Hill Of Beans

WRITER
RICHARD DINNICK

ARTIST
JESSICA MARTIN
AKA MAGS THE WEREWOLF!

COLORIST
CHARLIE KIRCHOFF

LETTERER
RICHARD STARKINGS
AND COMICRAFT'S JIMMY BETANCOURT

THE CHARACTER OF 'MAGS' APPEARS COURTESY OF **STEPHEN WYATT**.

TITAN
COMICS

BBC

BBC

DOCTOR WHO

THE SEVENTH DOCTOR

Character Bios

THE DOCTOR

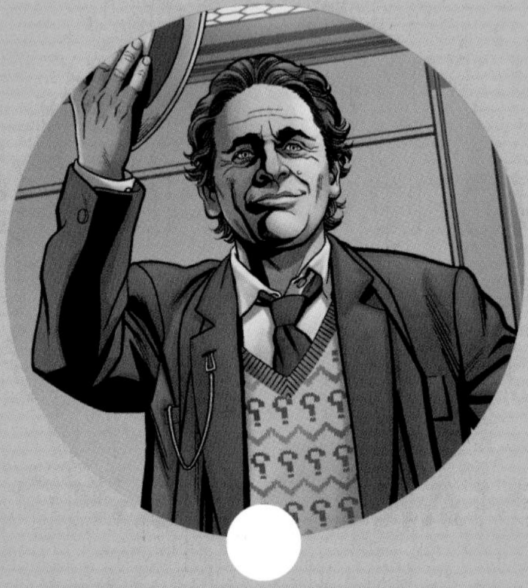

The Doctor is an alien – a Time Lord who has worn many faces in his long, long life.

Never cruel or cowardly, the Doctor champions the oppressed across time and space, often traveling with human friends and companions who offer him a new perspective on the universe.

The Doctor's Seventh incarnation is an inquisitive explorer, revelling in adventure. He might trick you into thinking he's a buffoon, playing the fool or muddling his words –but these traits disguise a sharp intelligence and a shrewd judge of character...

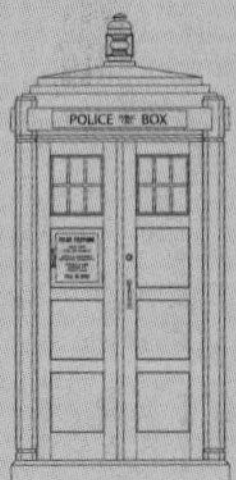
POLICE BOX

BBC
DOCTOR WHO
THE SEVENTH DOCTOR
Operation Volcano

"**The Seventh Doctor** feels like a natural progression of the ambitious episodes from McCoy's tenure. Couple Andrew Cartmel's authentic script and fun fan service with the screen-accurate, vibrant pencils and colors of Christopher Jones and Marco Lesko, and **Doctor Who: The Seventh Doctor** stands as an engrossing and worthy reintroduction for one of the most underrated Doctors."

Newsarama

"A fun and entertaining science fiction mystery. Check it out!"

Bleeding Cool

"Titan Comics continue to prove that they are the perfect publisher for new **Doctor Who**."

Pop Culture Uncovered

"Although not a direct sequel to 'Remembrance of the Daleks', this comic manages to recapture that magic. Simply a lovely item."

Blogtor Who

"It's all fast and funny, and an entertaining reprise of the classic cast! Recommended!"

Chuck's Comic of the Day

"If you've never experienced a **Seventh Doctor** story, this is a good one to start with. Would make for a great episode of the television series!"

Kabooooom

"The art is gorgeous as always. Titan Comics really know how to choose their artists and colorists, which gives all their comics such a complete, beautiful look." 10/10

Geeks Worldwide

"Visually impressive, complex, and feels like a quintessential **Seventh Doctor** tale. The Doctor and Ace are perfectly in character with their 80s heyday!"

Major Spoilers

"Recommended to fans both old and new!"

Doctor Who Watch

Editor
John Freeman

Assistant Editor
Jessica Burton

Senior Designer
Andrew Leung

Titan Comics

Managing and Launch Editor
Andrew James

Production Assistant
Rhiannon Roy

Production Controller
Peter James

Senior Production Controller
Jackie Flook

Art Director
Oz Browne

Circulation Executive
Frances Hallam

Sales & Circulation Manager
Steve Tothill

Press Officer
William O'Mullane

Publicist
Imogen Harris

Brand Manager
Chris Thompson

Ads & Marketing Assistant
Bella Hoy

Direct Sales & Marketing Manager
Ricky Claydon

Commercial Manager
Michelle Fairlamb

Head Of Rights
Jenny Boyce

Publishing Manager
Darryl Tothill

Publishing Director
Chris Teather

Operations Director
Leigh Baulch

Executive Director
Vivian Cheung

Publisher
Nick Landau

Special thanks to **Chris Chibnall, Matt Strevens, Sam Hoyle, Mandy Thwaites, Gabby De Matteis, Ross McGlinchey, David Wilson-Nunn, Kirsty Mullan, Kate Bush, and Ed Casey for their invaluable assistance.**

BBC Worldwide

Director of Editorial Governance
Nicolas Brett

Director of Consumer Products And Publishing
Andrew Moultrie

Head Of UK Publishing
Chris Kerwin

Publisher
Mandy Thwaites

Publishing Co-Ordinator
Eva Abramik

DOCTOR WHO: THE SEVENTH DOCTOR – OPERATION VOLCANO
ISBN: 9781785868221

Published by Titan Comics, a division of Titan Publishing Group, Ltd. 144 Southwark Street, London, SE1 0UP.
Titan Comics is a registered trademark. All rights reserved.

A CIP catalogue record for this title is available from the British Library.
First edition: January 2019

10 9 8 7 6 5 4 3 2 1

Printed in Spain.

Titan Comics does not read or accept unsolicited DOCTOR WHO submissions of ideas, stories or artwork.

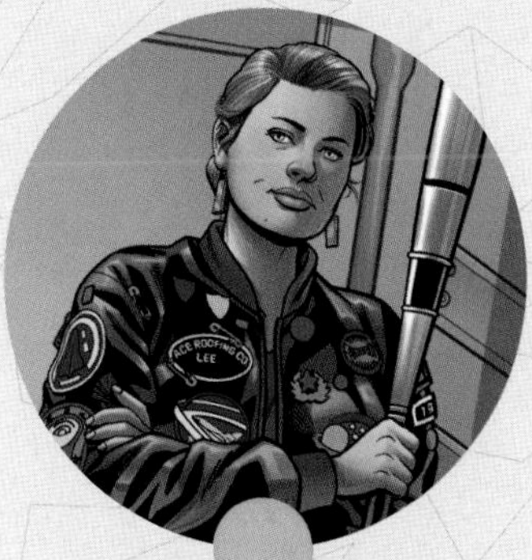

ACE

A trusted companion of the Seventh Doctor, Dorothy Gale 'Ace' McShane always fights for what she believes in. She's ready to take on anyone - or anything - that gets in her way... sometimes with a dose of home-made explosives!

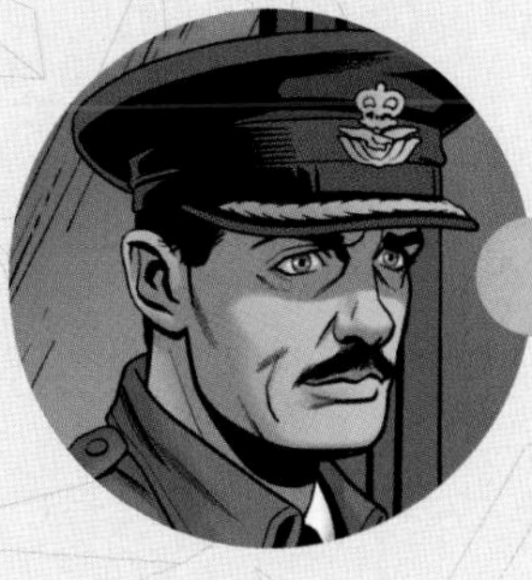

GILMORE

A Royal Air Force officer, the original leader of the Intrusion Countermeasures Group, Group Captain Ian Gilmore is a no nonsense military man, known for doing things by the book... so partnering with the Doctor never comes easily to him...

MAGS

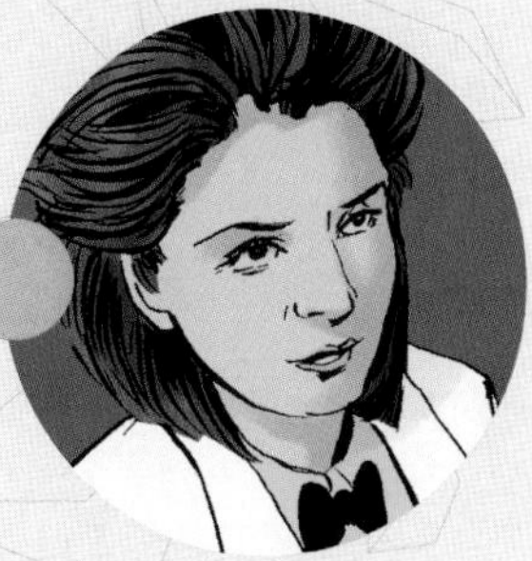

The Doctor encountered Mags when she was part of the Psychic Circus, also known as the Greatest Show in the Galaxy. Mags is an alien werewolf from the planet Vulpana, and on page 98, you can find out what she did next!

THE TARDIS

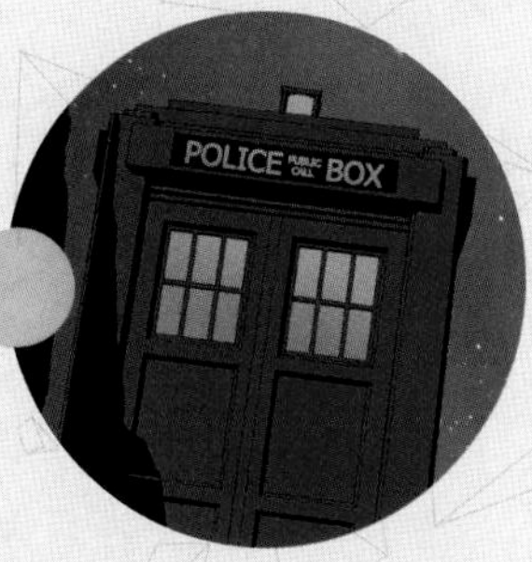
POLICE BOX

'Time and Relative Dimension in Space'. Bigger on the inside, this unassuming blue box is your ticket to unforgettable adventure! The TARDIS takes the Doctor where and when he needs to be – not always where or when he intended!

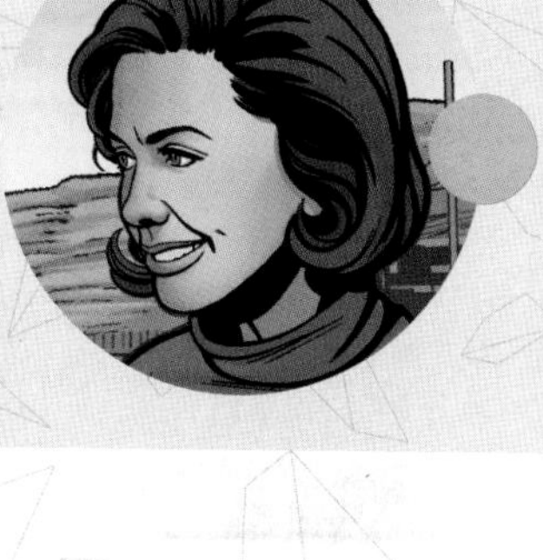

RACHEL

A computing pioneer during World War Two, Professor Rachel Jensen isn't keen on her continued research into Artificial Intelligence being sidelined by the work of the Intrusion Countermeasures Group... but some mysteries are just too enticing to be ignored!

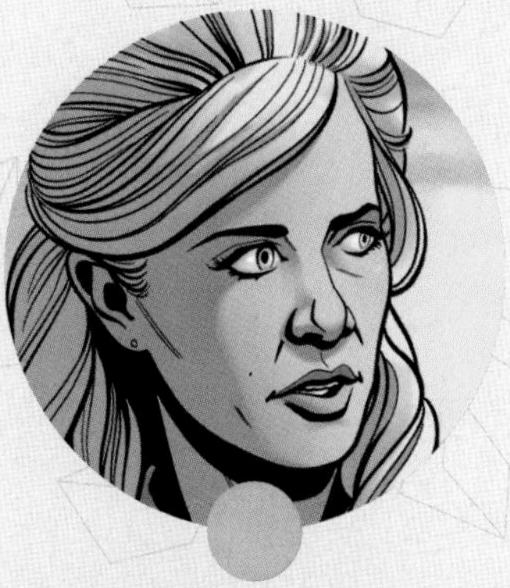

ALLISON

Cambridge graduate Allison Williams is used to being thrown in the deep end when it comes to working alongside Group Captain Gilmore and Rachel Jensen - and she's more than capable of taking care of herself in any battle - even tussles with invading aliens!

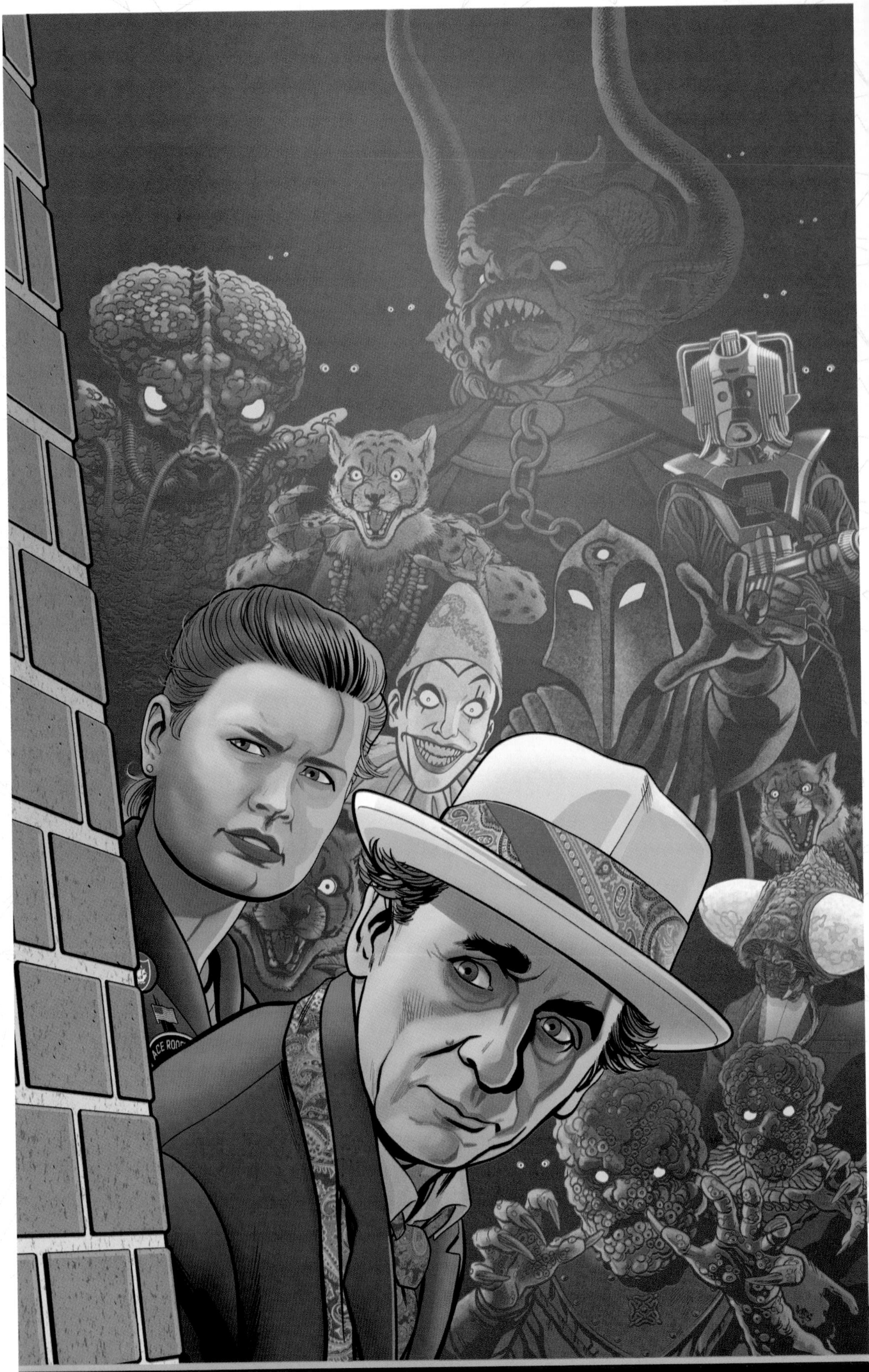

#3A Cover by Christopher Jones

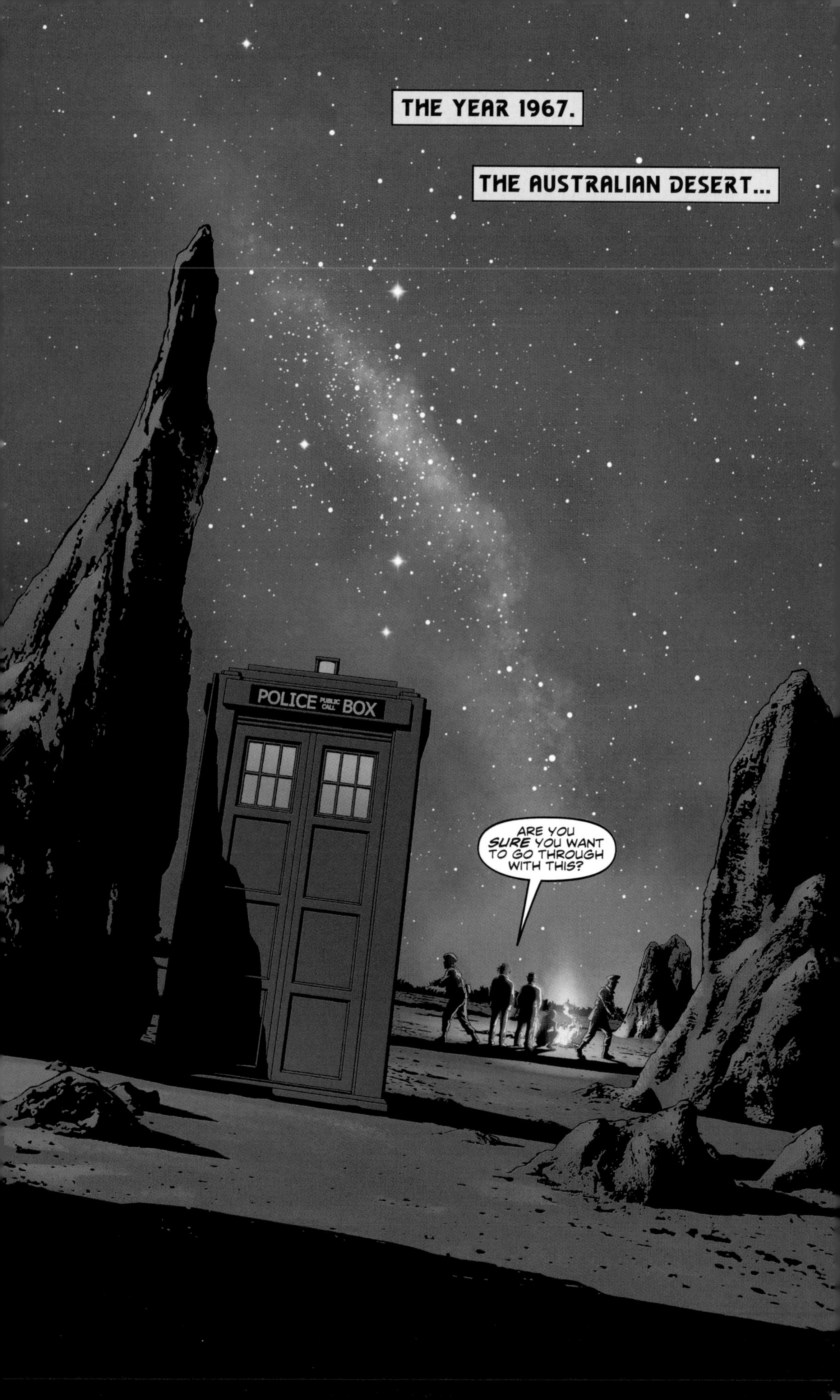
THE YEAR 1967.
THE AUSTRALIAN DESERT...
POLICE PUBLIC CALL BOX
ARE YOU SURE YOU WANT TO GO THROUGH WITH THIS?

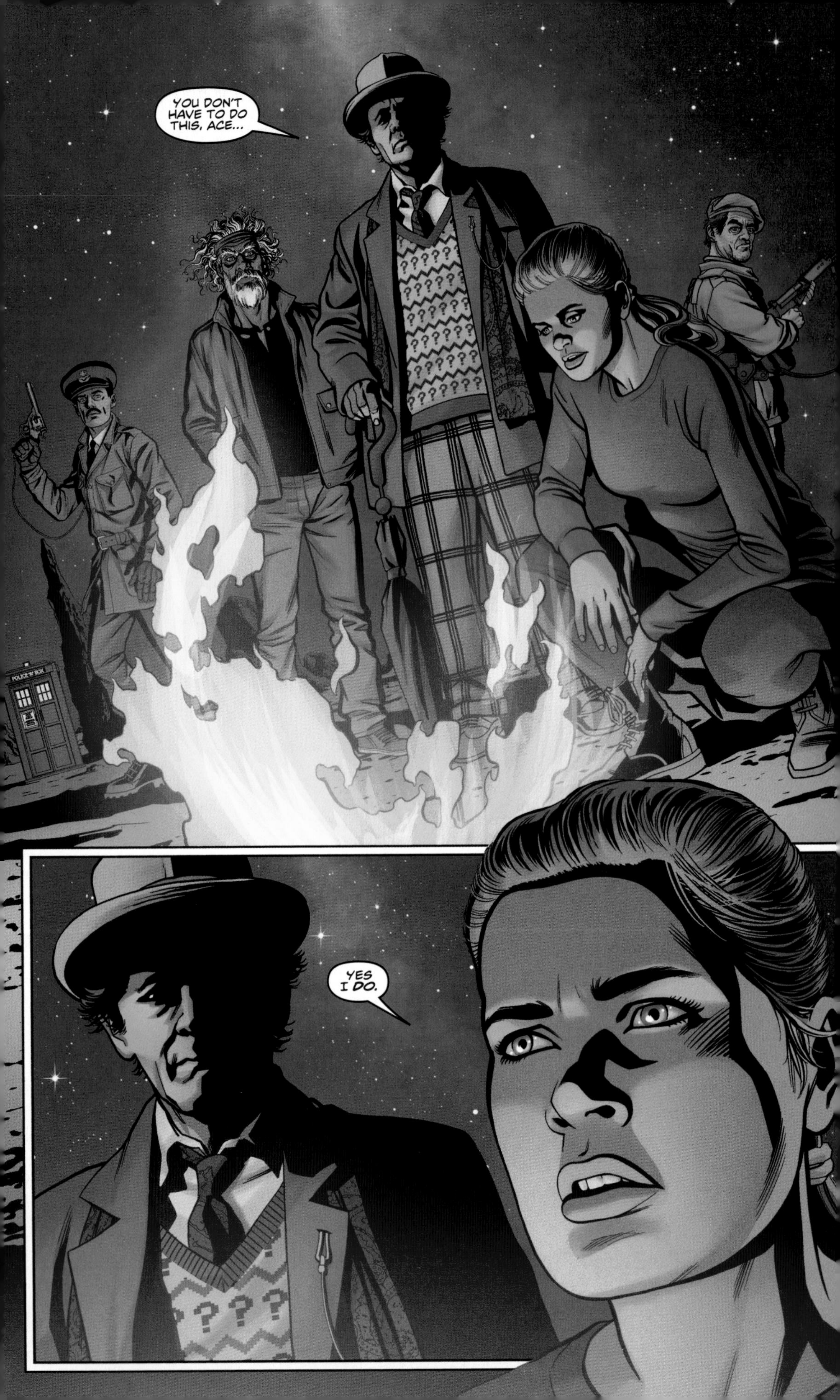
YOU DON'T HAVE TO DO THIS, ACE...
POLICE BOX
YES I DO.

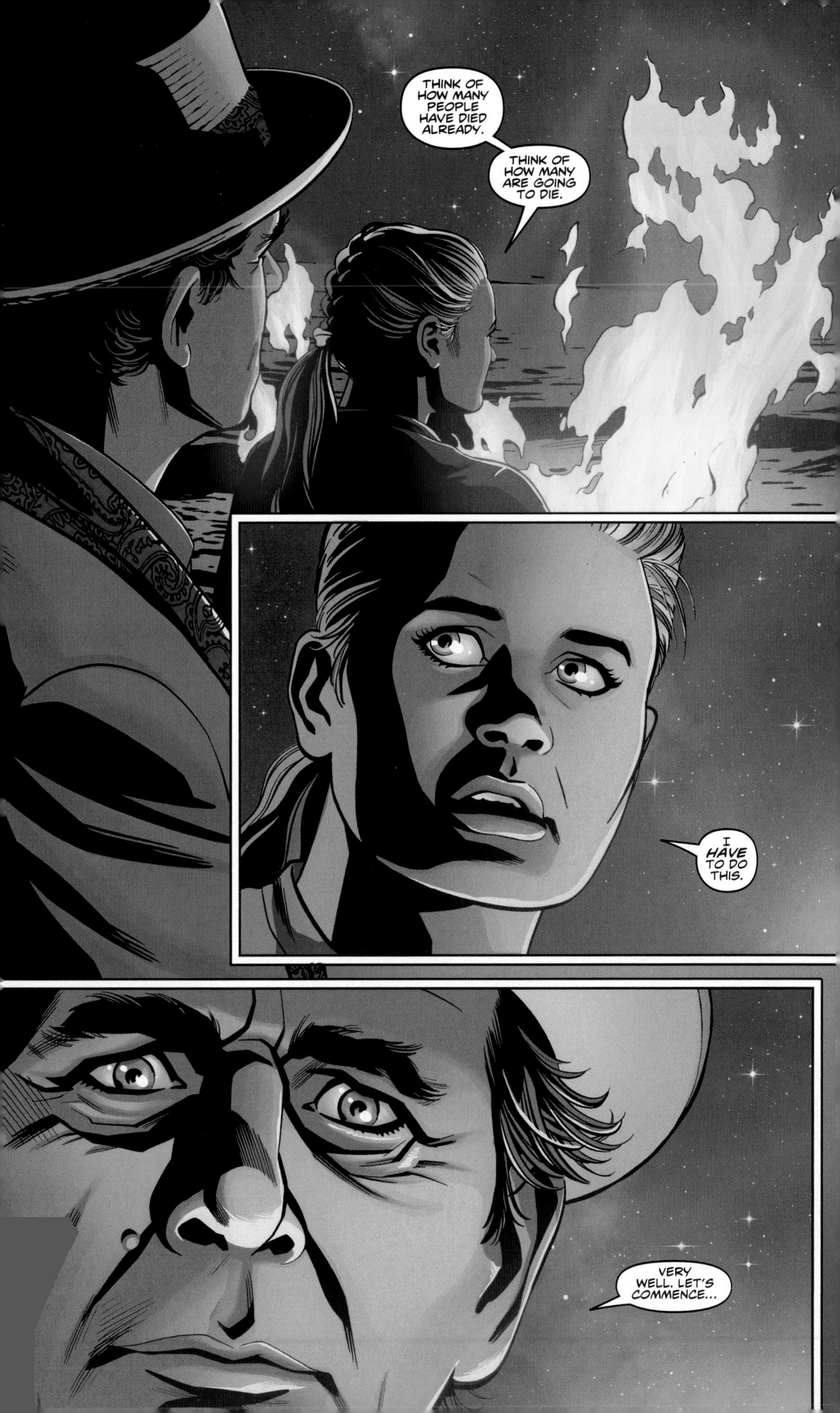
THINK OF HOW MANY PEOPLE HAVE DIED ALREADY.
THINK OF HOW MANY ARE GOING TO DIE.
I *HAVE* TO DO THIS.
VERY WELL. LET'S COMMENCE...

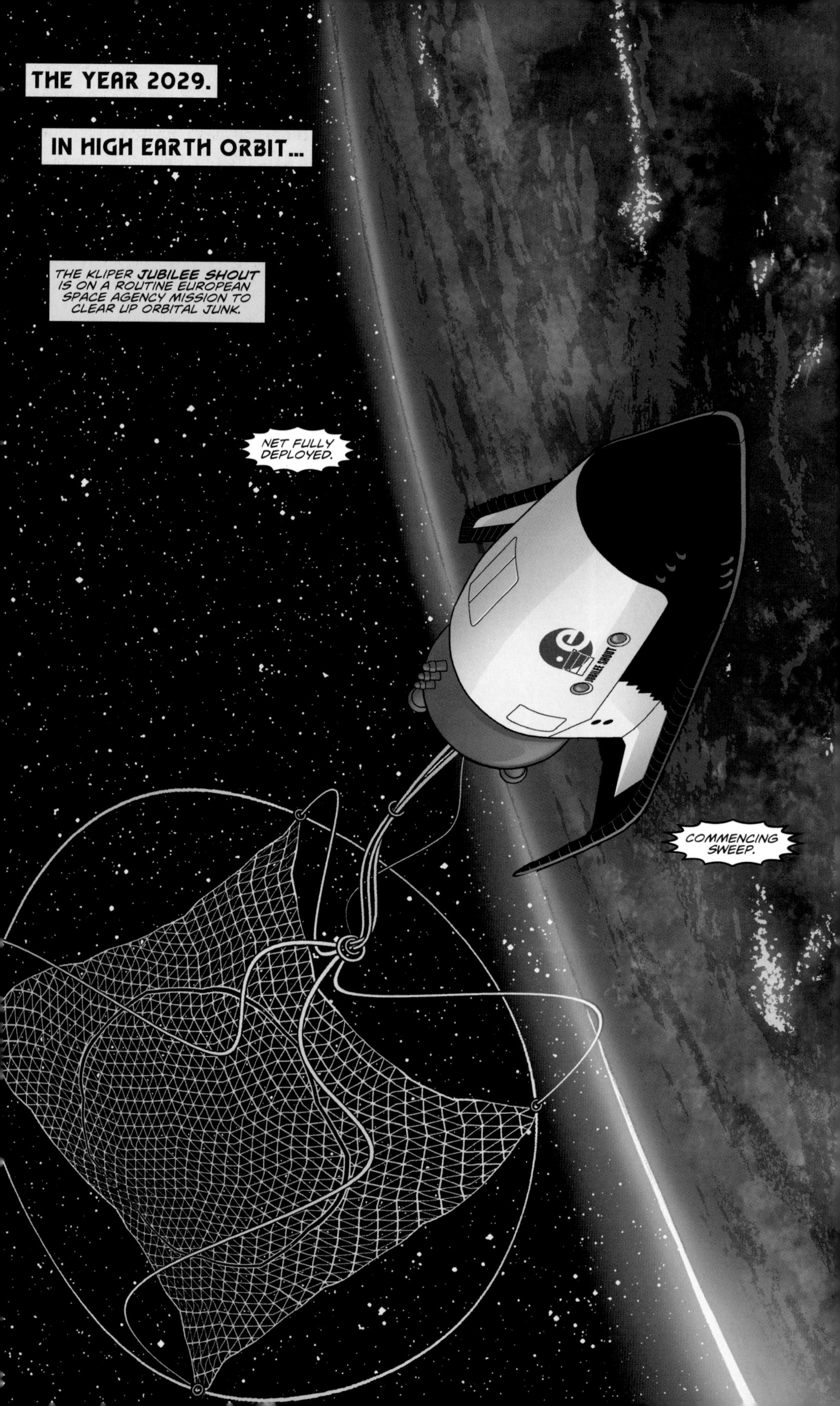
THE YEAR 2029.
IN HIGH EARTH ORBIT...
THE KLIPER JUBILEE SHOUT IS ON A ROUTINE EUROPEAN SPACE AGENCY MISSION TO CLEAR UP ORBITAL JUNK.
NET FULLY DEPLOYED.
JUBILEE SHOUT
COMMENCING SWEEP.

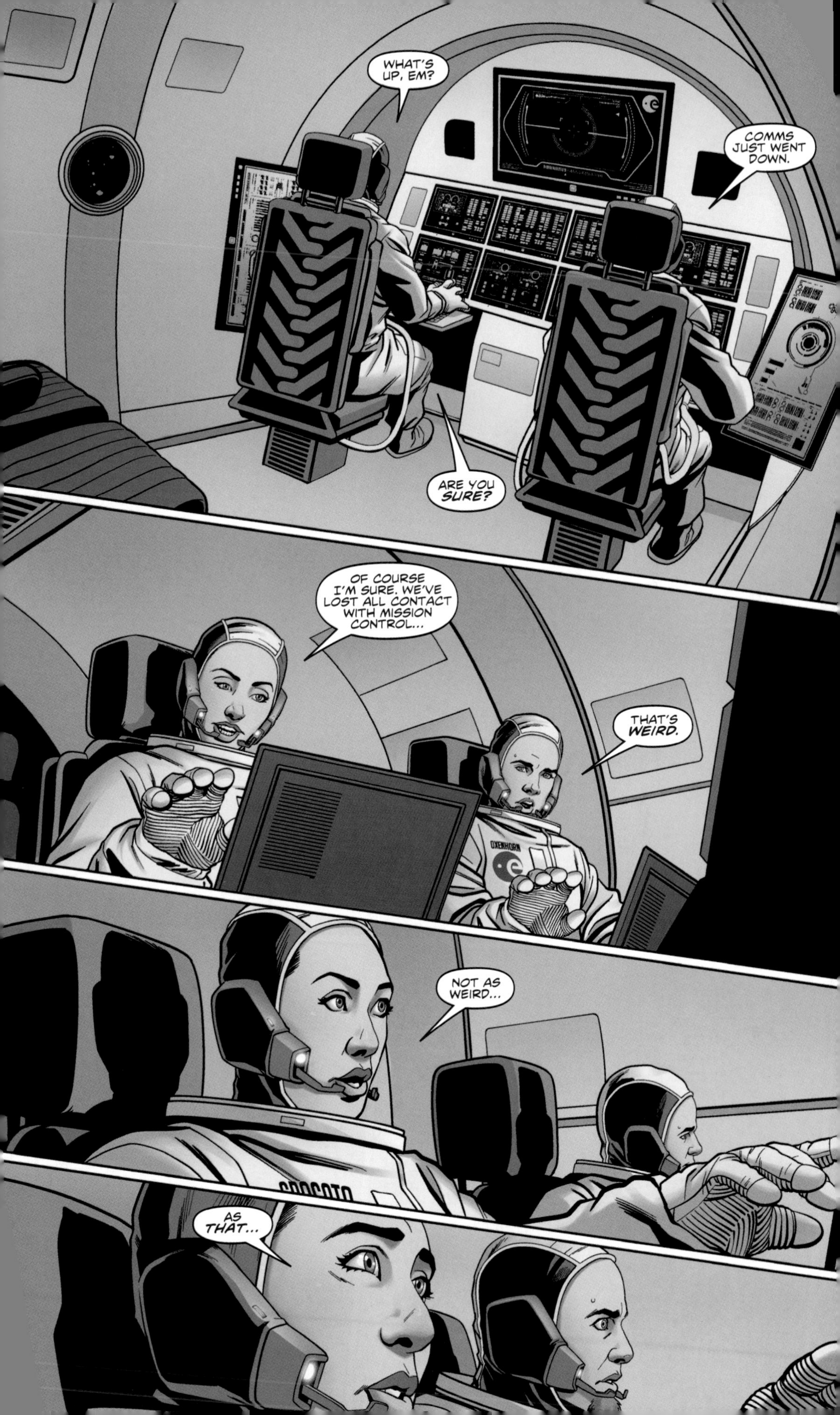
WHAT'S UP, EM?
COMMS JUST WENT DOWN.
ARE YOU *SURE?*
OF COURSE I'M SURE. WE'VE LOST ALL CONTACT WITH MISSION CONTROL...
THAT'S *WEIRD.*
OXENHORN
NOT AS WEIRD...
AS *THAT...*

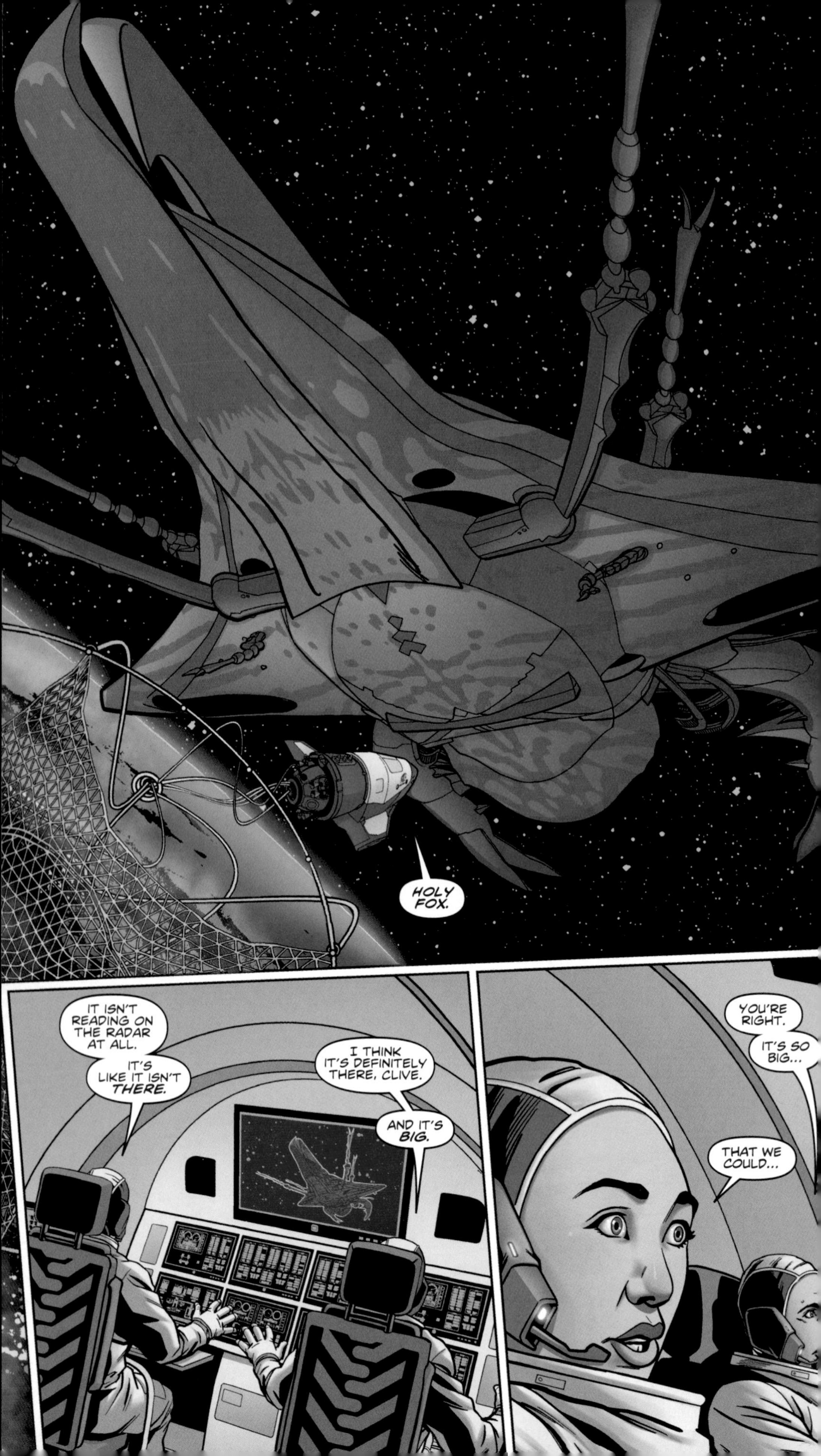
HOLY FOX.
IT ISN'T READING ON THE RADAR AT ALL.
IT'S LIKE IT ISN'T THERE.
I THINK IT'S DEFINITELY THERE, CLIVE.
AND IT'S BIG.
YOU'RE RIGHT.
IT'S SO BIG...
THAT WE COULD...

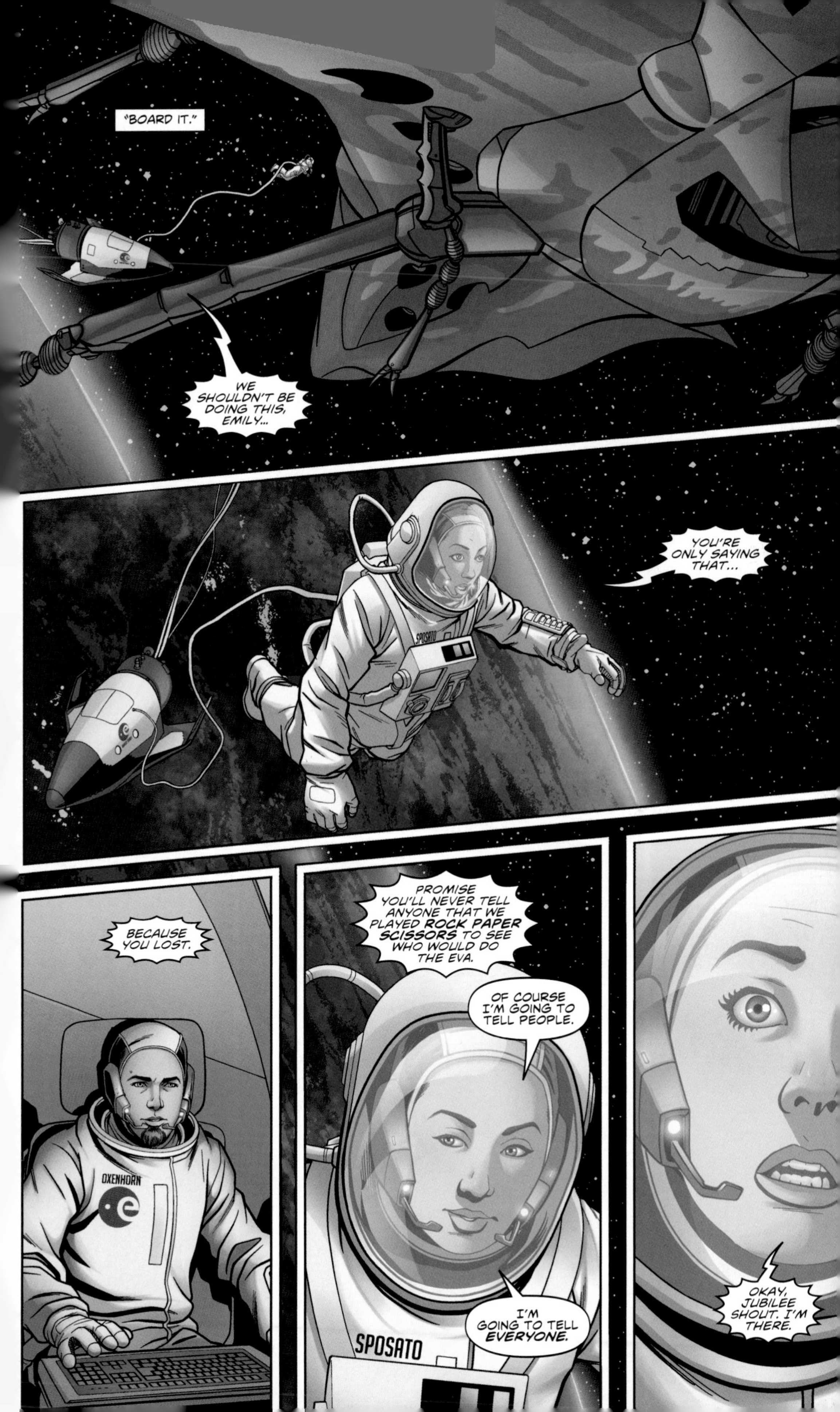

"BOARD IT."
WE SHOULDN'T BE DOING THIS, EMILY...
YOU'RE ONLY SAYING THAT...
BECAUSE YOU LOST.
PROMISE YOU'LL NEVER TELL ANYONE THAT WE PLAYED ROCK PAPER SCISSORS TO SEE WHO WOULD DO THE EVA.
OF COURSE I'M GOING TO TELL PEOPLE.
I'M GOING TO TELL EVERYONE.
OKAY, JUBILEE SHOUT. I'M THERE.

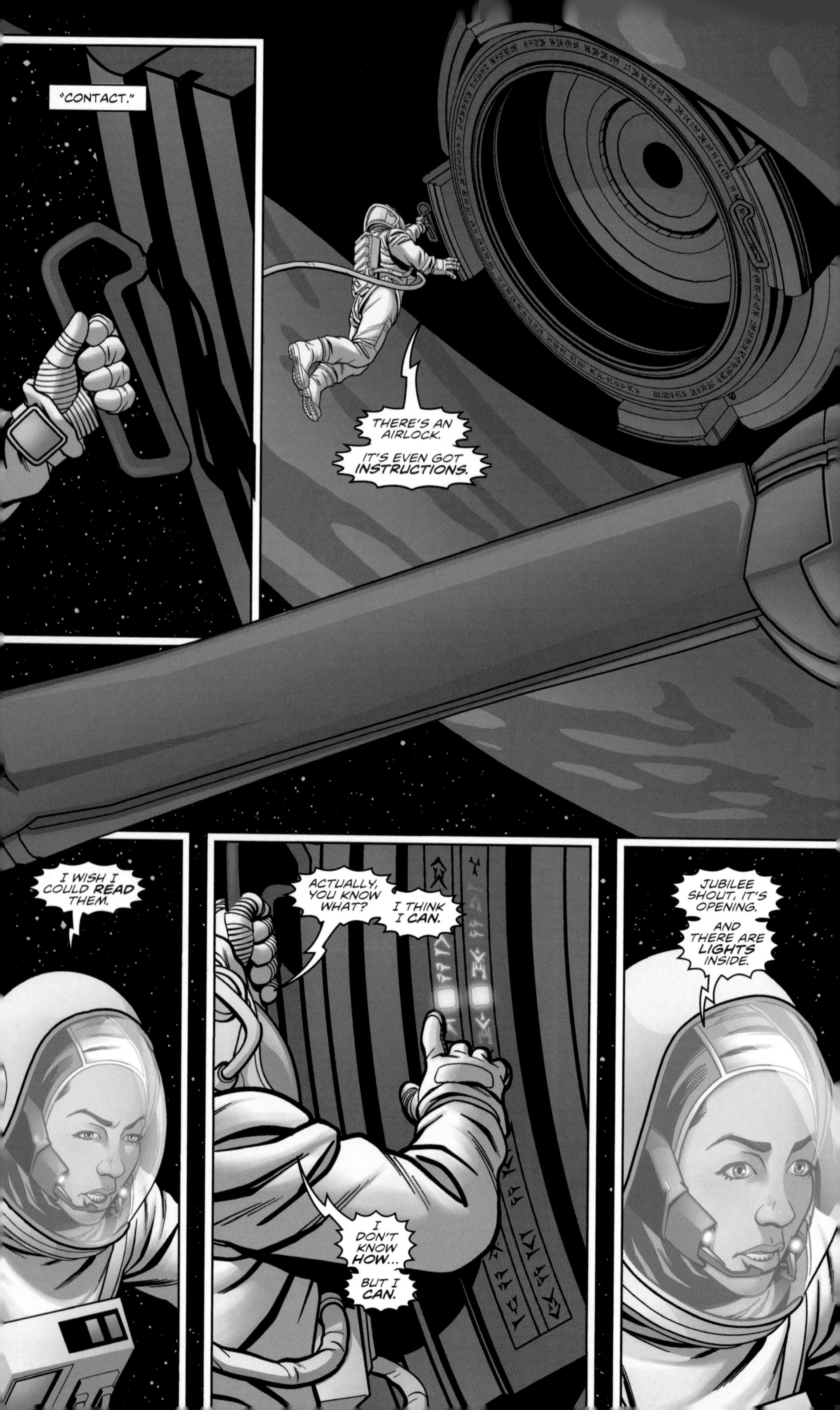
"CONTACT."
THERE'S AN AIRLOCK.
IT'S EVEN GOT INSTRUCTIONS.
I WISH I COULD READ THEM.
ACTUALLY, YOU KNOW WHAT?
I THINK I CAN.
I DON'T KNOW HOW...
BUT I CAN.
JUBILEE SHOUT, IT'S OPENING.
AND THERE ARE LIGHTS INSIDE.

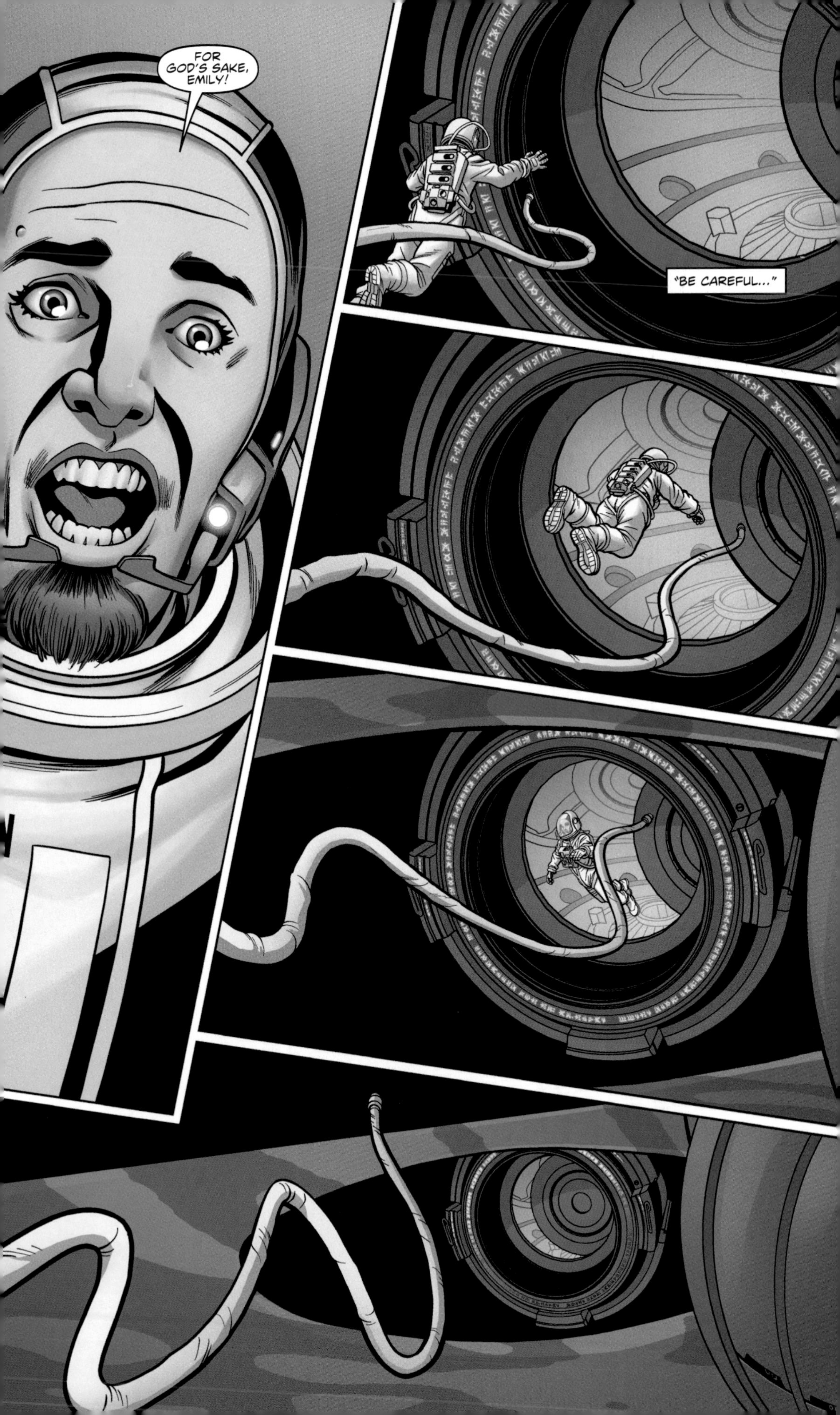
FOR GOD'S SAKE, EMILY!
"BE CAREFUL..."

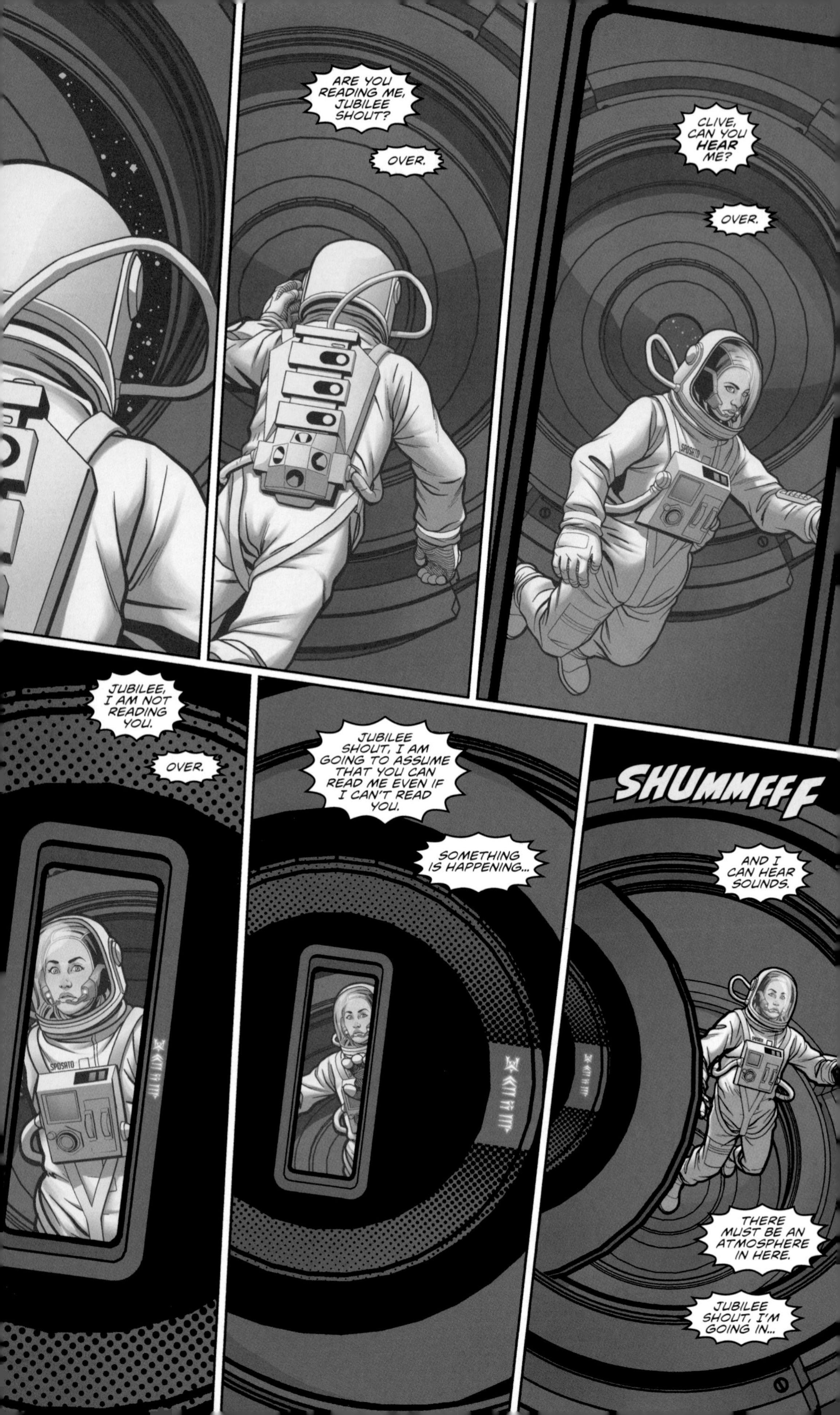
ARE YOU READING ME, JUBILEE SHOUT?
OVER.
CLIVE, CAN YOU HEAR ME?
OVER.
JUBILEE, I AM NOT READING YOU.
OVER.
JUBILEE SHOUT, I AM GOING TO ASSUME THAT YOU CAN READ ME EVEN IF I CAN'T READ YOU.
SOMETHING IS HAPPENING...
SHUMMFFF
AND I CAN HEAR SOUNDS.
THERE MUST BE AN ATMOSPHERE IN HERE.
JUBILEE SHOUT, I'M GOING IN...

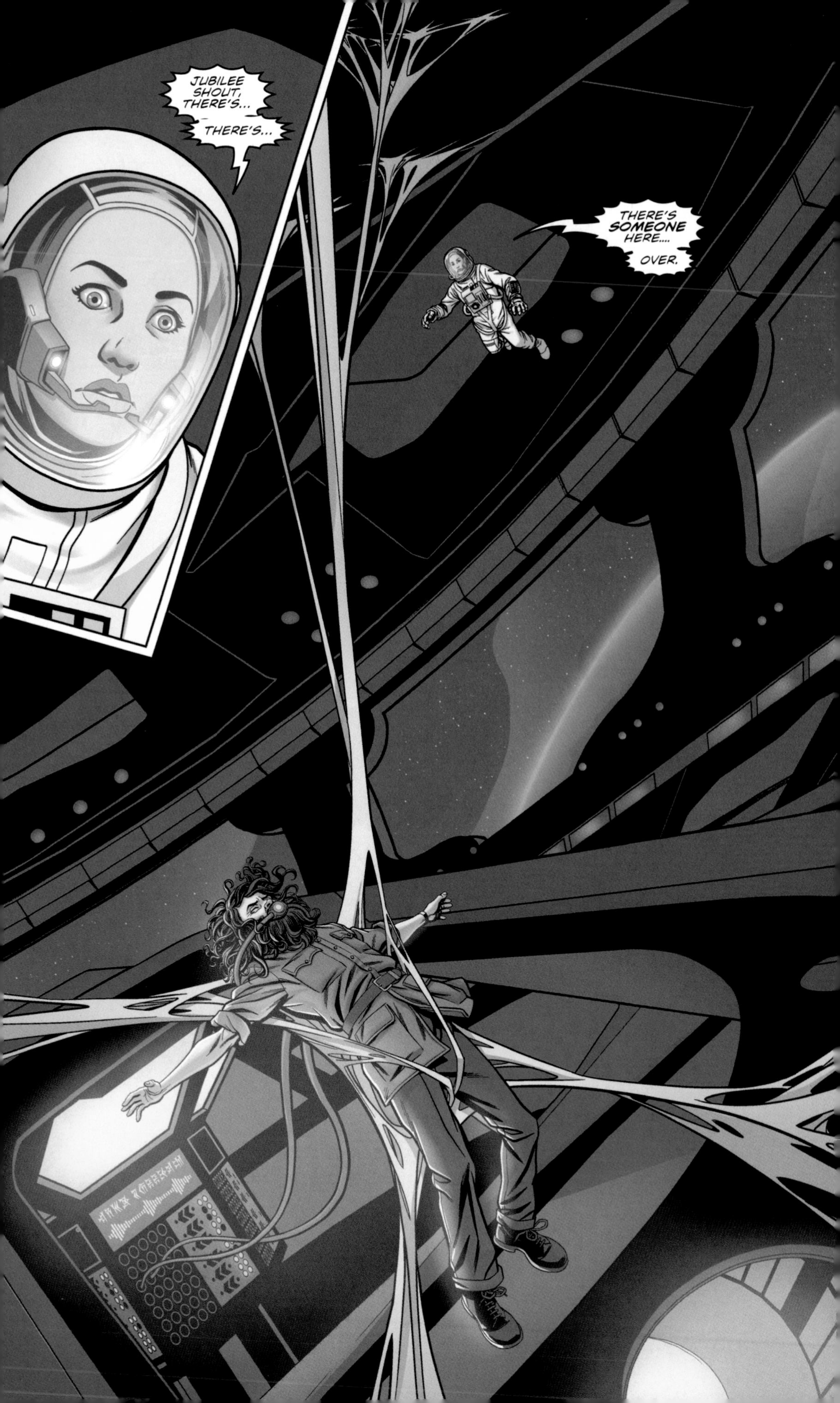
JUBILEE SHOUT, THERE'S...
THERE'S...
THERE'S SOMEONE HERE....
OVER.

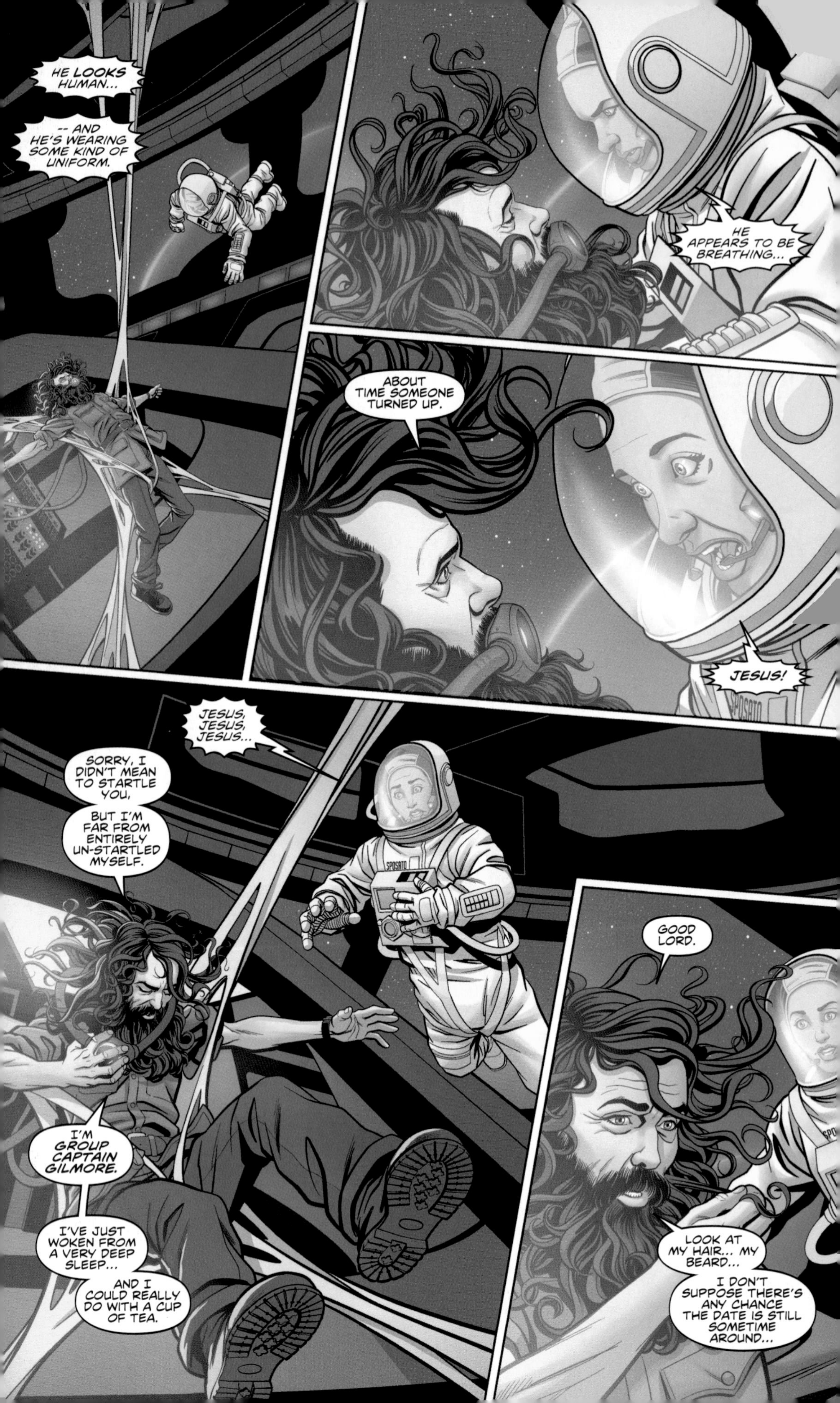

HE LOOKS HUMAN...
-- AND HE'S WEARING SOME KIND OF UNIFORM.
HE APPEARS TO BE BREATHING...
ABOUT TIME SOMEONE TURNED UP.
JESUS!
SPOSATO
JESUS, JESUS, JESUS...
SORRY, I DIDN'T MEAN TO STARTLE YOU,
BUT I'M FAR FROM ENTIRELY UN-STARTLED MYSELF.
SPOSATO
I'M GROUP CAPTAIN GILMORE.
I'VE JUST WOKEN FROM A VERY DEEP SLEEP...
AND I COULD REALLY DO WITH A CUP OF TEA.
GOOD LORD.
LOOK AT MY HAIR... MY BEARD...
I DON'T SUPPOSE THERE'S ANY CHANCE THE DATE IS STILL SOMETIME AROUND...

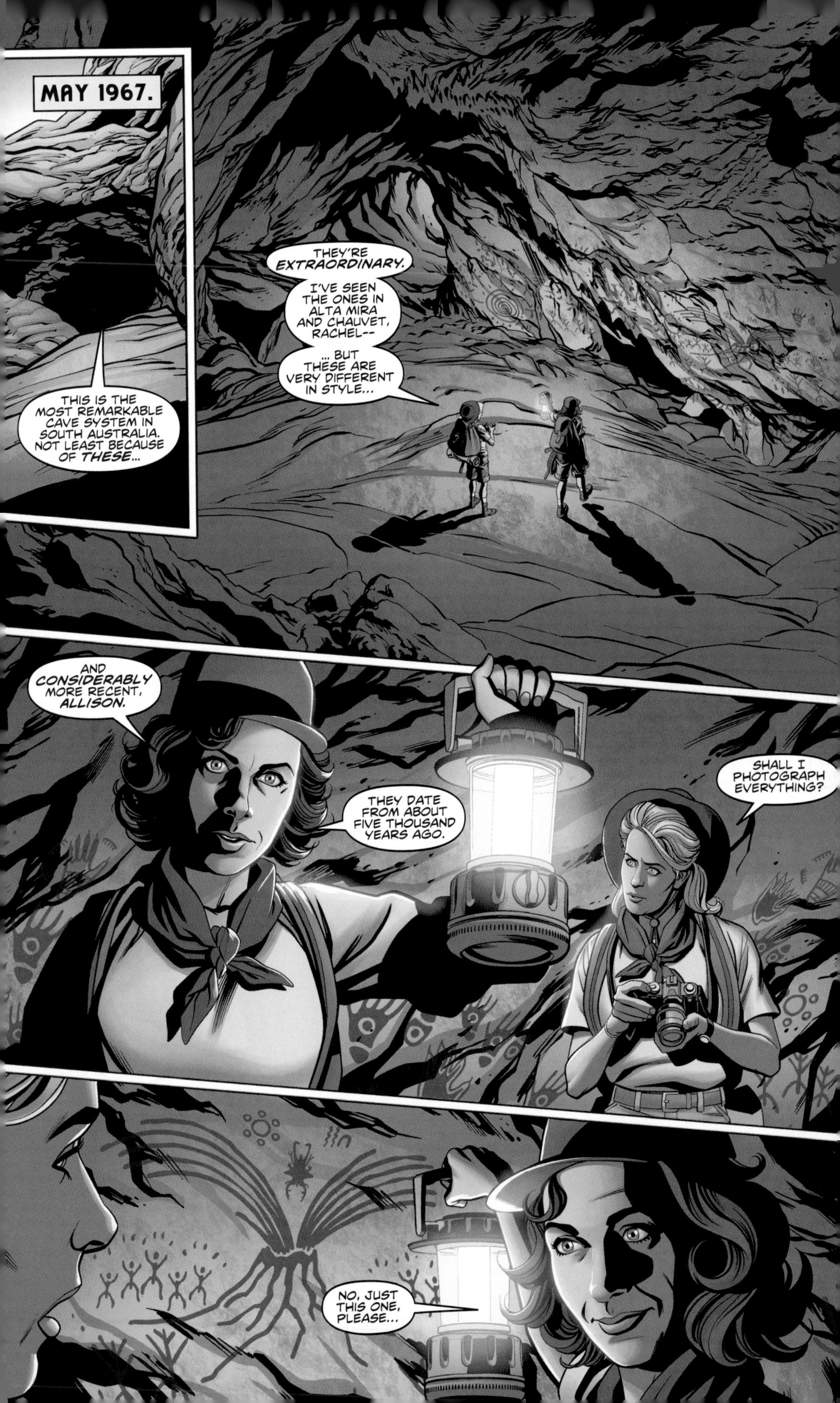

MAY 1967.
THIS IS THE MOST REMARKABLE CAVE SYSTEM IN SOUTH AUSTRALIA. NOT LEAST BECAUSE OF *THESE*...
THEY'RE *EXTRAORDINARY.*
I'VE SEEN THE ONES IN ALTA MIRA AND CHAUVET, RACHEL--
... BUT THESE ARE VERY DIFFERENT IN STYLE...
AND *CONSIDERABLY* MORE RECENT, *ALLISON.*
THEY DATE FROM ABOUT FIVE THOUSAND YEARS AGO.
SHALL I PHOTOGRAPH EVERYTHING?
NO, JUST THIS ONE, PLEASE...

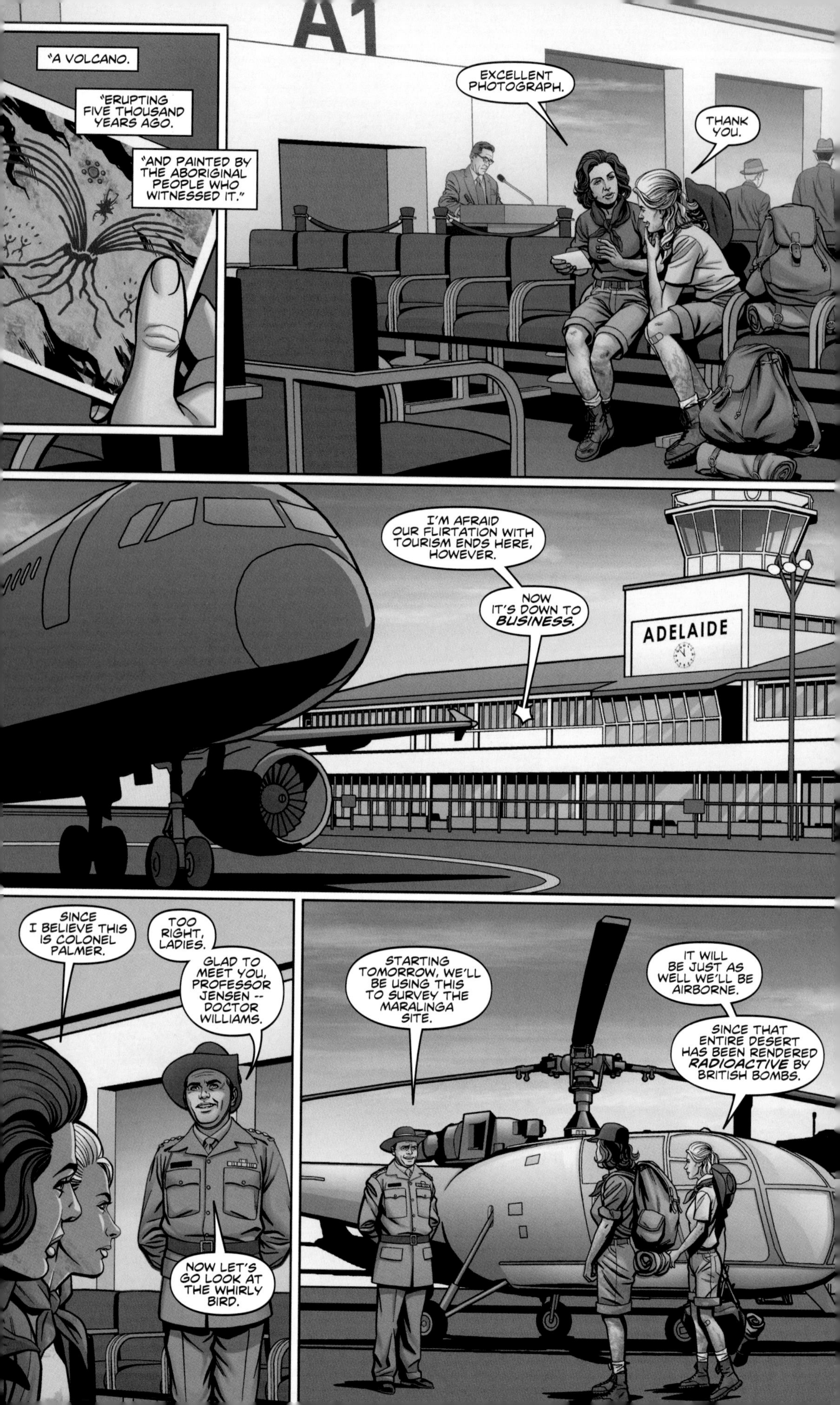
"A VOLCANO.
"ERUPTING FIVE THOUSAND YEARS AGO.
"AND PAINTED BY THE ABORIGINAL PEOPLE WHO WITNESSED IT."
EXCELLENT PHOTOGRAPH.
THANK YOU.
A1
I'M AFRAID OUR FLIRTATION WITH TOURISM ENDS HERE, HOWEVER.
NOW IT'S DOWN TO *BUSINESS.*
ADELAIDE
SINCE I BELIEVE THIS IS COLONEL PALMER.
TOO RIGHT, LADIES.
GLAD TO MEET YOU, PROFESSOR JENSEN -- DOCTOR WILLIAMS.
NOW LET'S GO LOOK AT THE WHIRLY BIRD.
STARTING TOMORROW, WE'LL BE USING THIS TO SURVEY THE MARALINGA SITE.
IT WILL BE JUST AS WELL WE'LL BE AIRBORNE.
SINCE THAT ENTIRE DESERT HAS BEEN RENDERED *RADIOACTIVE* BY BRITISH BOMBS.

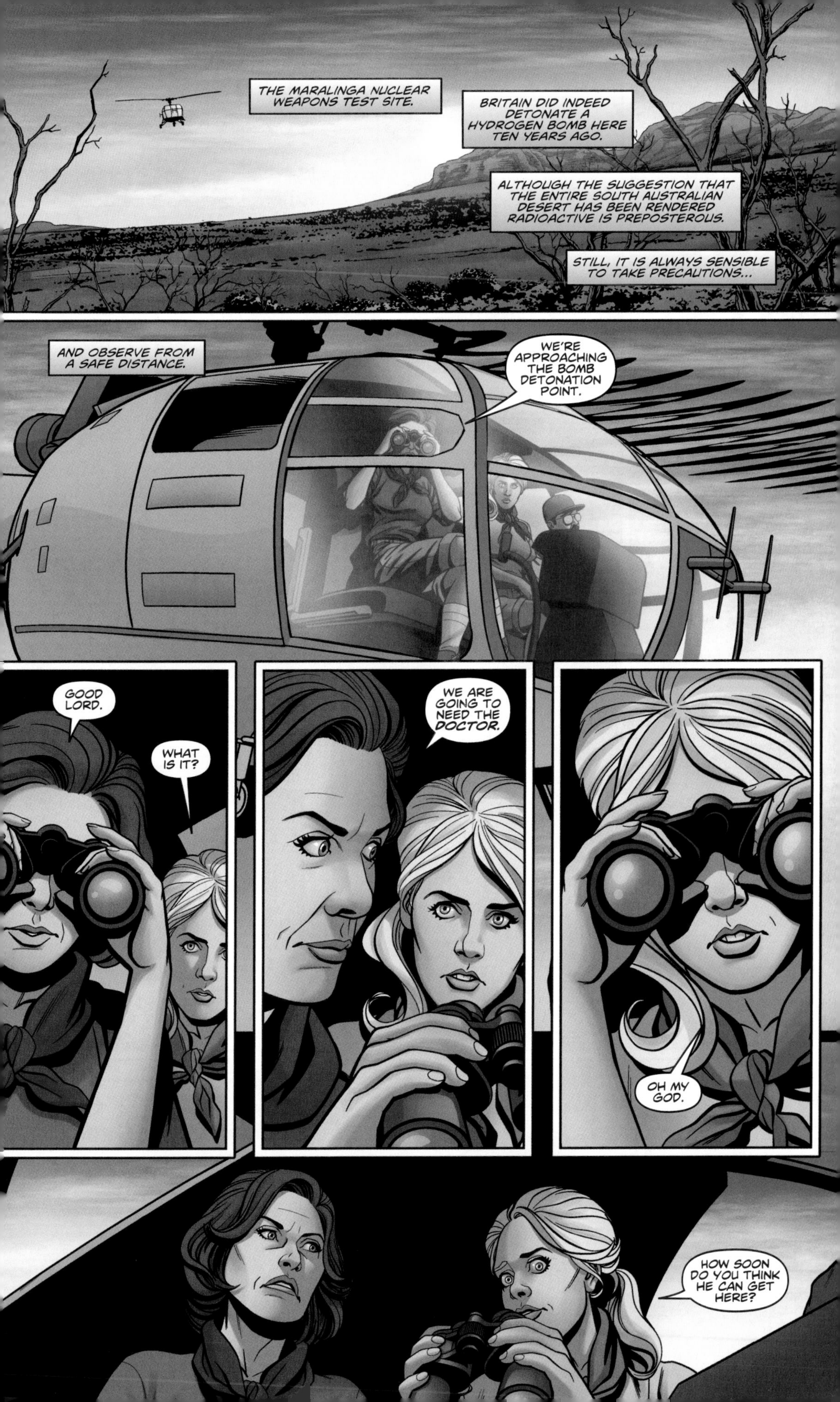
THE MARALINGA NUCLEAR WEAPONS TEST SITE.
BRITAIN DID INDEED DETONATE A HYDROGEN BOMB HERE TEN YEARS AGO.
ALTHOUGH THE SUGGESTION THAT THE ENTIRE SOUTH AUSTRALIAN DESERT HAS BEEN RENDERED RADIOACTIVE IS PREPOSTEROUS.
STILL, IT IS ALWAYS SENSIBLE TO TAKE PRECAUTIONS...
AND OBSERVE FROM A SAFE DISTANCE.
WE'RE APPROACHING THE BOMB DETONATION POINT.
GOOD LORD.
WHAT IS IT?
WE ARE GOING TO NEED THE *DOCTOR*.
OH MY GOD.
HOW SOON DO YOU THINK HE CAN GET HERE?

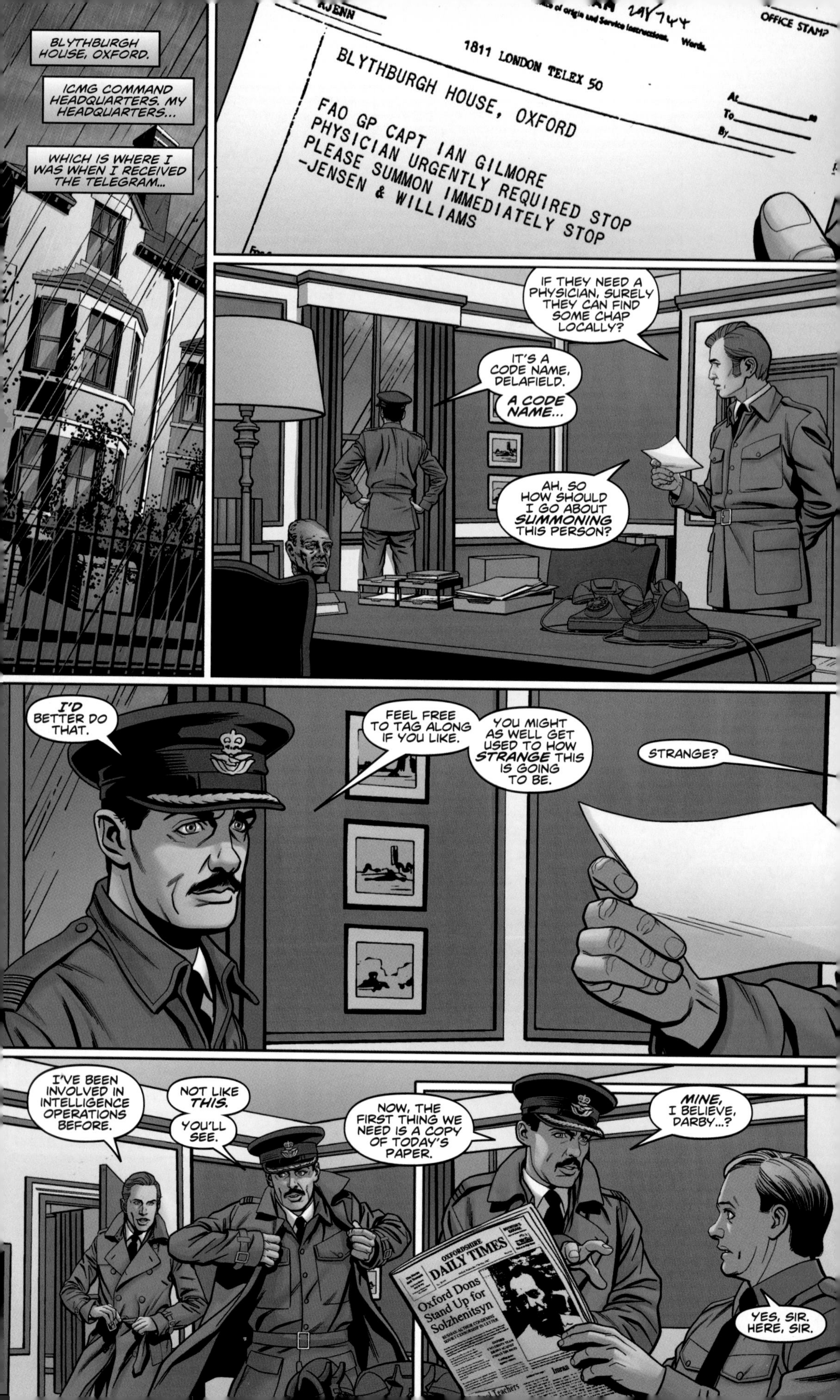
BLYTHBURGH HOUSE, OXFORD.
ICMG COMMAND HEADQUARTERS. MY HEADQUARTERS...
WHICH IS WHERE I WAS WHEN I RECEIVED THE TELEGRAM...
OFFICE STAMP
1811 LONDON TELEX 50
BLYTHBURGH HOUSE, OXFORD
FAO GP CAPT IAN GILMORE
PHYSICIAN URGENTLY REQUIRED STOP
PLEASE SUMMON IMMEDIATELY STOP
-JENSEN & WILLIAMS
IF THEY NEED A PHYSICIAN, SURELY THEY CAN FIND SOME CHAP LOCALLY?
IT'S A CODE NAME, DELAFIELD.
A CODE NAME...
AH, SO HOW SHOULD I GO ABOUT SUMMONING THIS PERSON?
I'D BETTER DO THAT.
FEEL FREE TO TAG ALONG IF YOU LIKE.
YOU MIGHT AS WELL GET USED TO HOW STRANGE THIS IS GOING TO BE.
STRANGE?
I'VE BEEN INVOLVED IN INTELLIGENCE OPERATIONS BEFORE.
NOT LIKE THIS.
YOU'LL SEE.
NOW, THE FIRST THING WE NEED IS A COPY OF TODAY'S PAPER.
MINE, I BELIEVE, DARBY...?
OXFORDSHIRE DAILY TIMES
Oxford Dons Stand Up for Solzhenitsyn
YES, SIR. HERE, SIR.

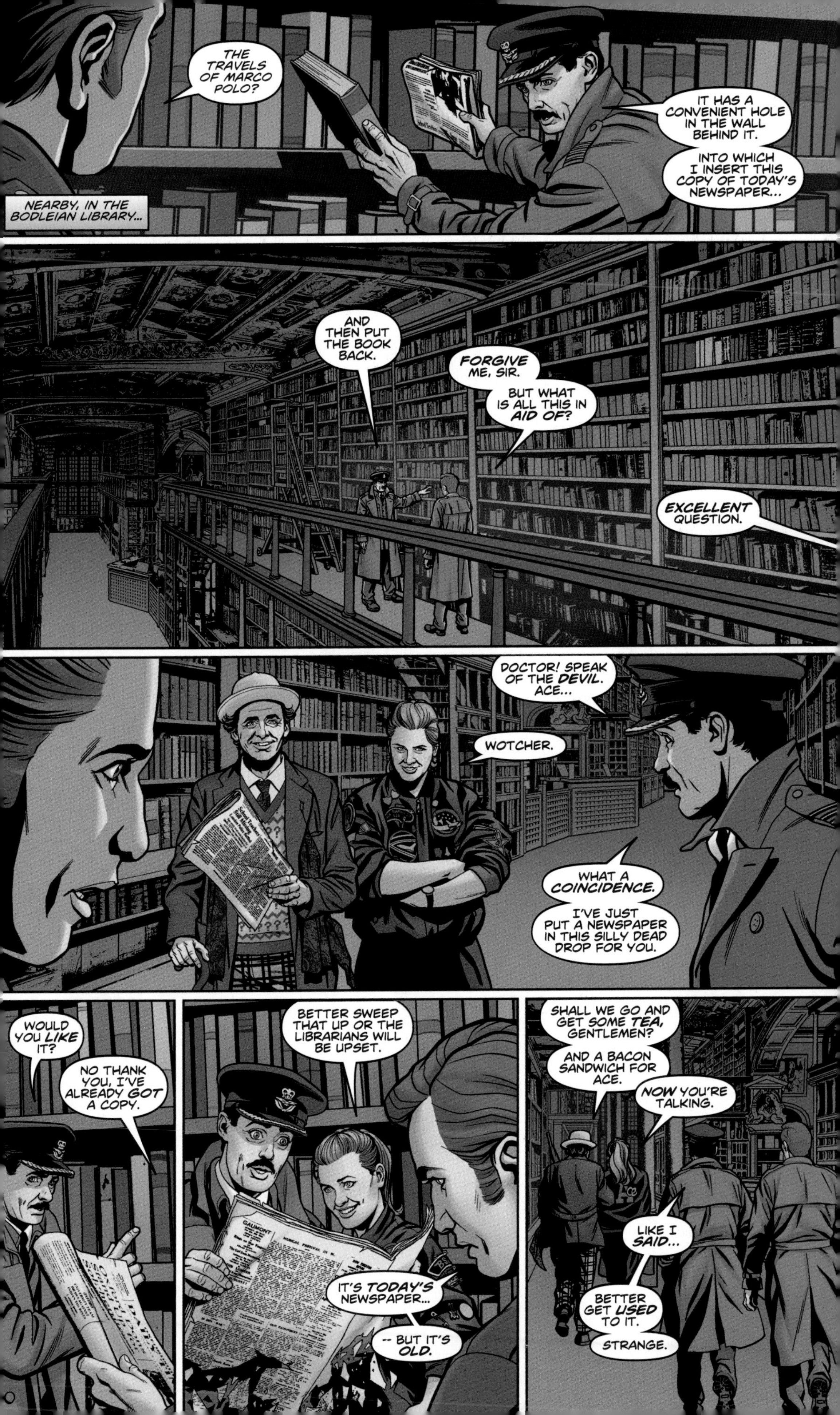

THE TRAVELS OF MARCO POLO?
IT HAS A CONVENIENT HOLE IN THE WALL BEHIND IT.
INTO WHICH I INSERT THIS COPY OF TODAY'S NEWSPAPER...
NEARBY, IN THE BODLEIAN LIBRARY...
AND THEN PUT THE BOOK BACK.
FORGIVE ME, SIR.
BUT WHAT IS ALL THIS IN AID OF?
EXCELLENT QUESTION.
DOCTOR! SPEAK OF THE DEVIL. ACE...
WOTCHER.
WHAT A COINCIDENCE.
I'VE JUST PUT A NEWSPAPER IN THIS SILLY DEAD DROP FOR YOU.
WOULD YOU LIKE IT?
NO THANK YOU, I'VE ALREADY GOT A COPY.
BETTER SWEEP THAT UP OR THE LIBRARIANS WILL BE UPSET.
IT'S TODAY'S NEWSPAPER...
-- BUT IT'S OLD.
SHALL WE GO AND GET SOME TEA, GENTLEMEN?
AND A BACON SANDWICH FOR ACE.
NOW YOU'RE TALKING.
LIKE I SAID...
BETTER GET USED TO IT.
STRANGE.

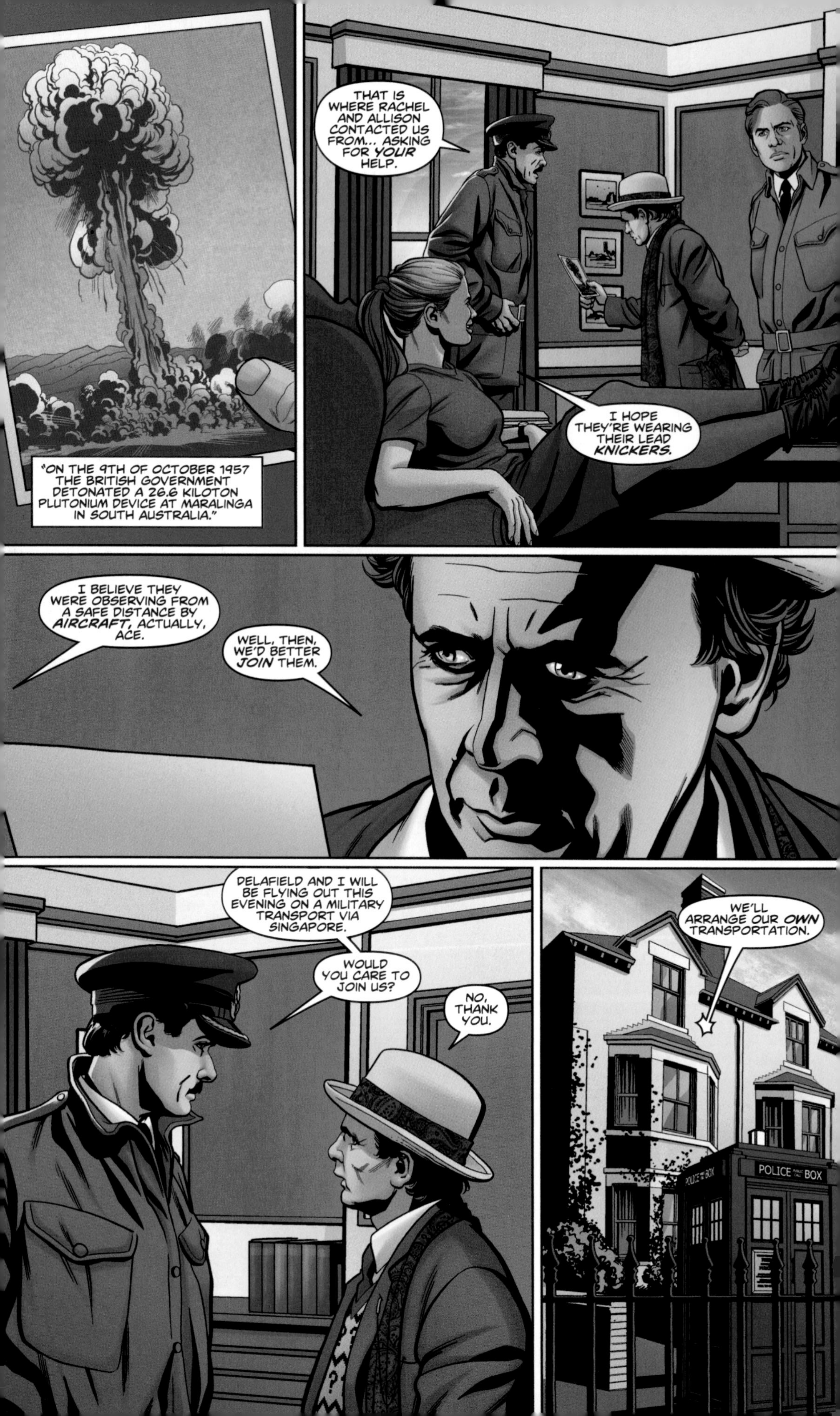
"ON THE 9TH OF OCTOBER 1957 THE BRITISH GOVERNMENT DETONATED A 26.6 KILOTON PLUTONIUM DEVICE AT MARALINGA IN SOUTH AUSTRALIA."
THAT IS WHERE RACHEL AND ALLISON CONTACTED US FROM... ASKING FOR *YOUR* HELP.
I HOPE THEY'RE WEARING THEIR LEAD *KNICKERS*.
I BELIEVE THEY WERE OBSERVING FROM A SAFE DISTANCE BY *AIRCRAFT*, ACTUALLY, ACE.
WELL, THEN, WE'D BETTER *JOIN* THEM.
DELAFIELD AND I WILL BE FLYING OUT THIS EVENING ON A MILITARY TRANSPORT VIA SINGAPORE.
WOULD YOU CARE TO JOIN US?
NO, THANK YOU.
WE'LL ARRANGE OUR *OWN* TRANSPORTATION.
POLICE BOX
POLICE BOX

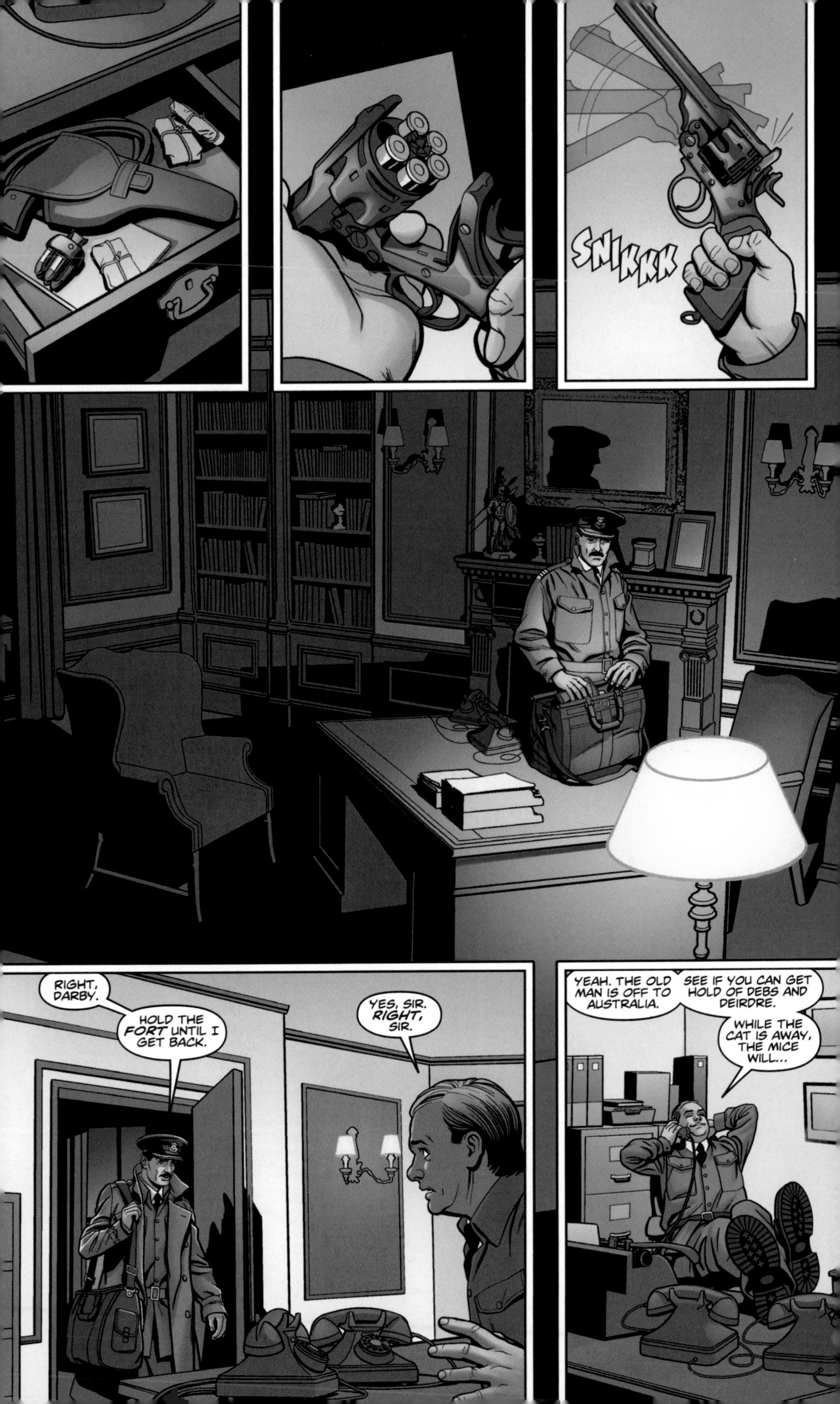
SNIKKK
RIGHT, DARBY.
HOLD THE FORT UNTIL I GET BACK.
YES, SIR. RIGHT, SIR.
YEAH. THE OLD MAN IS OFF TO AUSTRALIA.
SEE IF YOU CAN GET HOLD OF DEBS AND DEIRDRE.
WHILE THE CAT IS AWAY, THE MICE WILL...

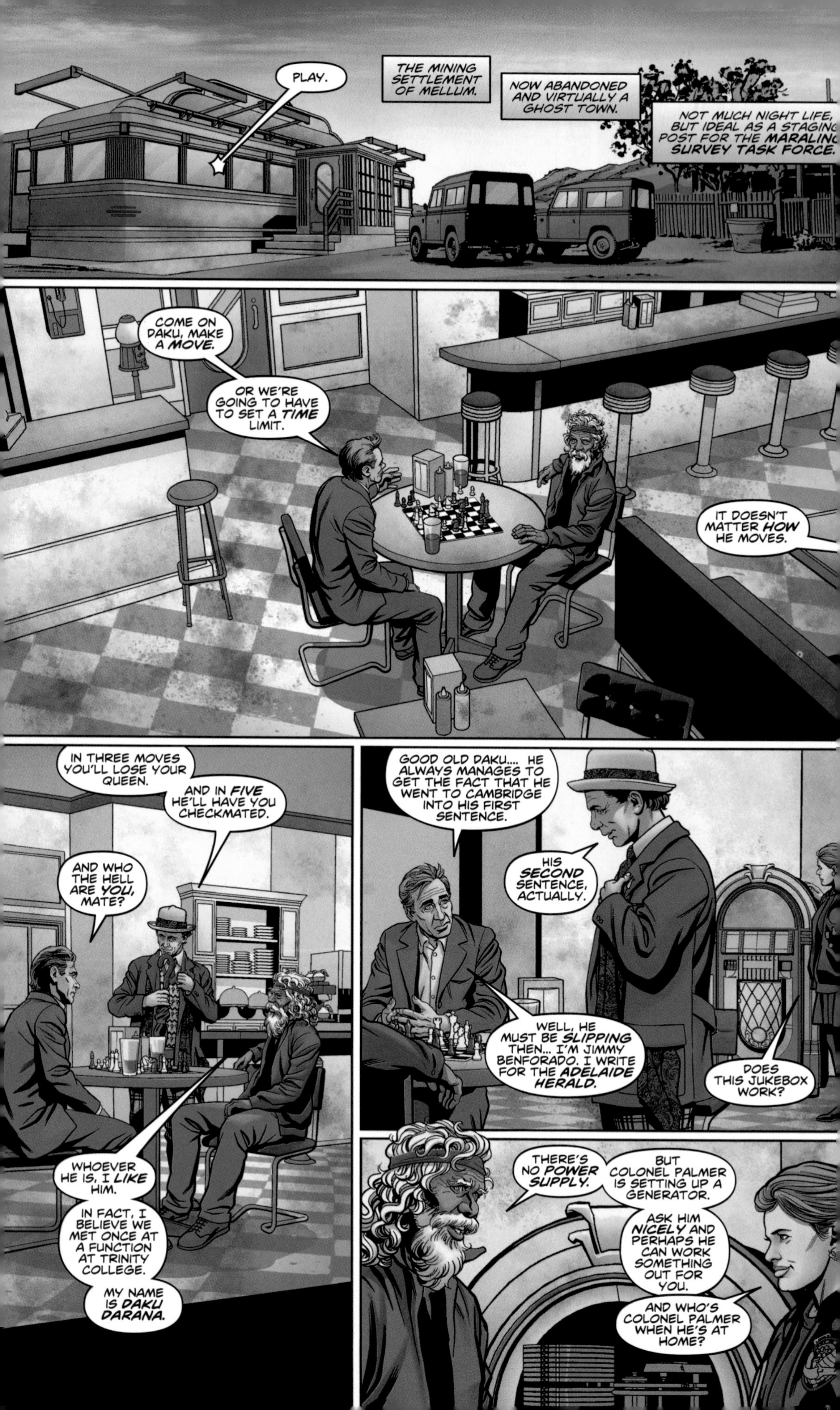
PLAY.
THE MINING SETTLEMENT OF MELLUM.
NOW ABANDONED AND VIRTUALLY A GHOST TOWN.
NOT MUCH NIGHT LIFE, BUT IDEAL AS A STAGING POST FOR THE MARALING SURVEY TASK FORCE.
COME ON DAKU, MAKE A MOVE.
OR WE'RE GOING TO HAVE TO SET A TIME LIMIT.
IT DOESN'T MATTER HOW HE MOVES.
IN THREE MOVES YOU'LL LOSE YOUR QUEEN.
AND IN FIVE HE'LL HAVE YOU CHECKMATED.
AND WHO THE HELL ARE YOU, MATE?
WHOEVER HE IS, I LIKE HIM.
IN FACT, I BELIEVE WE MET ONCE AT A FUNCTION AT TRINITY COLLEGE.
MY NAME IS DAKU DARANA.
GOOD OLD DAKU.... HE ALWAYS MANAGES TO GET THE FACT THAT HE WENT TO CAMBRIDGE INTO HIS FIRST SENTENCE.
HIS SECOND SENTENCE, ACTUALLY.
WELL, HE MUST BE SLIPPING THEN... I'M JIMMY BENFORADO. I WRITE FOR THE ADELAIDE HERALD.
DOES THIS JUKEBOX WORK?
THERE'S NO POWER SUPPLY.
BUT COLONEL PALMER IS SETTING UP A GENERATOR.
ASK HIM NICELY AND PERHAPS HE CAN WORK SOMETHING OUT FOR YOU.
AND WHO'S COLONEL PALMER WHEN HE'S AT HOME?

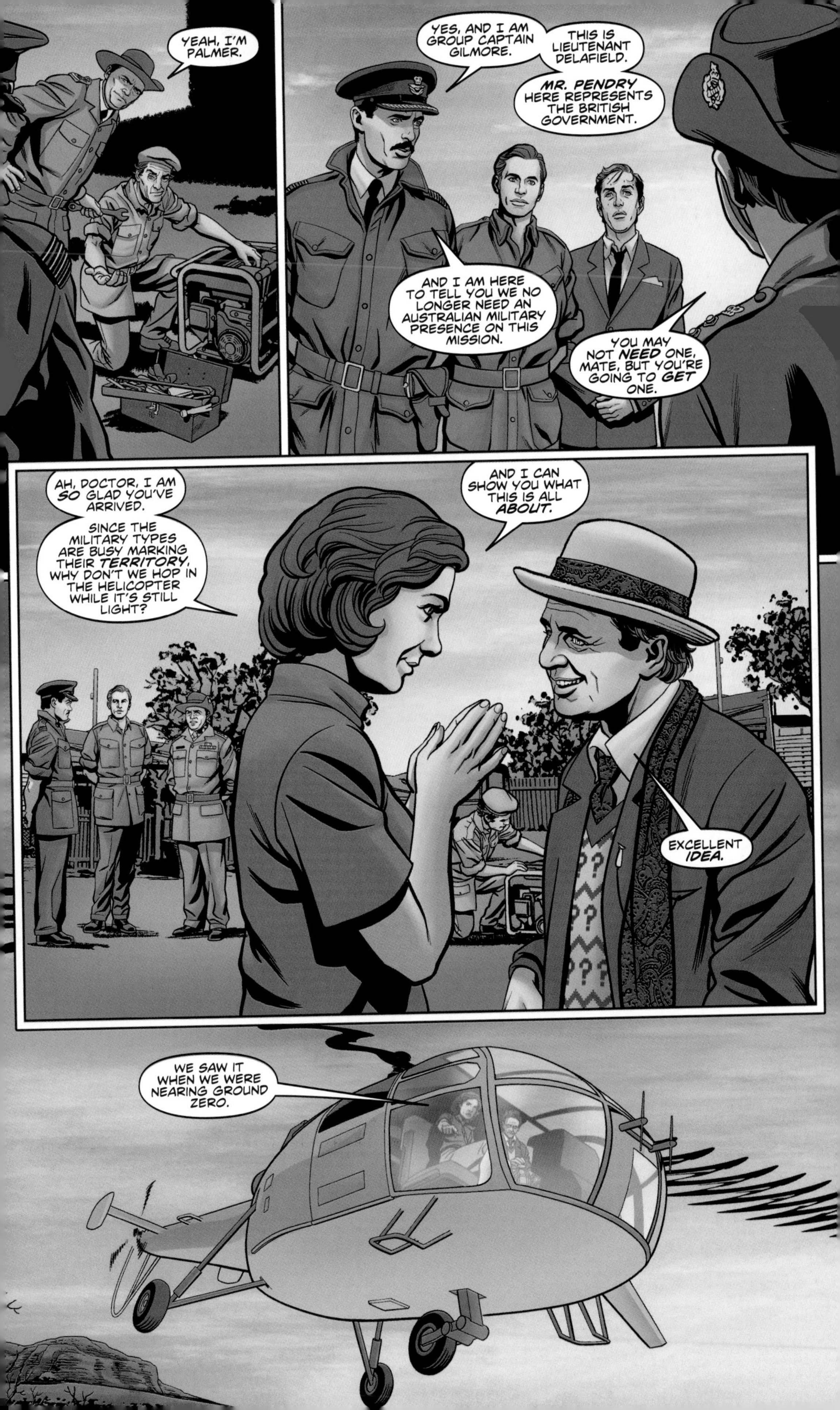

YEAH, I'M PALMER.
YES, AND I AM GROUP CAPTAIN GILMORE.
THIS IS LIEUTENANT DELAFIELD.
MR. PENDRY HERE REPRESENTS THE BRITISH GOVERNMENT.
AND I AM HERE TO TELL YOU WE NO LONGER NEED AN AUSTRALIAN MILITARY PRESENCE ON THIS MISSION.
YOU MAY NOT NEED ONE, MATE, BUT YOU'RE GOING TO GET ONE.
AH, DOCTOR, I AM SO GLAD YOU'VE ARRIVED.
SINCE THE MILITARY TYPES ARE BUSY MARKING THEIR TERRITORY, WHY DON'T WE HOP IN THE HELICOPTER WHILE IT'S STILL LIGHT?
AND I CAN SHOW YOU WHAT THIS IS ALL ABOUT.
EXCELLENT IDEA.
WE SAW IT WHEN WE WERE NEARING GROUND ZERO.

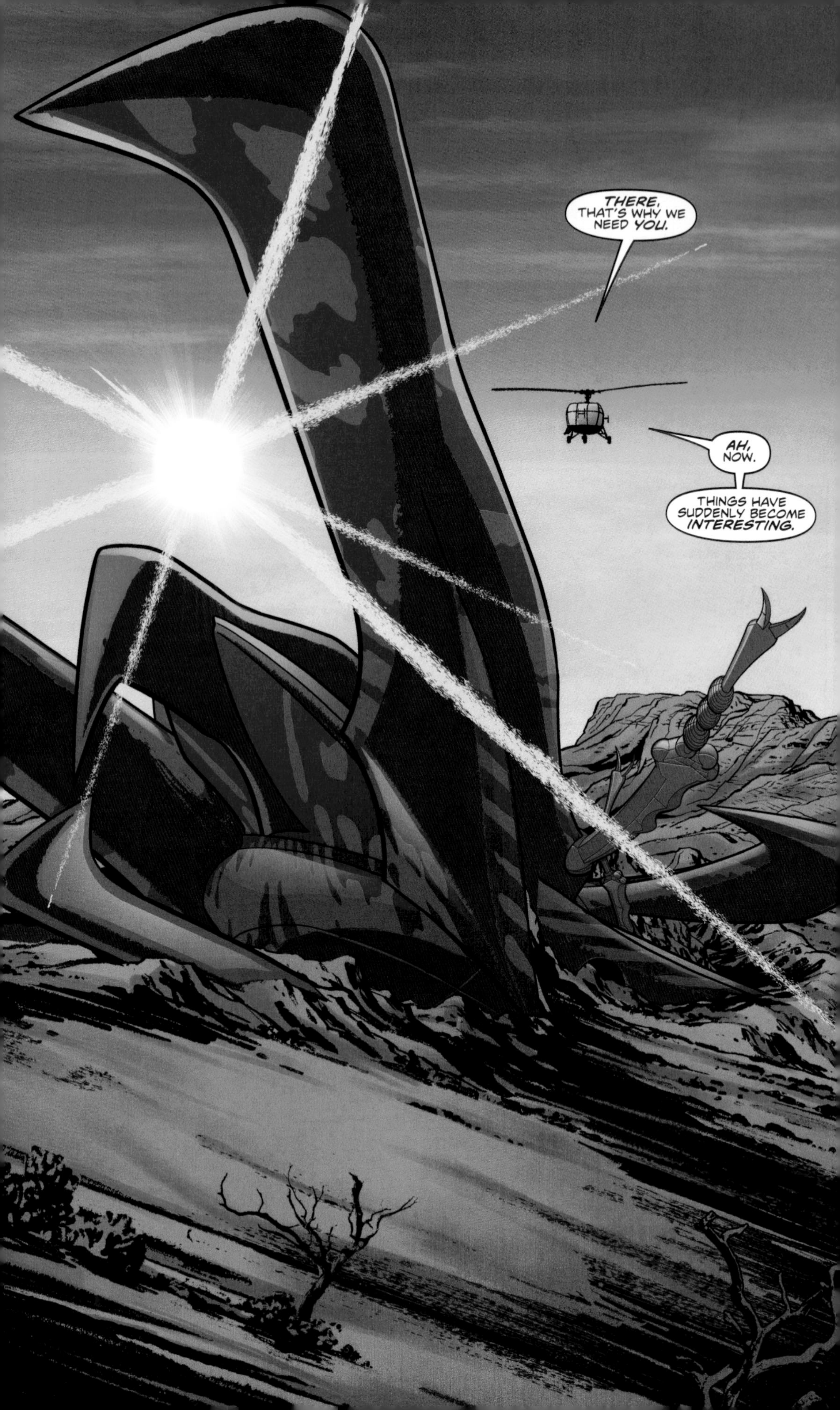
THERE, THAT'S WHY WE NEED YOU.
AH, NOW.
THINGS HAVE SUDDENLY BECOME INTERESTING.

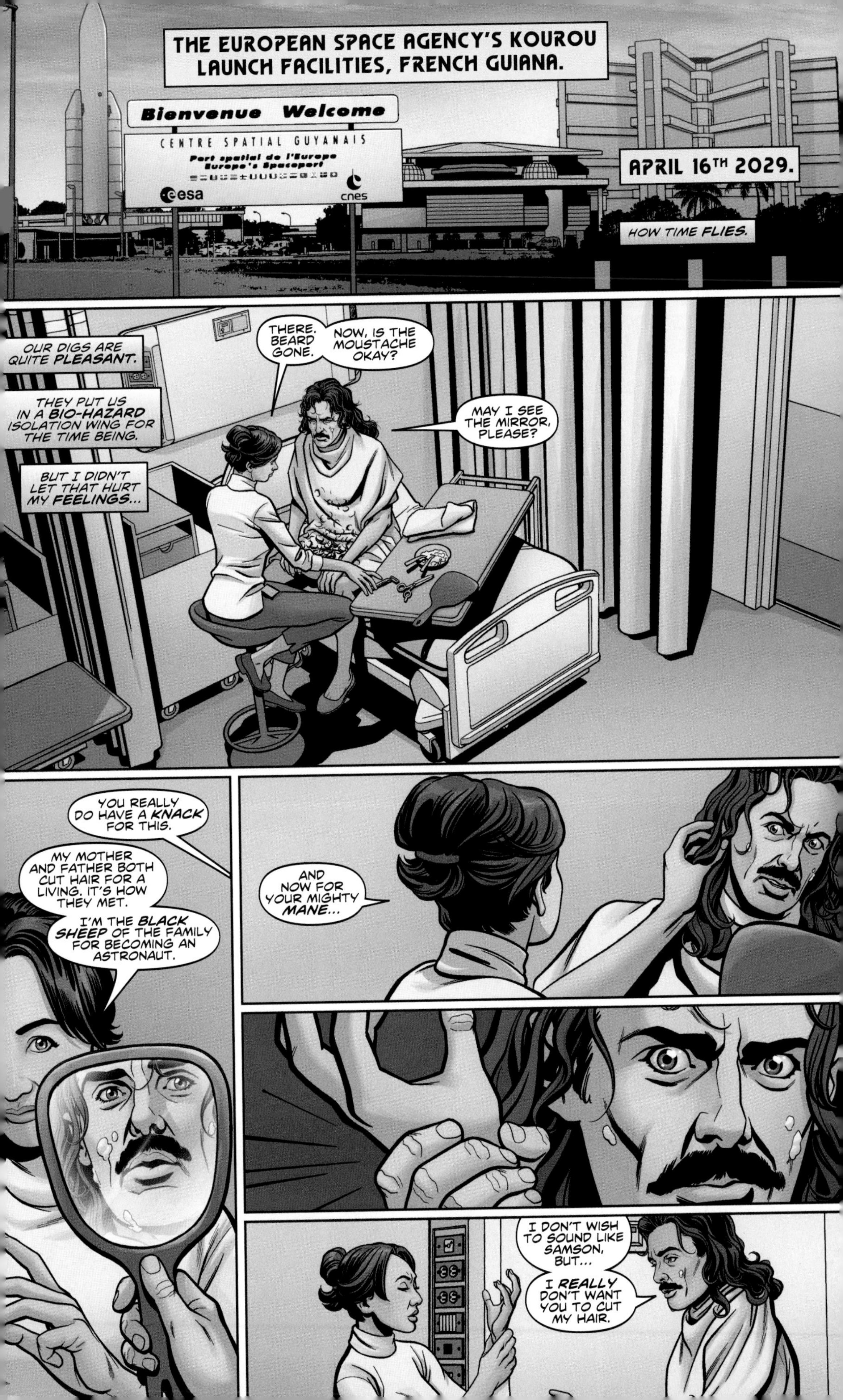
THE EUROPEAN SPACE AGENCY'S KOUROU LAUNCH FACILITIES, FRENCH GUIANA.
Bienvenue Welcome
CENTRE SPATIAL GUYANAIS
Port spatial de l'Europe
Europe's Spaceport
esa
cnes
APRIL 16TH 2029.
HOW TIME FLIES.
OUR DIGS ARE QUITE PLEASANT.
THEY PUT US IN A BIO-HAZARD ISOLATION WING FOR THE TIME BEING.
BUT I DIDN'T LET THAT HURT MY FEELINGS...
THERE. BEARD GONE.
NOW, IS THE MOUSTACHE OKAY?
MAY I SEE THE MIRROR, PLEASE?
YOU REALLY DO HAVE A KNACK FOR THIS.
MY MOTHER AND FATHER BOTH CUT HAIR FOR A LIVING. IT'S HOW THEY MET.
I'M THE BLACK SHEEP OF THE FAMILY FOR BECOMING AN ASTRONAUT.
AND NOW FOR YOUR MIGHTY MANE...
I DON'T WISH TO SOUND LIKE SAMSON, BUT...
I REALLY DON'T WANT YOU TO CUT MY HAIR.

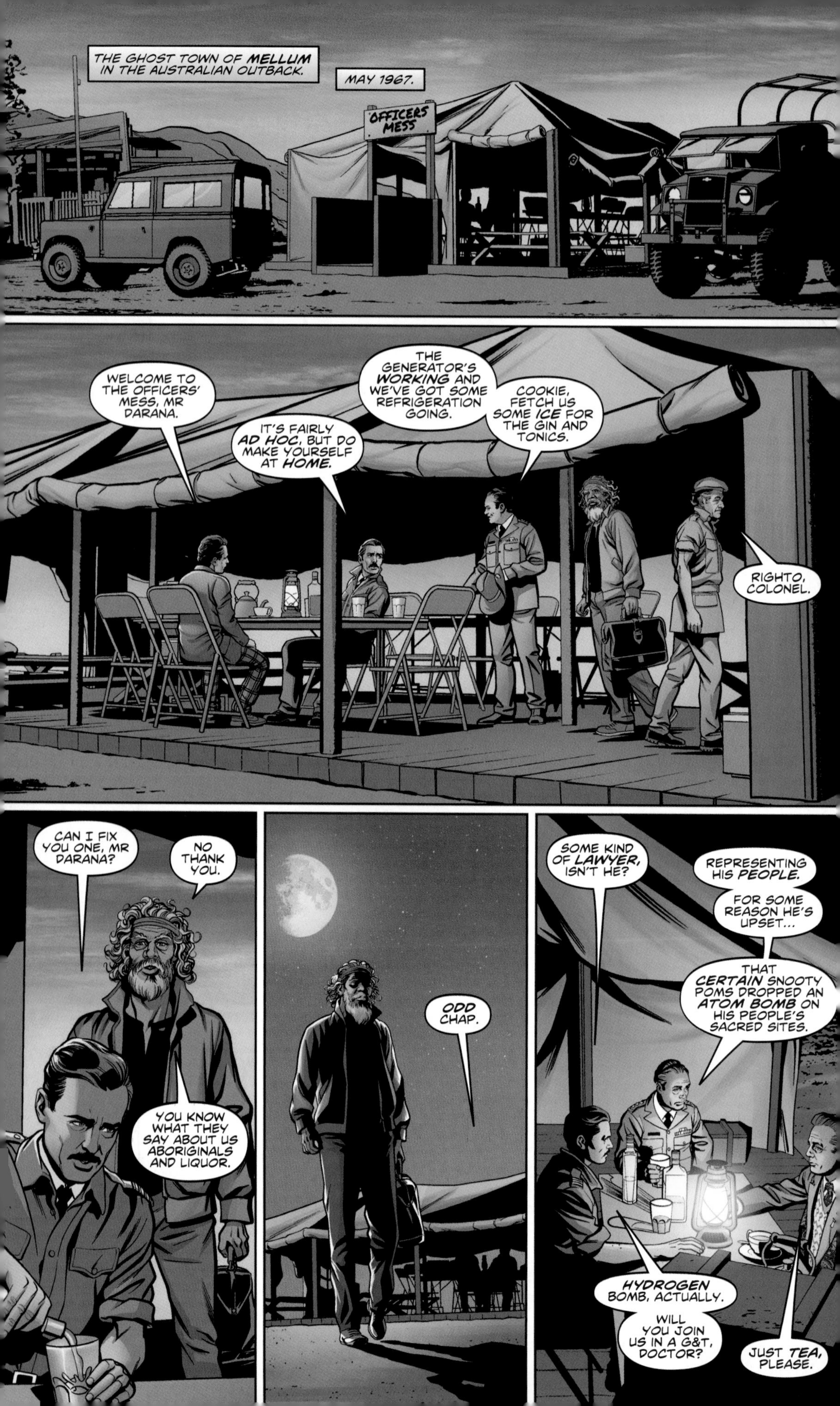
THE GHOST TOWN OF MELLUM IN THE AUSTRALIAN OUTBACK.
MAY 1967.
OFFICERS MESS
WELCOME TO THE OFFICERS' MESS, MR DARANA.
IT'S FAIRLY AD HOC, BUT DO MAKE YOURSELF AT HOME.
THE GENERATOR'S WORKING AND WE'VE GOT SOME REFRIGERATION GOING.
COOKIE, FETCH US SOME ICE FOR THE GIN AND TONICS.
RIGHTO, COLONEL.
CAN I FIX YOU ONE, MR DARANA?
NO THANK YOU.
YOU KNOW WHAT THEY SAY ABOUT US ABORIGINALS AND LIQUOR.
ODD CHAP.
SOME KIND OF LAWYER, ISN'T HE?
REPRESENTING HIS PEOPLE.
FOR SOME REASON HE'S UPSET...
THAT CERTAIN SNOOTY POMS DROPPED AN ATOM BOMB ON HIS PEOPLE'S SACRED SITES.
HYDROGEN BOMB, ACTUALLY.
WILL YOU JOIN US IN A G&T, DOCTOR?
JUST TEA, PLEASE.

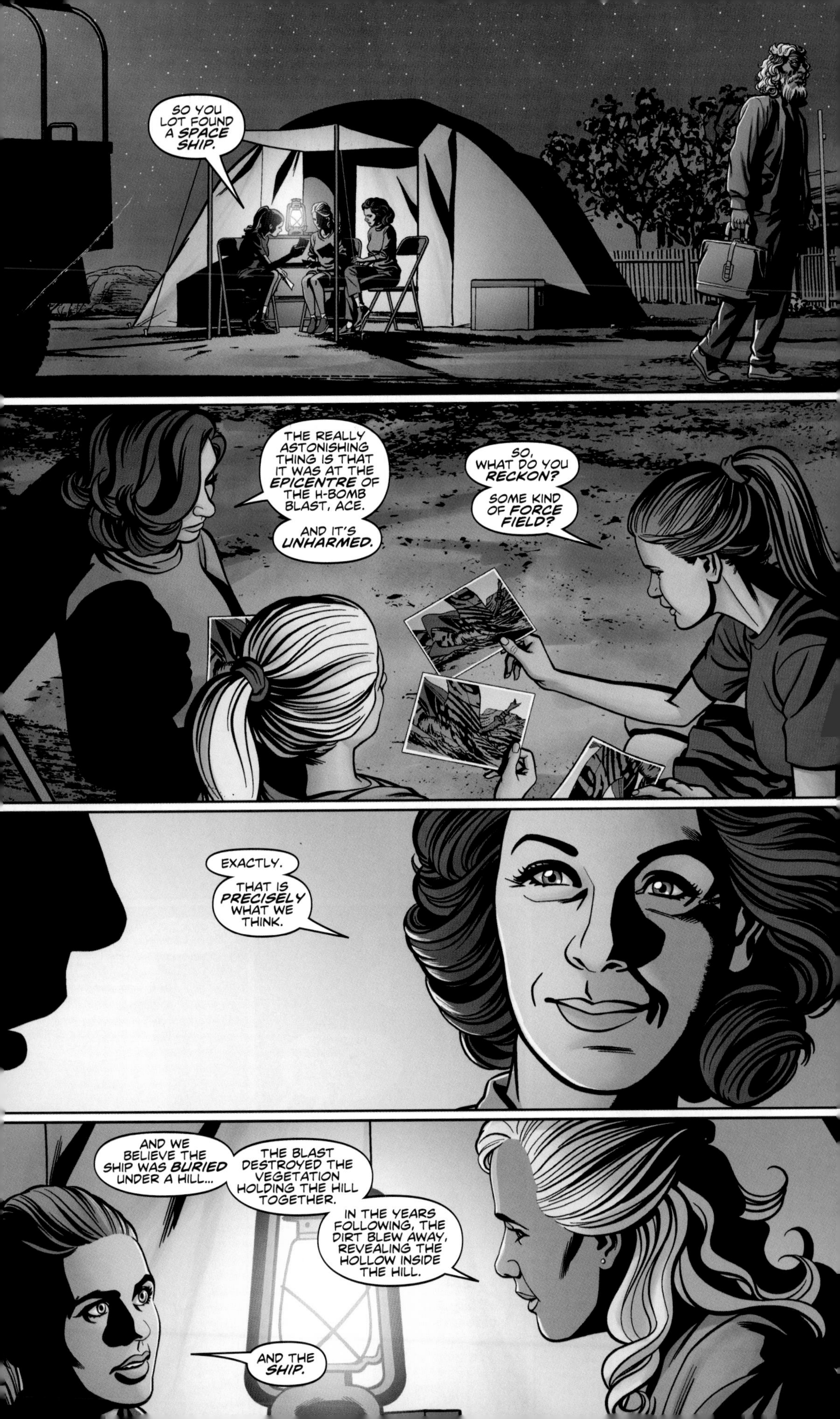
SO YOU LOT FOUND A SPACE SHIP.
THE REALLY ASTONISHING THING IS THAT IT WAS AT THE EPICENTRE OF THE H-BOMB BLAST, ACE.
AND IT'S UNHARMED.
SO, WHAT DO YOU RECKON?
SOME KIND OF FORCE FIELD?
EXACTLY.
THAT IS PRECISELY WHAT WE THINK.
AND WE BELIEVE THE SHIP WAS BURIED UNDER A HILL...
THE BLAST DESTROYED THE VEGETATION HOLDING THE HILL TOGETHER.
IN THE YEARS FOLLOWING, THE DIRT BLEW AWAY, REVEALING THE HOLLOW INSIDE THE HILL.
AND THE SHIP.

AMAZING HOW *FAST* WORD GETS AROUND ABOUT GIN AND TONIC.

AND LET'S NOT FORGET THE *ICE*. ANOTHER TRIUMPH FOR *AUSTRALIAN* MILITARY EFFICIENCY.

THANK YOU FOR ALLOWING ME TO INVADE YOUR *MALE* ENCLAVE, GENTLEMEN.

OUR PLEASURE.

I UNDERSTAND YOU ARE A *PEACE* ACTIVIST, MISS SHARROW?

THAT'S WHY I'M *HERE*.

DEBUTANTE TURNED ANTI-NUCLEAR CAMPAIGNER?

YES.

SO YOU WANT TO DISMANTLE THE VERY SYSTEM WHICH KEEPS YOU *SAFE*?

THE WAY IT DID DURING THE *CUBAN MISSILE CRISIS*?

PRECISELY.

YOU'RE A SOLDIER. YOU FOLLOW *ORDERS*. EVEN IF YOU'RE TOLD TO INCINERATE A MILLION *CHILDREN*.

YOU'D AGREE *BLINDLY*.

IF YOU'LL *EXCUSE ME* GENTLEMEN... I'M RATHER *TIRED*.

GOOD NIGHT.

"INCINERATE A MILLION CHILDREN." *REALLY*, DOCTOR.

THAT GIRL IS A DEBUTANTE AND A *DILETTANTE*.

THEY'RE ALL *COMMIES*, ANYWAY, THAT BAN-THE-BOMB MOB.

WELL, FOR *ONCE* I DON'T ENTIRELY DISAGREE WITH YOU, COLONEL.

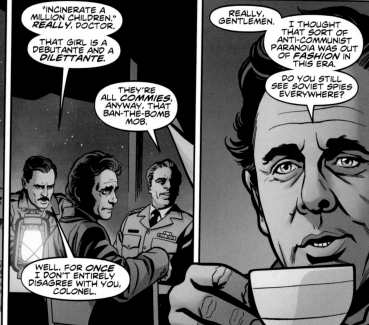

REALLY, GENTLEMEN. I THOUGHT THAT SORT OF ANTI-COMMUNIST PARANOIA WAS OUT OF *FASHION* IN THIS ERA.

DO YOU STILL SEE SOVIET SPIES EVERYWHERE?

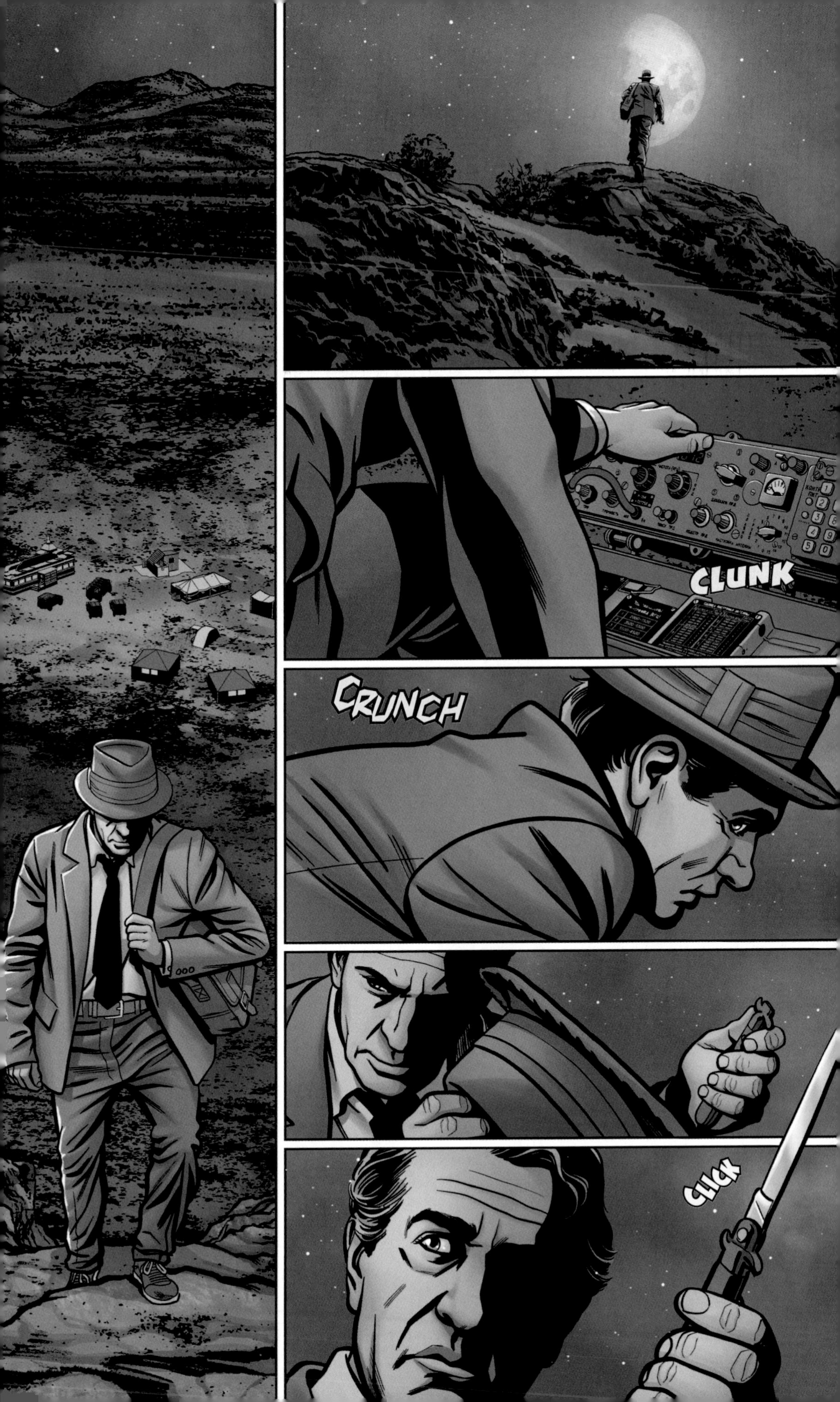
CLUNK
CRUNCH
CLICK

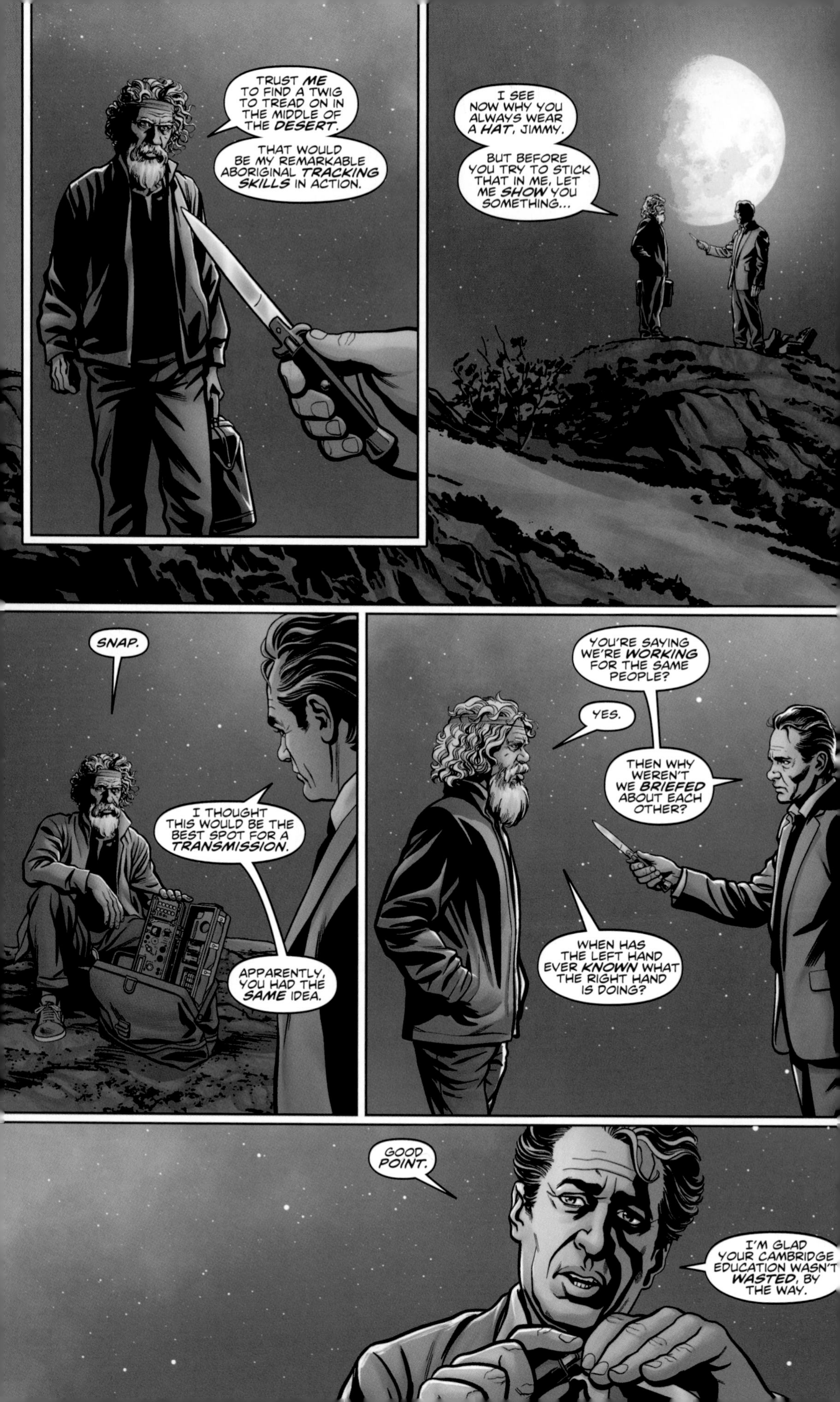

TRUST ME TO FIND A TWIG TO TREAD ON IN THE MIDDLE OF THE DESERT.
THAT WOULD BE MY REMARKABLE ABORIGINAL TRACKING SKILLS IN ACTION.
I SEE NOW WHY YOU ALWAYS WEAR A HAT, JIMMY.
BUT BEFORE YOU TRY TO STICK THAT IN ME, LET ME SHOW YOU SOMETHING...
SNAP.
I THOUGHT THIS WOULD BE THE BEST SPOT FOR A TRANSMISSION.
APPARENTLY, YOU HAD THE SAME IDEA.
YOU'RE SAYING WE'RE WORKING FOR THE SAME PEOPLE?
YES.
THEN WHY WEREN'T WE BRIEFED ABOUT EACH OTHER?
WHEN HAS THE LEFT HAND EVER KNOWN WHAT THE RIGHT HAND IS DOING?
GOOD POINT.
I'M GLAD YOUR CAMBRIDGE EDUCATION WASN'T WASTED, BY THE WAY.

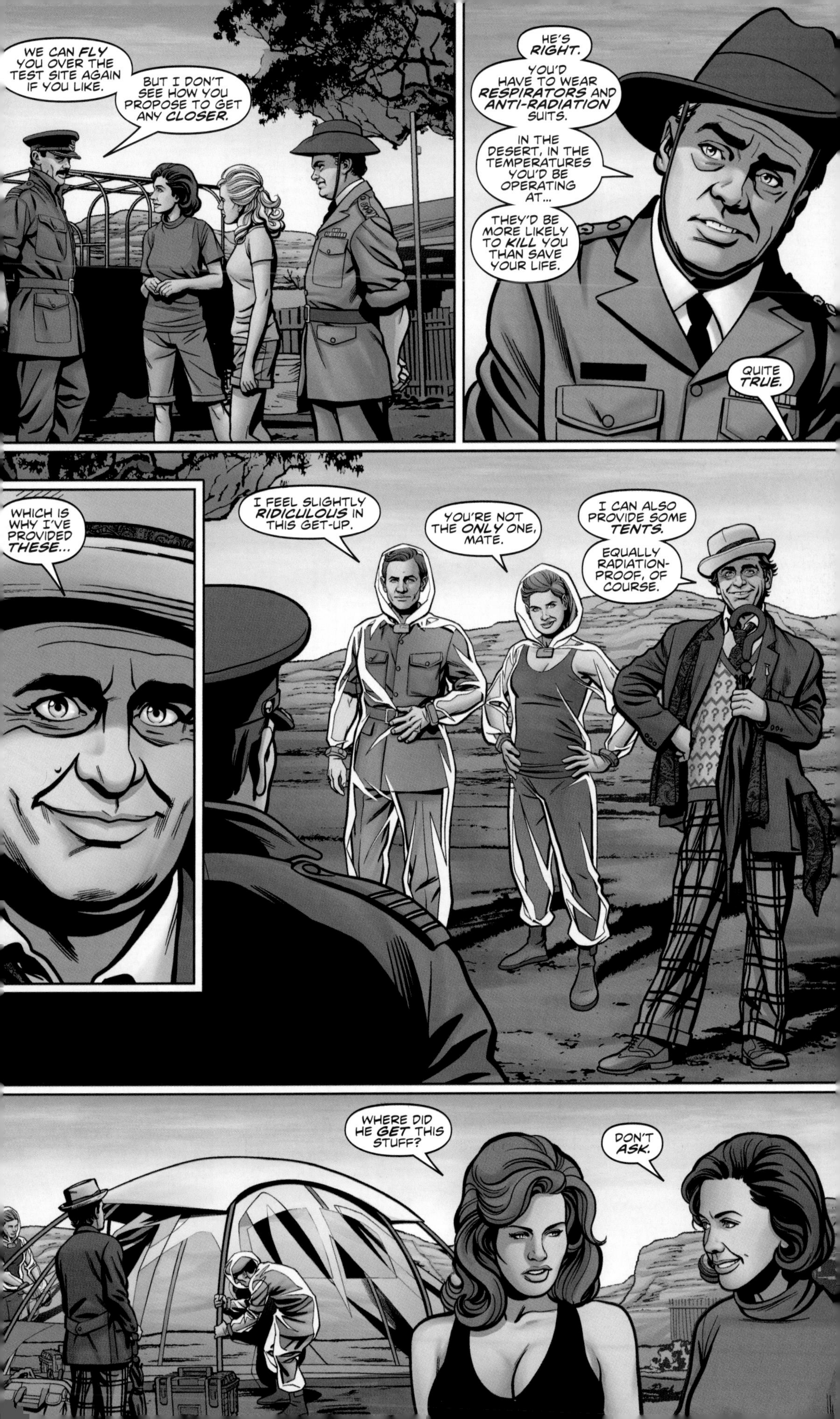
WE CAN FLY YOU OVER THE TEST SITE AGAIN IF YOU LIKE.
BUT I DON'T SEE HOW YOU PROPOSE TO GET ANY CLOSER.
HE'S RIGHT.
YOU'D HAVE TO WEAR RESPIRATORS AND ANTI-RADIATION SUITS.
IN THE DESERT, IN THE TEMPERATURES YOU'D BE OPERATING AT...
THEY'D BE MORE LIKELY TO KILL YOU THAN SAVE YOUR LIFE.
QUITE TRUE.
WHICH IS WHY I'VE PROVIDED THESE...
I FEEL SLIGHTLY RIDICULOUS IN THIS GET-UP.
YOU'RE NOT THE ONLY ONE, MATE.
I CAN ALSO PROVIDE SOME TENTS.
EQUALLY RADIATION-PROOF, OF COURSE.
WHERE DID HE GET THIS STUFF?
DON'T ASK.

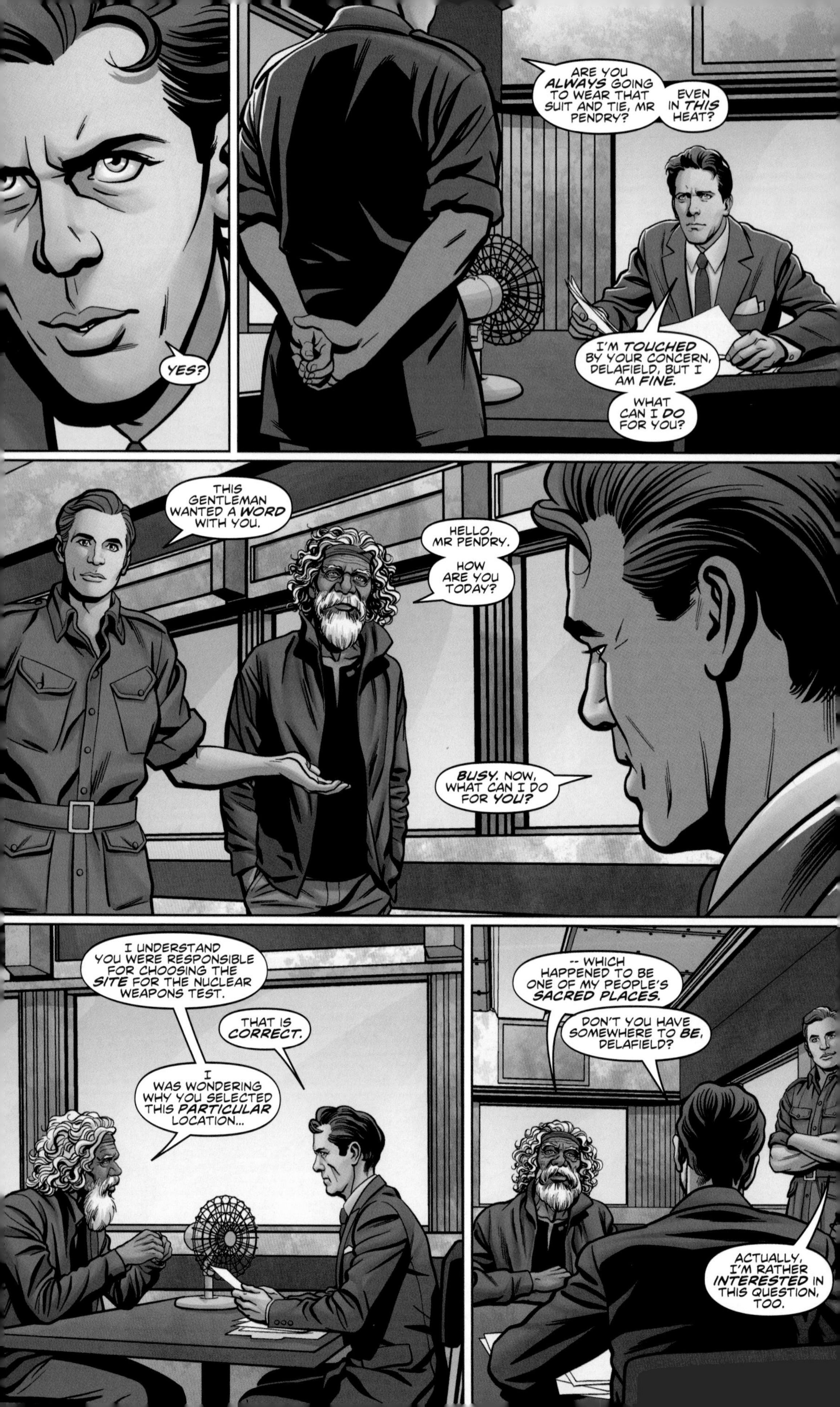
YES?
ARE YOU ALWAYS GOING TO WEAR THAT SUIT AND TIE, MR PENDRY?
EVEN IN THIS HEAT?
I'M TOUCHED BY YOUR CONCERN, DELAFIELD, BUT I AM FINE.
WHAT CAN I DO FOR YOU?
THIS GENTLEMAN WANTED A WORD WITH YOU.
HELLO, MR PENDRY.
HOW ARE YOU TODAY?
BUSY. NOW, WHAT CAN I DO FOR YOU?
I UNDERSTAND YOU WERE RESPONSIBLE FOR CHOOSING THE SITE FOR THE NUCLEAR WEAPONS TEST.
THAT IS CORRECT.
I WAS WONDERING WHY YOU SELECTED THIS PARTICULAR LOCATION...
-- WHICH HAPPENED TO BE ONE OF MY PEOPLE'S SACRED PLACES.
DON'T YOU HAVE SOMEWHERE TO BE, DELAFIELD?
ACTUALLY, I'M RATHER INTERESTED IN THIS QUESTION, TOO.

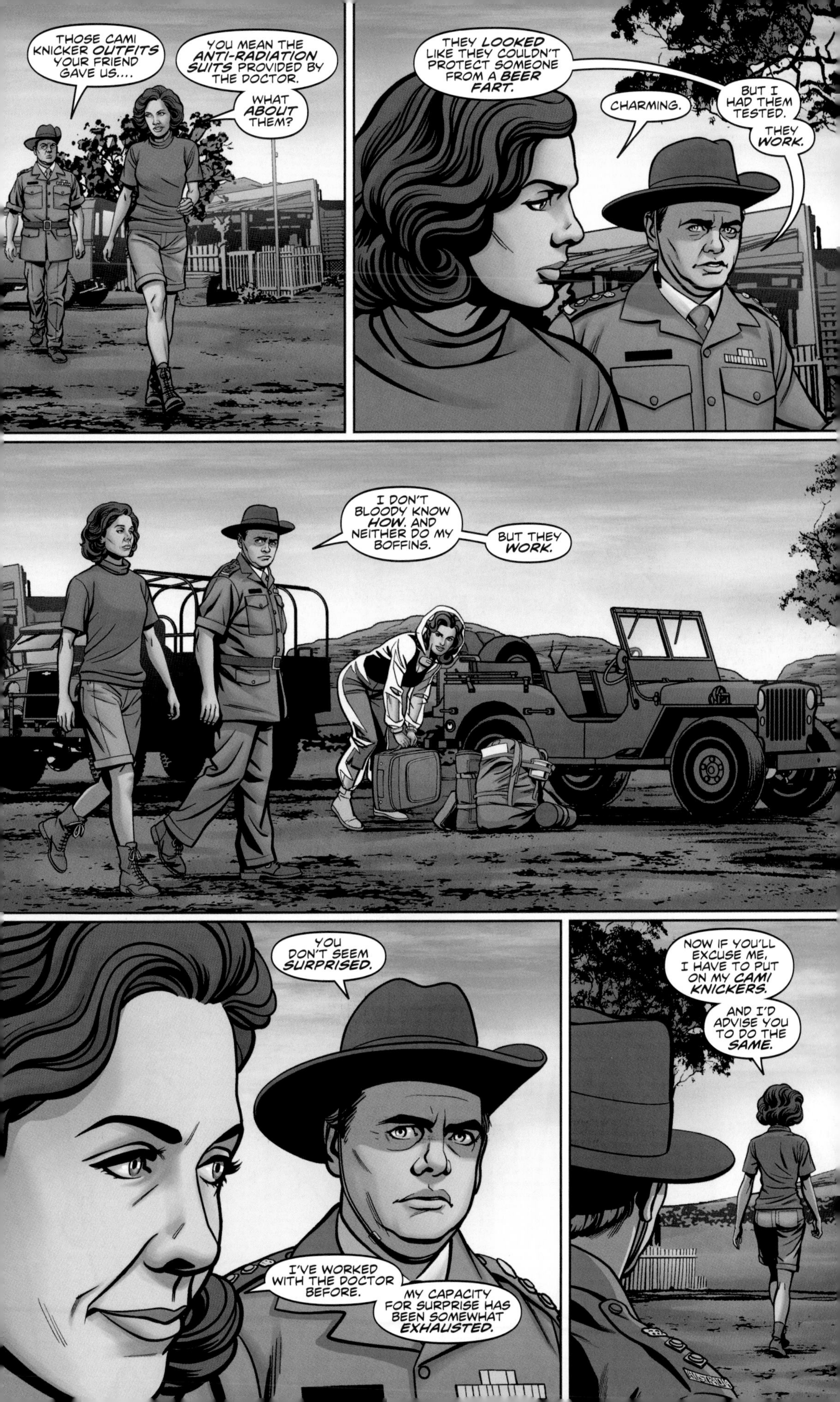

THOSE CAMI KNICKER OUTFITS YOUR FRIEND GAVE US....
YOU MEAN THE ANTI-RADIATION SUITS PROVIDED BY THE DOCTOR.
WHAT ABOUT THEM?
THEY LOOKED LIKE THEY COULDN'T PROTECT SOMEONE FROM A BEER FART.
CHARMING.
BUT I HAD THEM TESTED.
THEY WORK.
I DON'T BLOODY KNOW HOW. AND NEITHER DO MY BOFFINS.
BUT THEY WORK.
YOU DON'T SEEM SURPRISED.
I'VE WORKED WITH THE DOCTOR BEFORE.
MY CAPACITY FOR SURPRISE HAS BEEN SOMEWHAT EXHAUSTED.
NOW IF YOU'LL EXCUSE ME, I HAVE TO PUT ON MY CAMI KNICKERS.
AND I'D ADVISE YOU TO DO THE SAME.

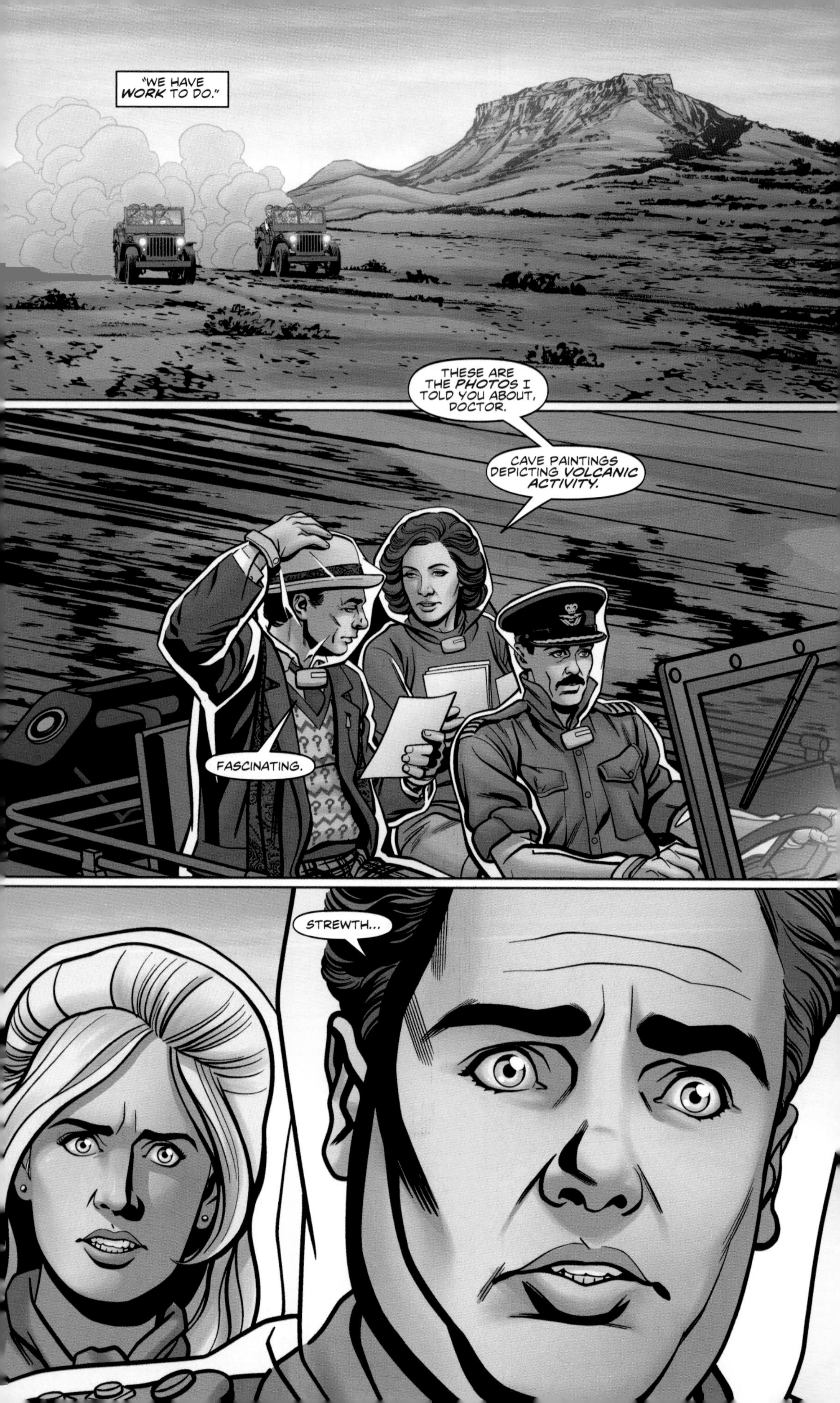

"WE HAVE WORK TO DO."
THESE ARE THE PHOTOS I TOLD YOU ABOUT, DOCTOR.
CAVE PAINTINGS DEPICTING VOLCANIC ACTIVITY.
FASCINATING.
STREWTH...

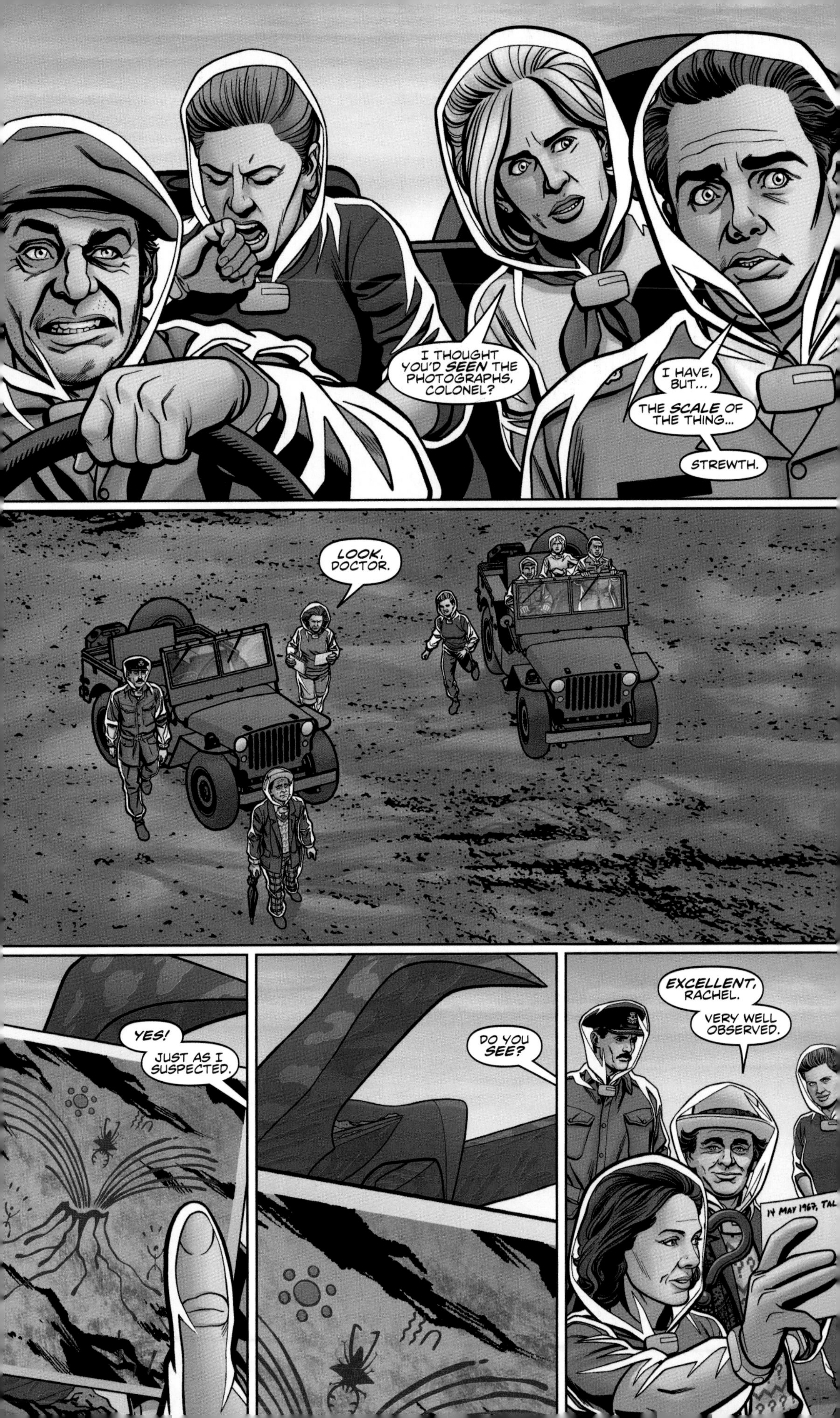
I THOUGHT YOU'D *SEEN* THE PHOTOGRAPHS, COLONEL?
I HAVE, BUT...
THE *SCALE* OF THE THING...
STREWTH.
LOOK, DOCTOR.
YES!
JUST AS I SUSPECTED.
DO YOU *SEE?*
EXCELLENT, RACHEL.
VERY WELL OBSERVED.
14 MAY 1967, TAL

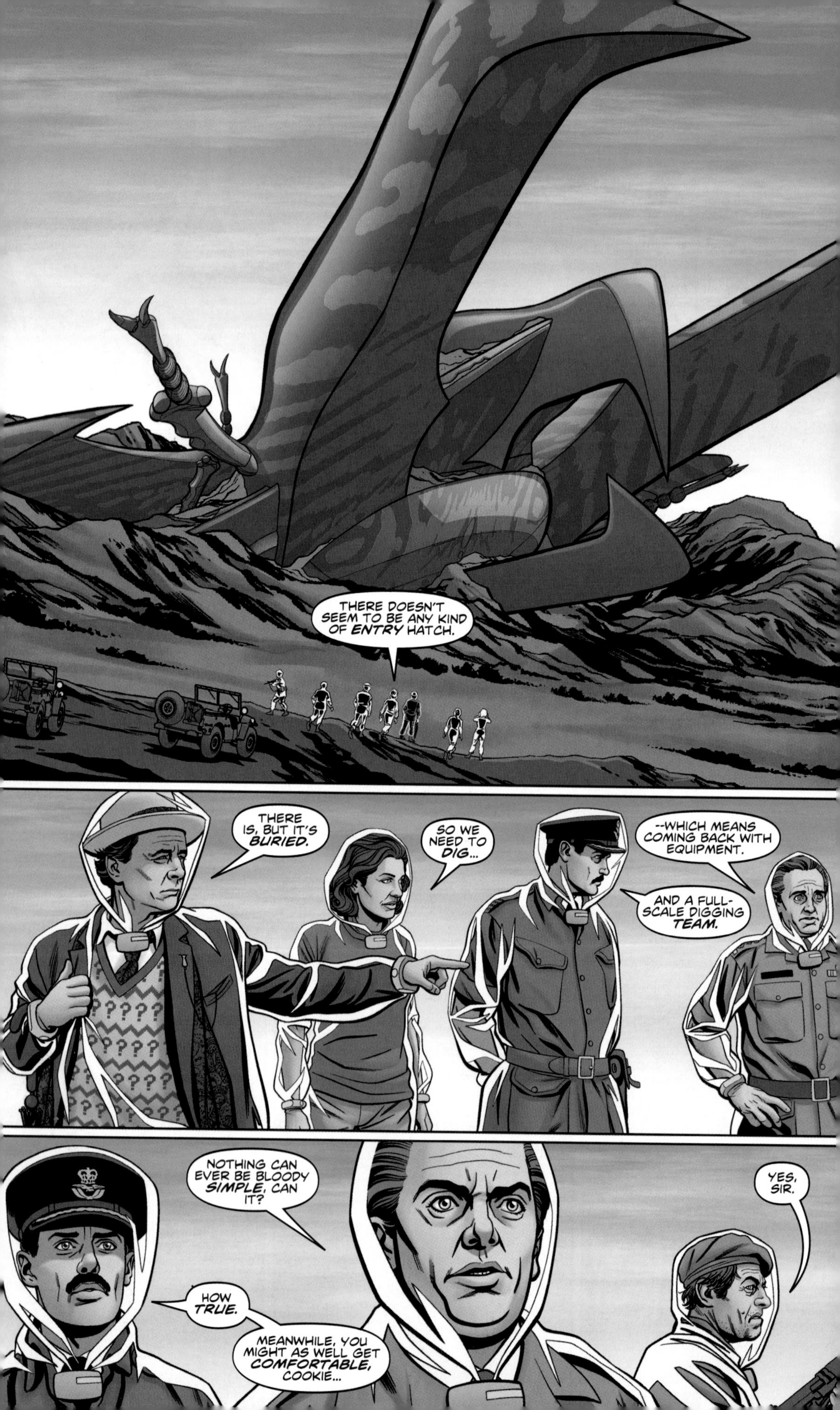
THERE DOESN'T SEEM TO BE ANY KIND OF ENTRY HATCH.
THERE IS, BUT IT'S BURIED.
SO WE NEED TO DIG...
--WHICH MEANS COMING BACK WITH EQUIPMENT.
AND A FULL-SCALE DIGGING TEAM.
NOTHING CAN EVER BE BLOODY SIMPLE, CAN IT?
HOW TRUE.
MEANWHILE, YOU MIGHT AS WELL GET COMFORTABLE, COOKIE...
YES, SIR.

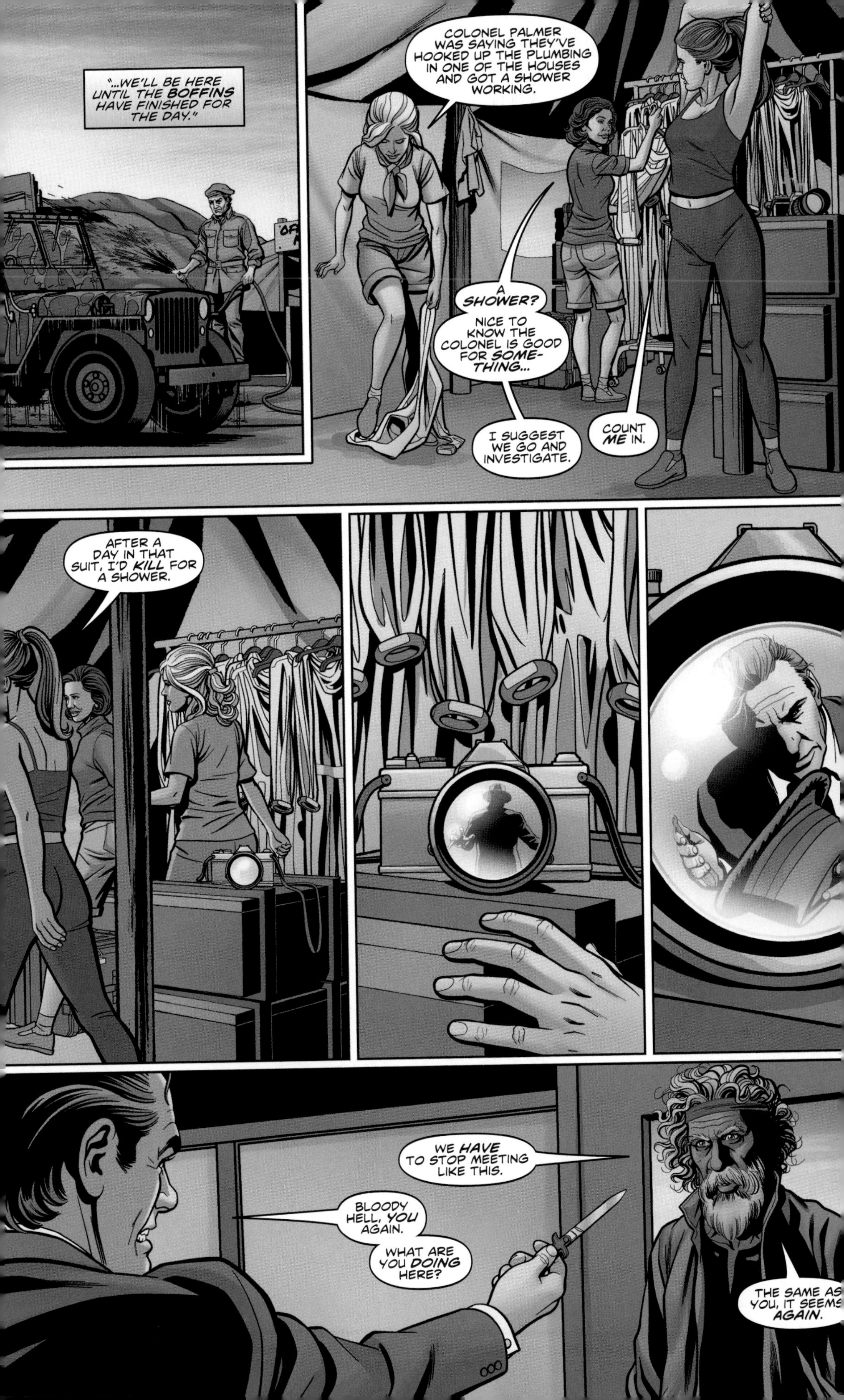
"...WE'LL BE HERE UNTIL THE BOFFINS HAVE FINISHED FOR THE DAY."
COLONEL PALMER WAS SAYING THEY'VE HOOKED UP THE PLUMBING IN ONE OF THE HOUSES AND GOT A SHOWER WORKING.
A SHOWER?
NICE TO KNOW THE COLONEL IS GOOD FOR SOME-THING...
I SUGGEST WE GO AND INVESTIGATE.
COUNT ME IN.
AFTER A DAY IN THAT SUIT, I'D KILL FOR A SHOWER.
WE HAVE TO STOP MEETING LIKE THIS.
BLOODY HELL, YOU AGAIN.
WHAT ARE YOU DOING HERE?
THE SAME AS YOU, IT SEEMS AGAIN.

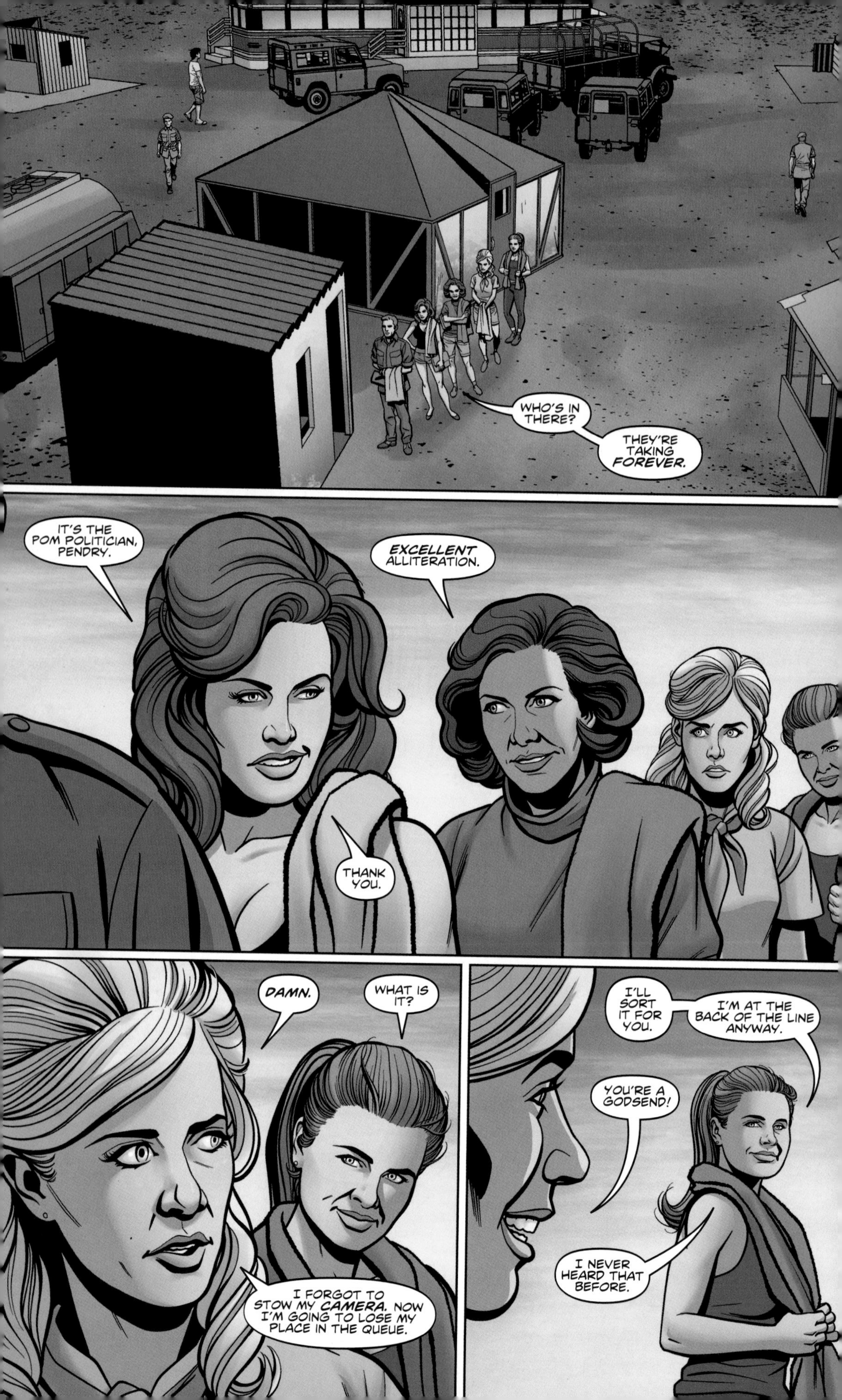
WHO'S IN THERE?
THEY'RE TAKING *FOREVER.*
IT'S THE POM POLITICIAN, PENDRY.
EXCELLENT ALLITERATION.
THANK YOU.
DAMN.
WHAT IS IT?
I FORGOT TO STOW MY *CAMERA.* NOW I'M GOING TO LOSE MY PLACE IN THE QUEUE.
I'LL SORT IT FOR YOU.
I'M AT THE BACK OF THE LINE ANYWAY.
YOU'RE A GODSEND!
I NEVER HEARD THAT BEFORE.

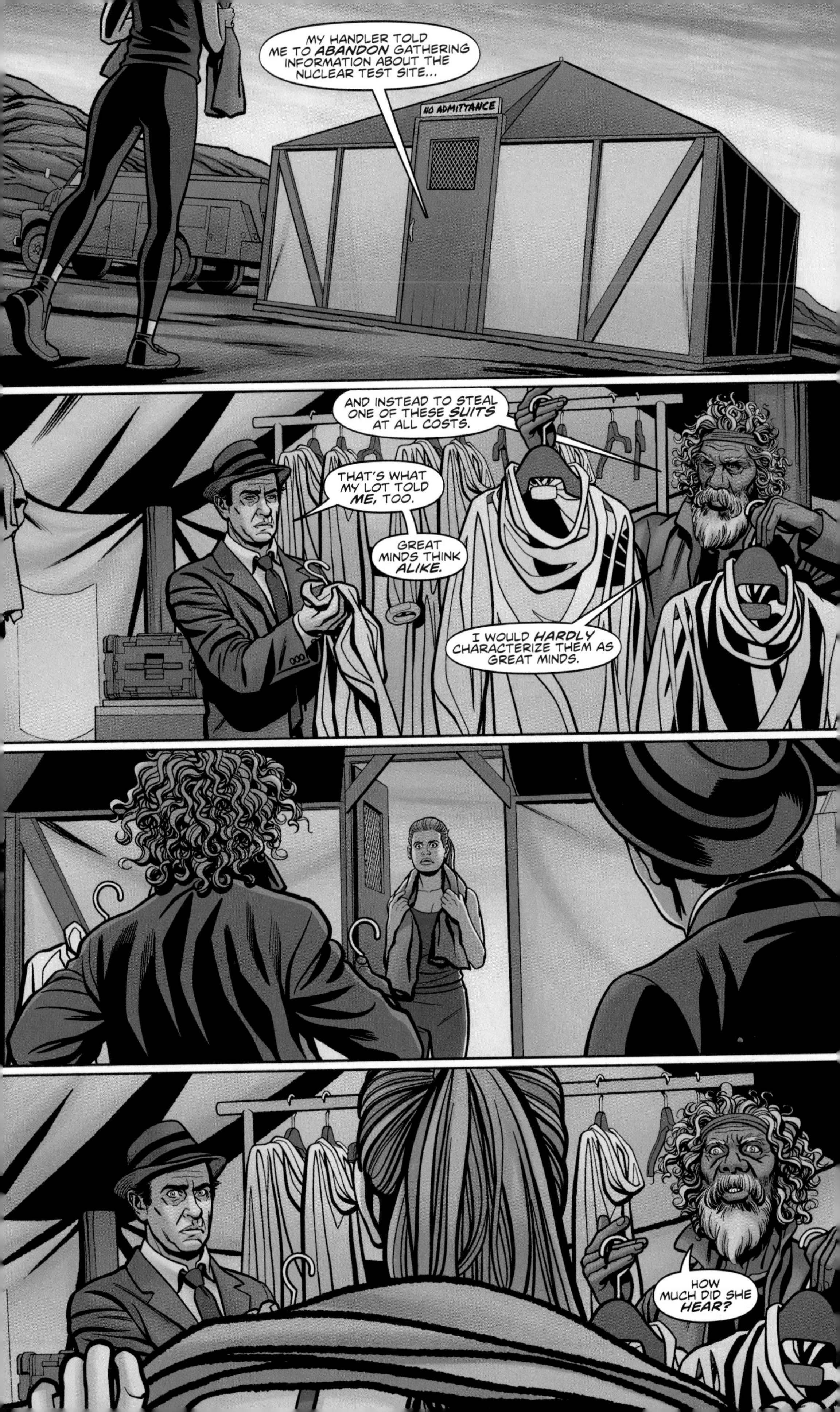

MY HANDLER TOLD ME TO ABANDON GATHERING INFORMATION ABOUT THE NUCLEAR TEST SITE...
NO ADMITTANCE
AND INSTEAD TO STEAL ONE OF THESE SUITS AT ALL COSTS.
THAT'S WHAT MY LOT TOLD ME, TOO.
GREAT MINDS THINK ALIKE.
I WOULD HARDLY CHARACTERIZE THEM AS GREAT MINDS.
HOW MUCH DID SHE HEAR?

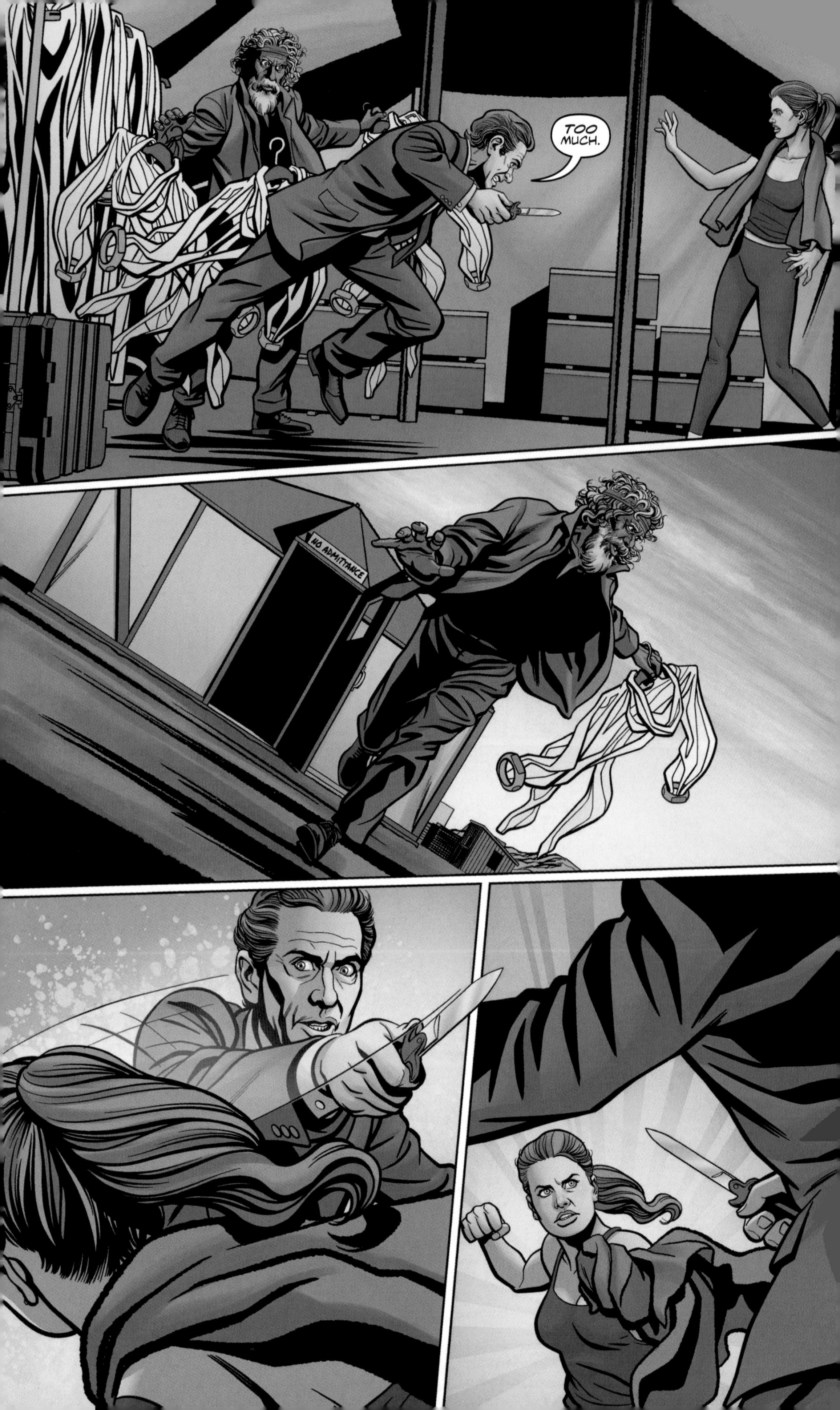
TOO MUCH.
NO ADMITTANCE

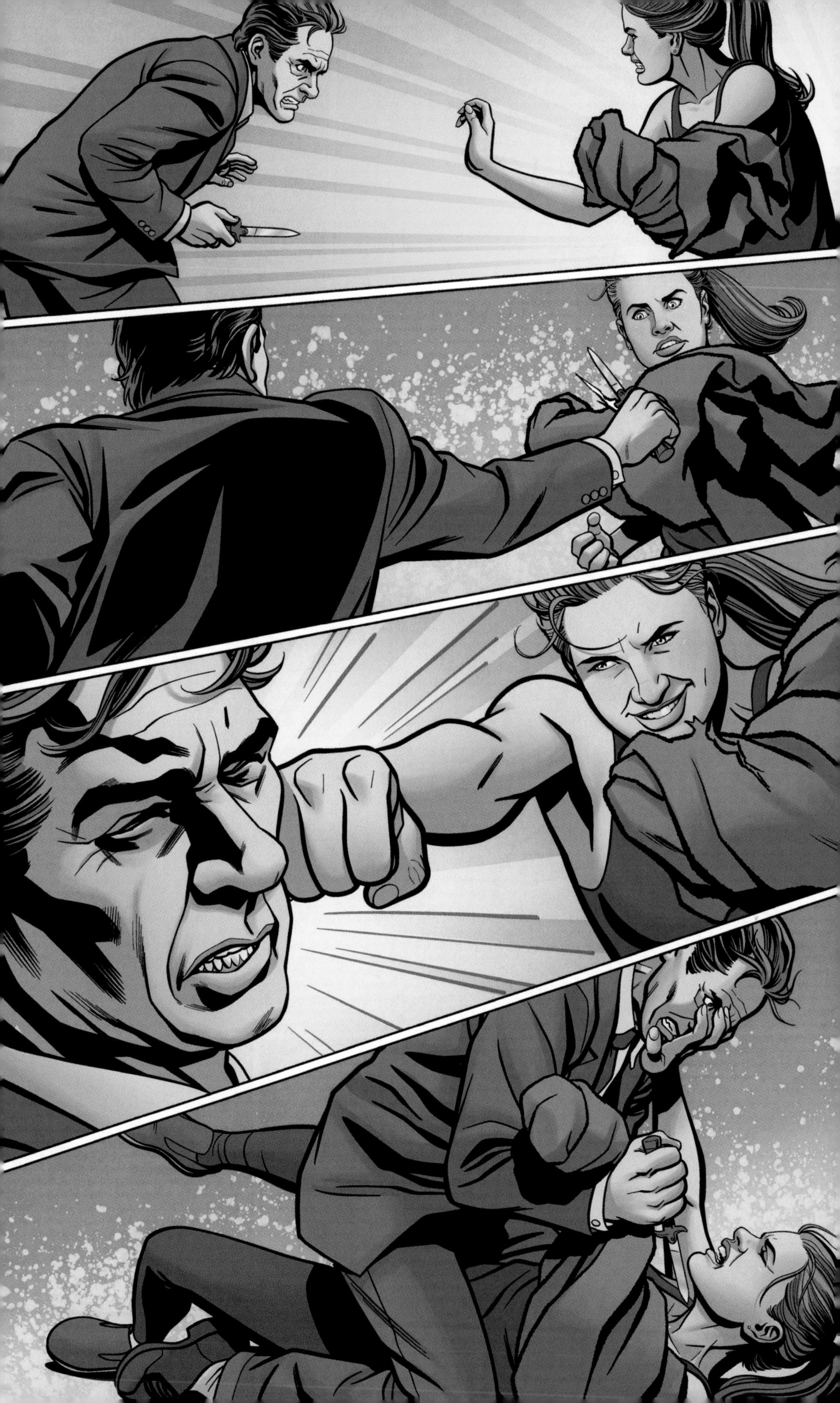

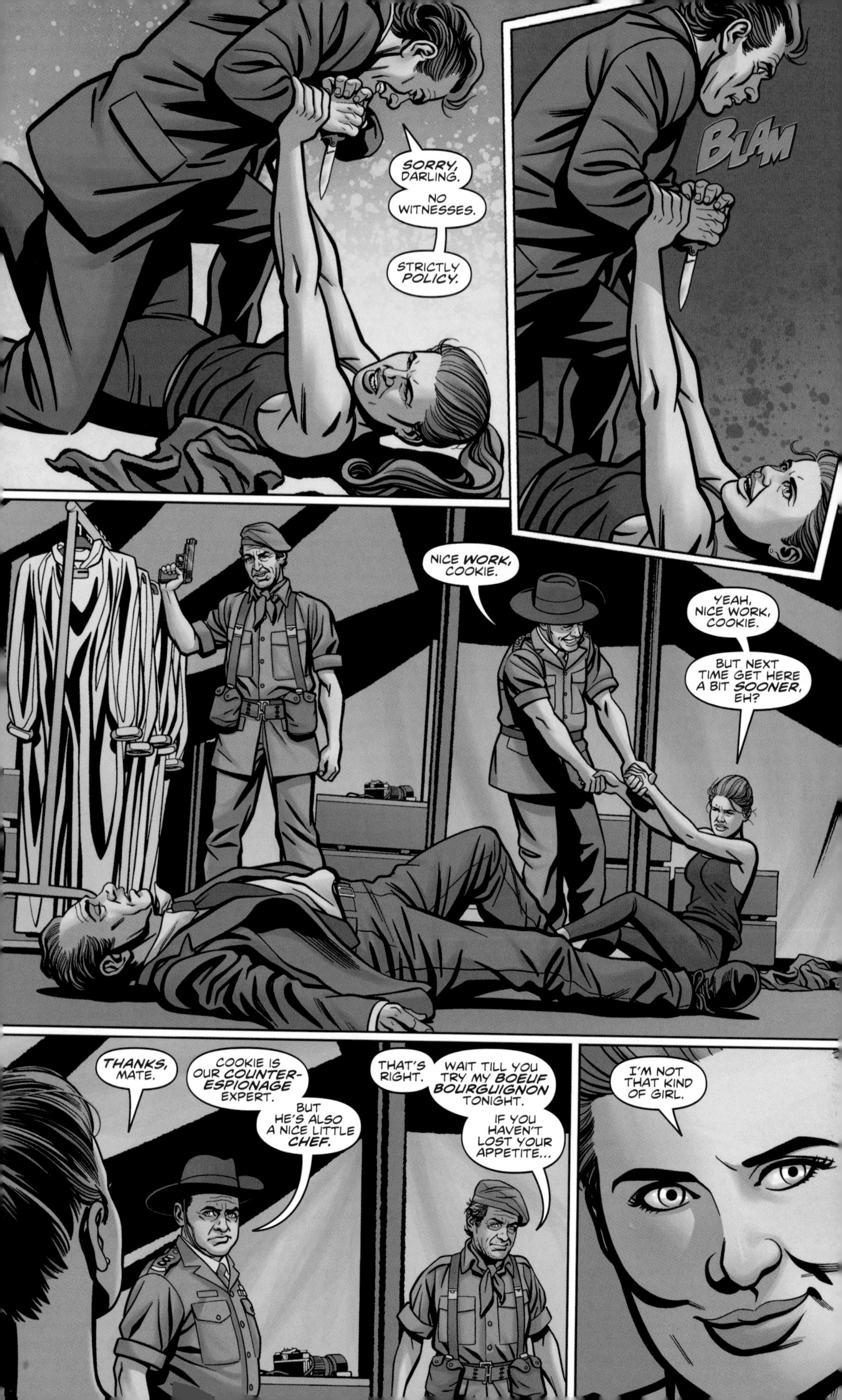
SORRY, DARLING.
NO WITNESSES.
STRICTLY POLICY.
BLAM
NICE WORK, COOKIE.
YEAH, NICE WORK, COOKIE.
BUT NEXT TIME GET HERE A BIT SOONER, EH?
THANKS, MATE.
COOKIE IS OUR COUNTER-ESPIONAGE EXPERT.
BUT HE'S ALSO A NICE LITTLE CHEF.
THAT'S RIGHT.
WAIT TILL YOU TRY MY BOEUF BOURGUIGNON TONIGHT.
IF YOU HAVEN'T LOST YOUR APPETITE...
I'M NOT THAT KIND OF GIRL.

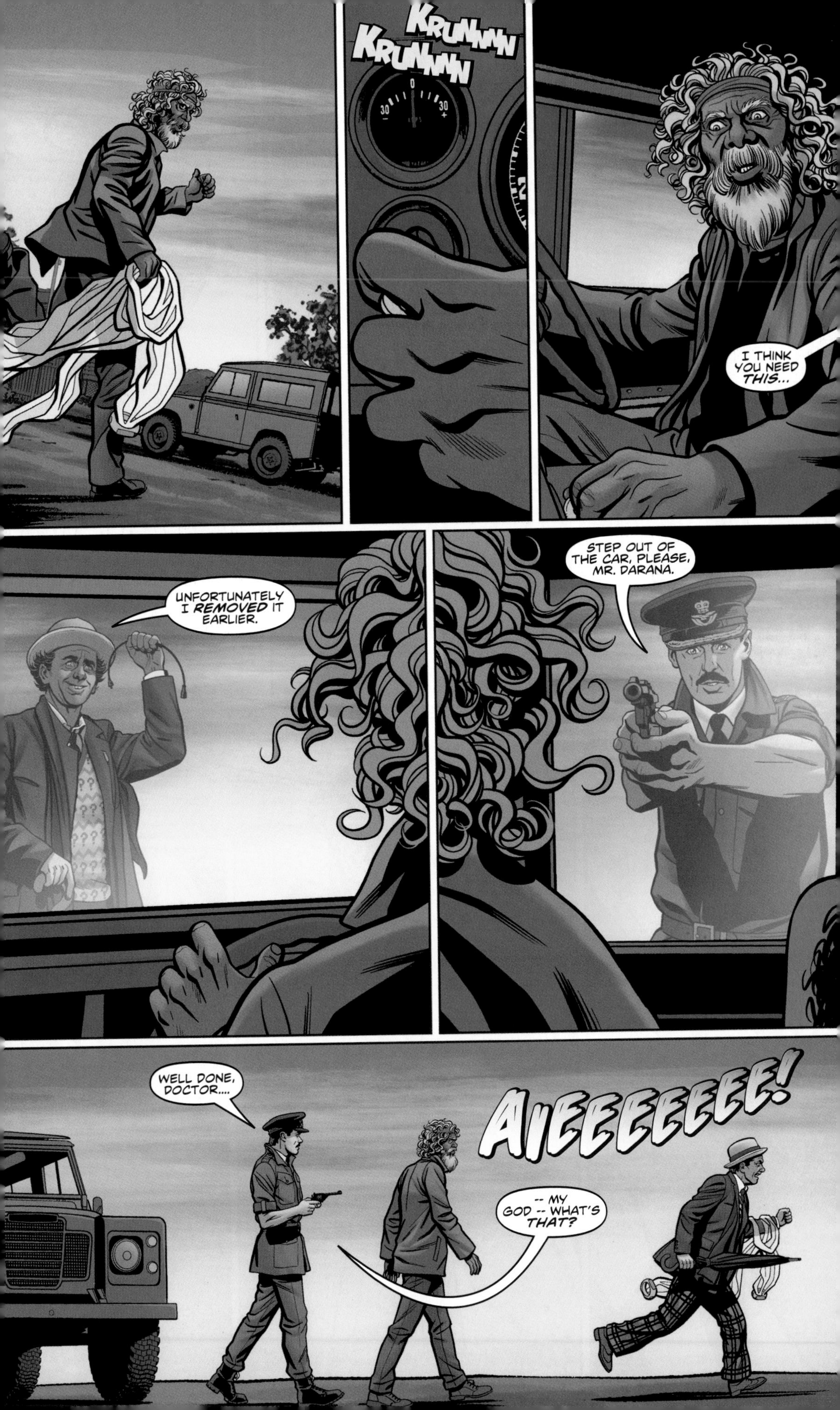
KRUNNNN
KRUNNNN
I THINK YOU NEED THIS...
UNFORTUNATELY I REMOVED IT EARLIER.
STEP OUT OF THE CAR, PLEASE, MR. DARANA.
WELL DONE, DOCTOR....
AIEEEEEEE!
-- MY GOD -- WHAT'S THAT?

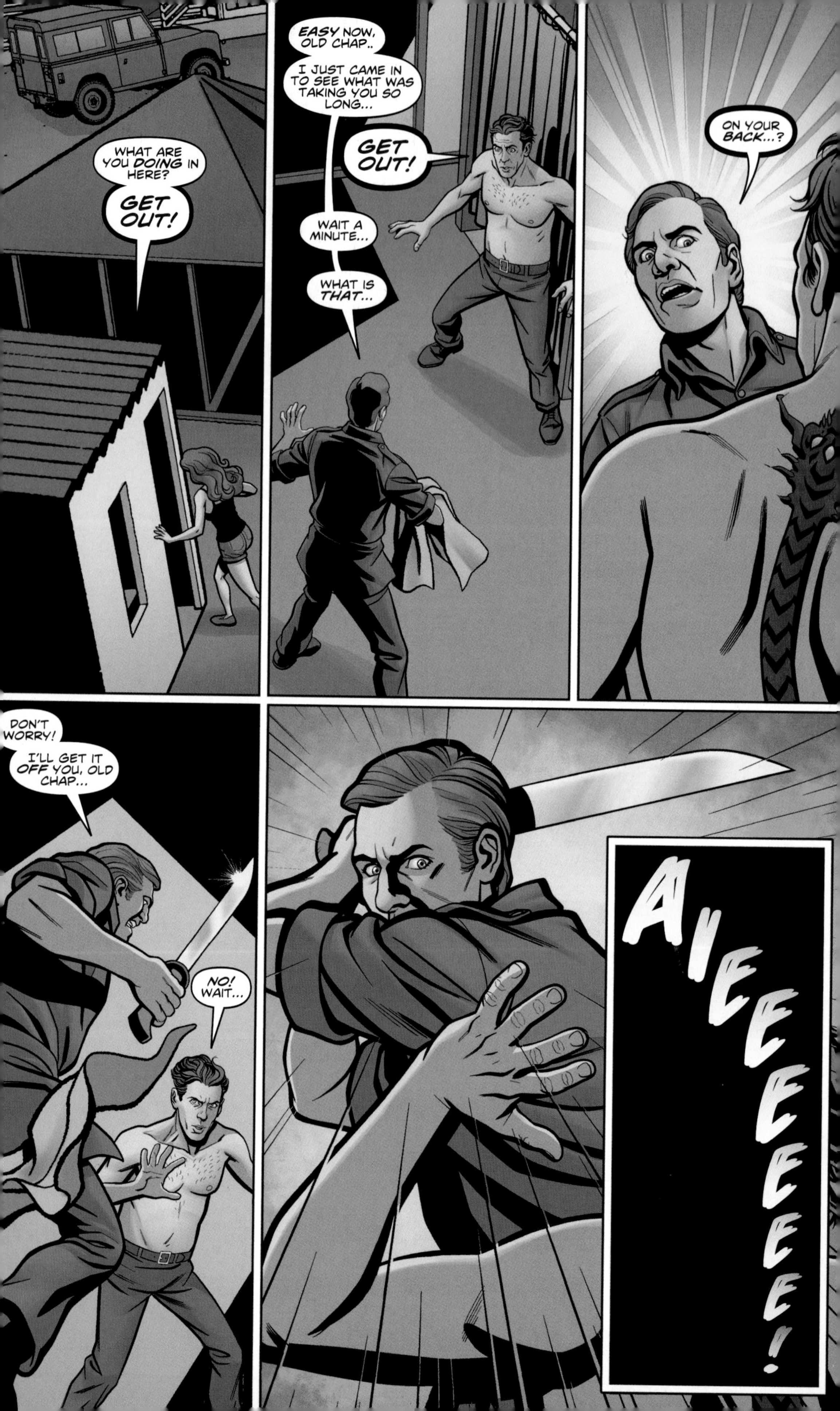
WHAT ARE YOU DOING IN HERE?
GET OUT!
EASY NOW, OLD CHAP..
I JUST CAME IN TO SEE WHAT WAS TAKING YOU SO LONG...
GET OUT!
WAIT A MINUTE...
WHAT IS THAT...
ON YOUR BACK...?
DON'T WORRY!
I'LL GET IT OFF YOU, OLD CHAP...
NO! WAIT...
AIEEEEEEEE!

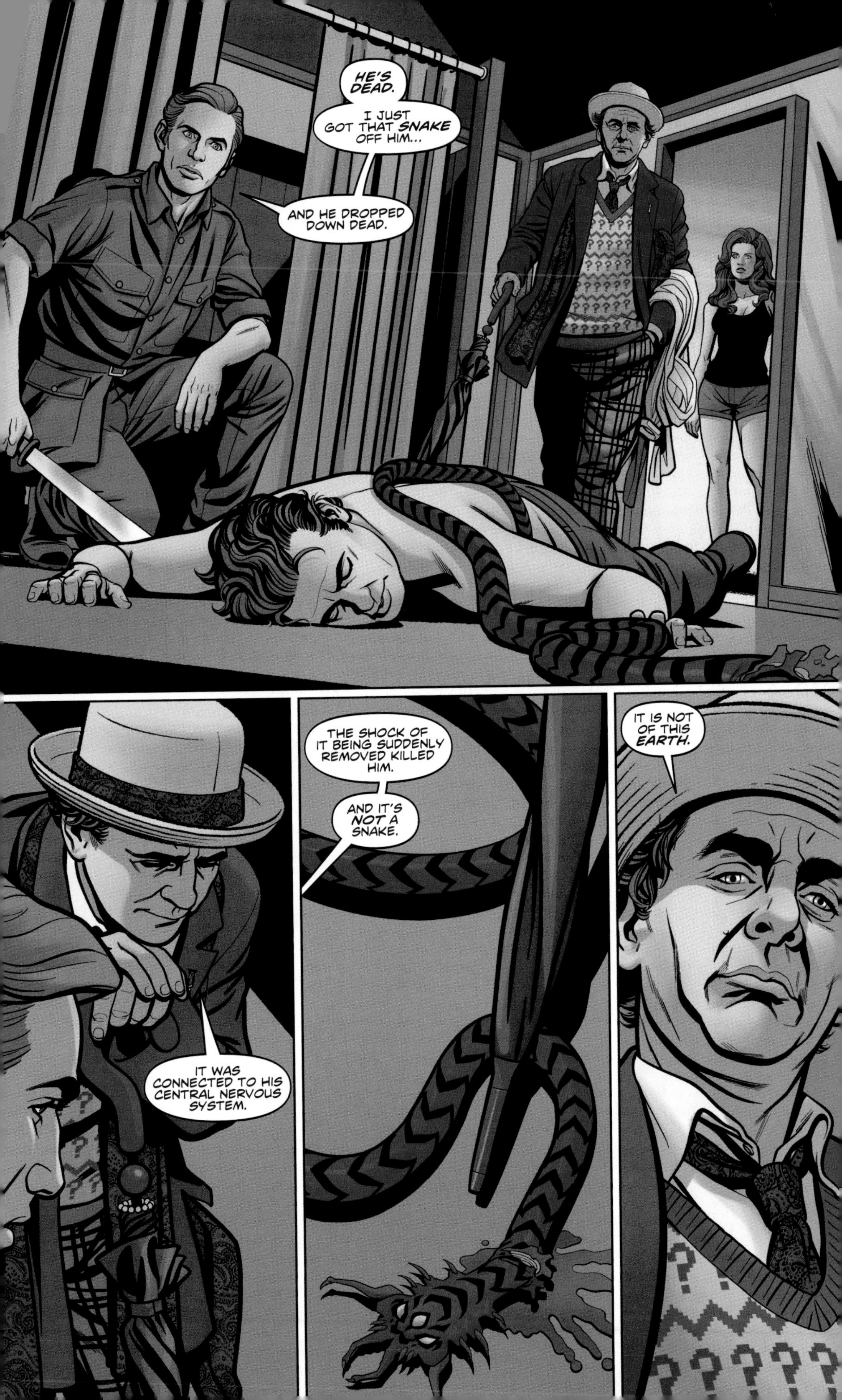
HE'S DEAD.
I JUST GOT THAT SNAKE OFF HIM...
AND HE DROPPED DOWN DEAD.
IT WAS CONNECTED TO HIS CENTRAL NERVOUS SYSTEM.
THE SHOCK OF IT BEING SUDDENLY REMOVED KILLED HIM.
AND IT'S NOT A SNAKE.
IT IS NOT OF THIS EARTH.

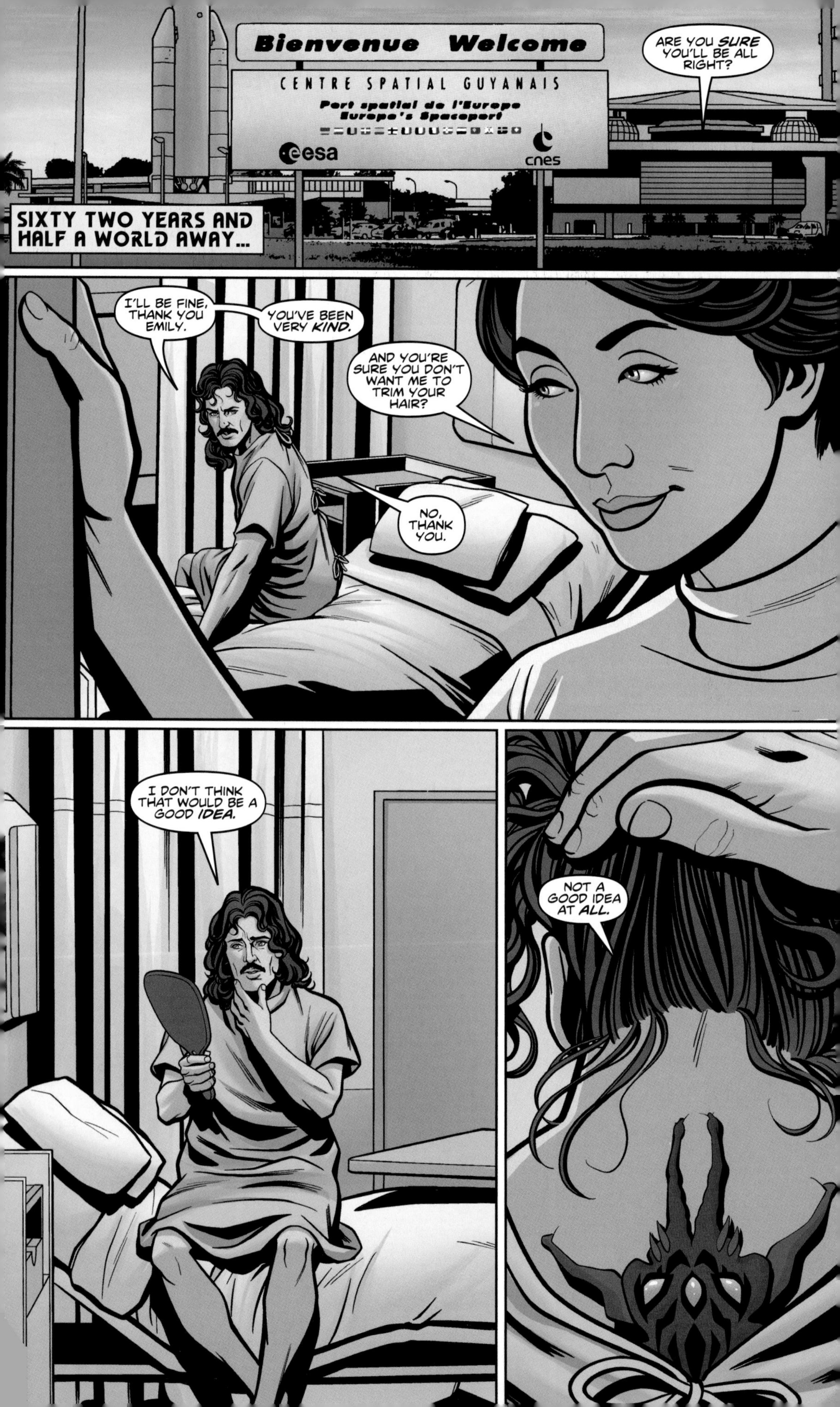
Bienvenue Welcome
CENTRE SPATIAL GUYANAIS
Port spatial de l'Europe
Europe's Spaceport
esa
cnes
SIXTY TWO YEARS AND HALF A WORLD AWAY...
ARE YOU SURE YOU'LL BE ALL RIGHT?
I'LL BE FINE, THANK YOU EMILY.
YOU'VE BEEN VERY KIND.
AND YOU'RE SURE YOU DON'T WANT ME TO TRIM YOUR HAIR?
NO, THANK YOU.
I DON'T THINK THAT WOULD BE A GOOD IDEA.
NOT A GOOD IDEA AT ALL.

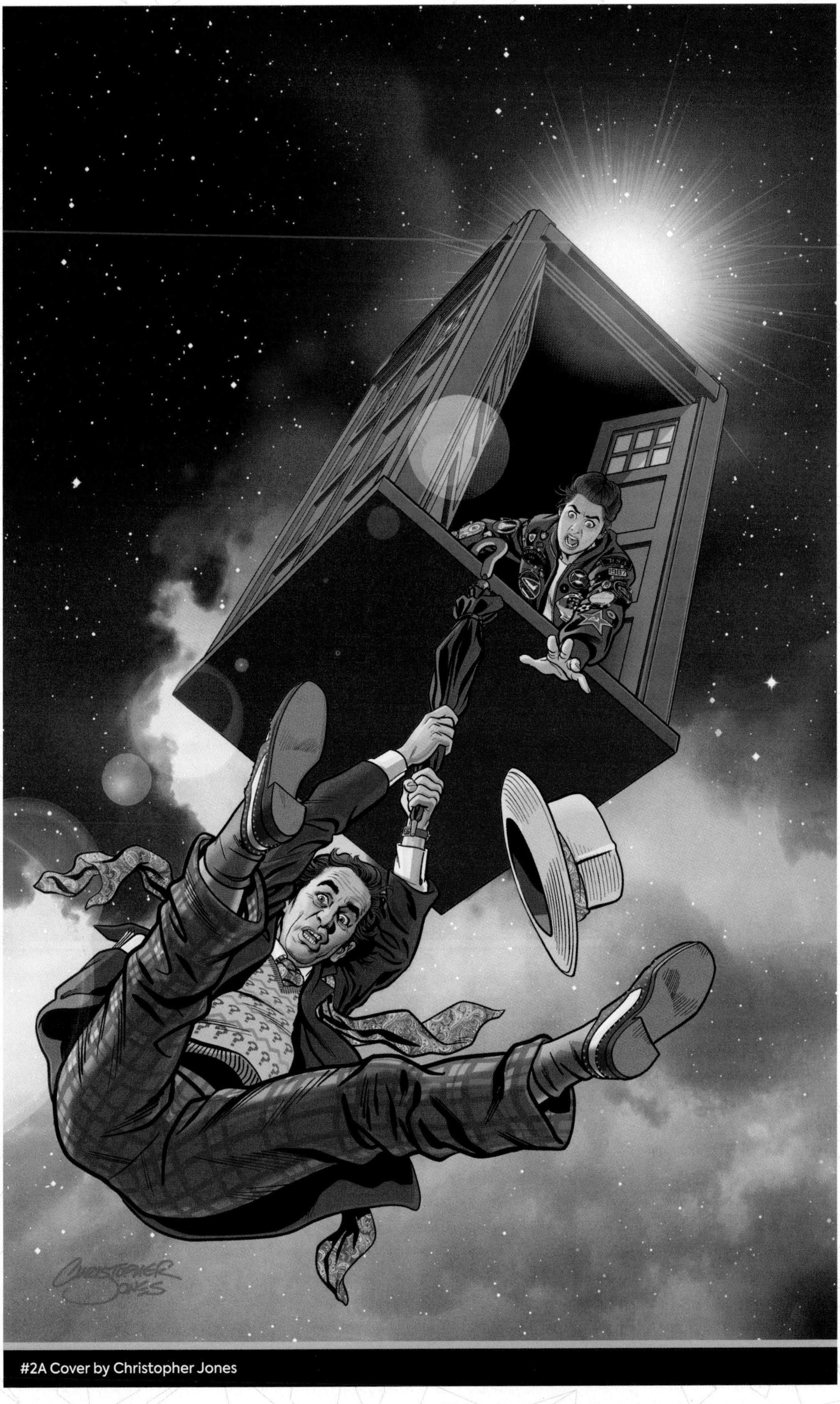
CHRISTOPHER JONES

#2A Cover by Christopher Jones

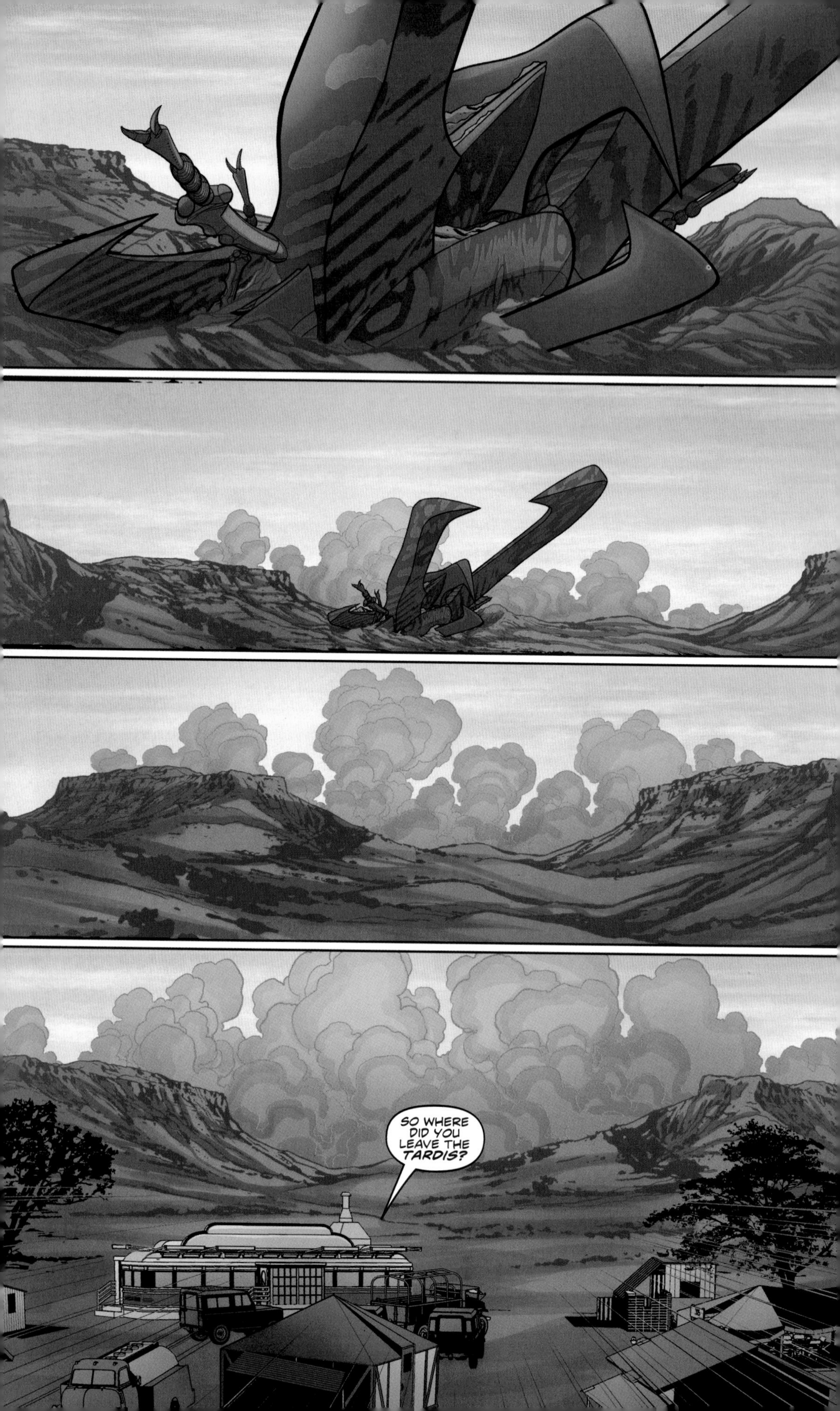
SO WHERE DID YOU LEAVE THE TARDIS?

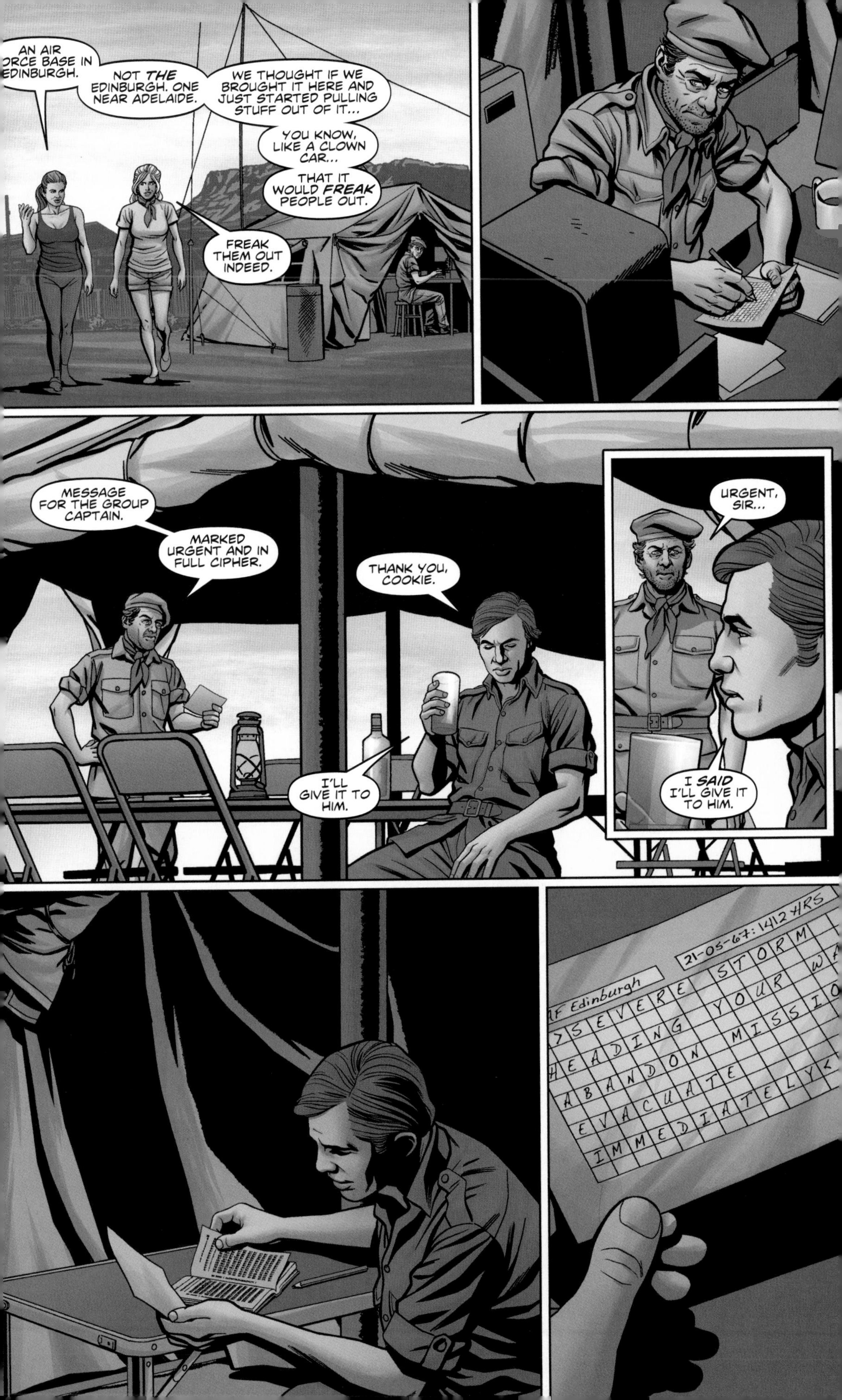
AN AIR FORCE BASE IN EDINBURGH.
NOT THE EDINBURGH. ONE NEAR ADELAIDE.
WE THOUGHT IF WE BROUGHT IT HERE AND JUST STARTED PULLING STUFF OUT OF IT...
YOU KNOW, LIKE A CLOWN CAR...
THAT IT WOULD FREAK PEOPLE OUT.
FREAK THEM OUT INDEED.
MESSAGE FOR THE GROUP CAPTAIN.
MARKED URGENT AND IN FULL CIPHER.
THANK YOU, COOKIE.
I'LL GIVE IT TO HIM.
URGENT, SIR...
I SAID I'LL GIVE IT TO HIM.
21-05-67: 1412 HRS
AF Edinburgh
SEVERE STORM
HEADING YOUR WA
ABANDON MISSIO
EVACUATE
IMMEDIATELY

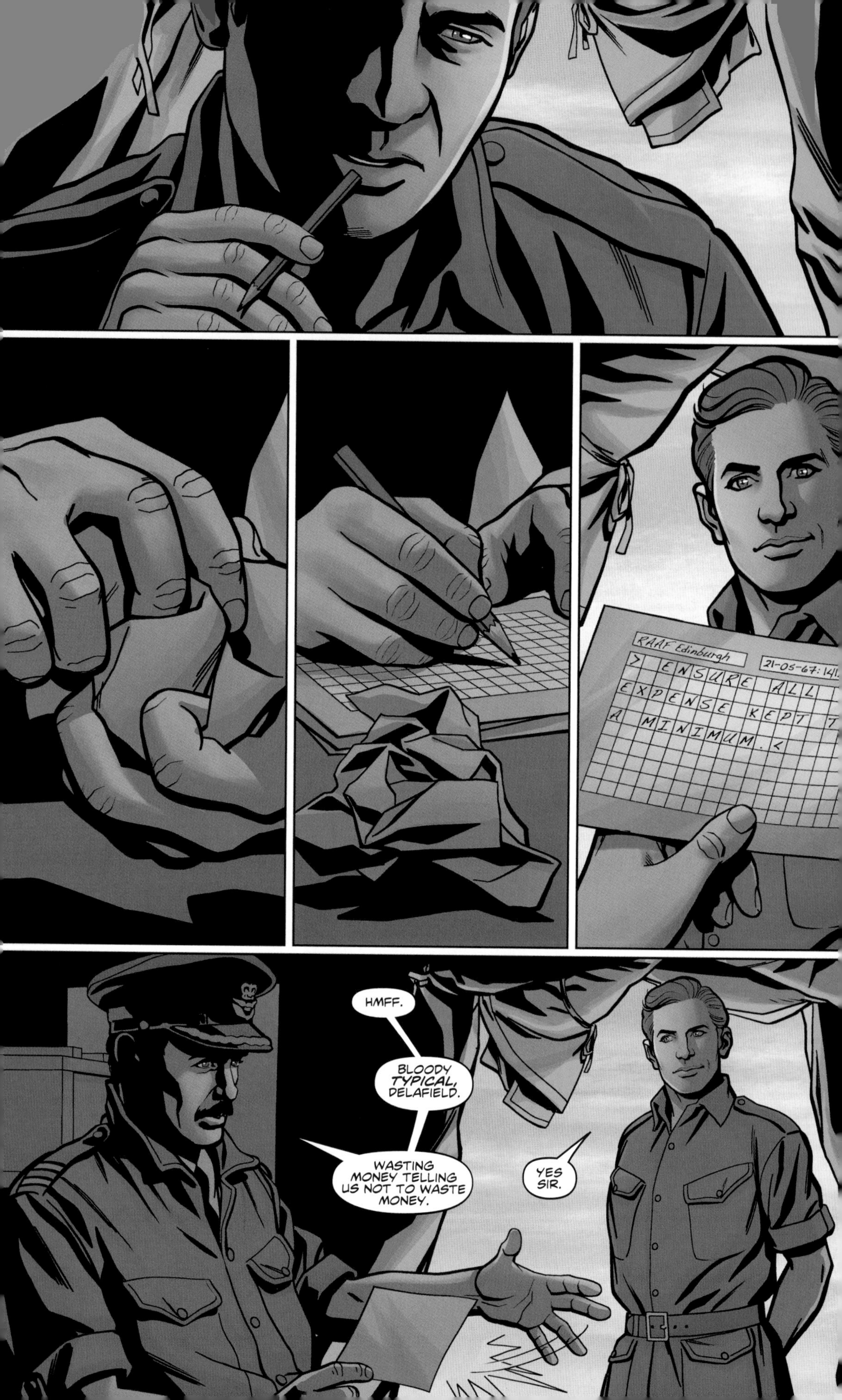
RAAF Edinburgh
21-05-67:14
> ENSURE ALL
EXPENSE KEPT
A MINIMUM. <
HMFF.
BLOODY *TYPICAL*, DELAFIELD.
WASTING MONEY TELLING US NOT TO WASTE MONEY.
YES SIR.

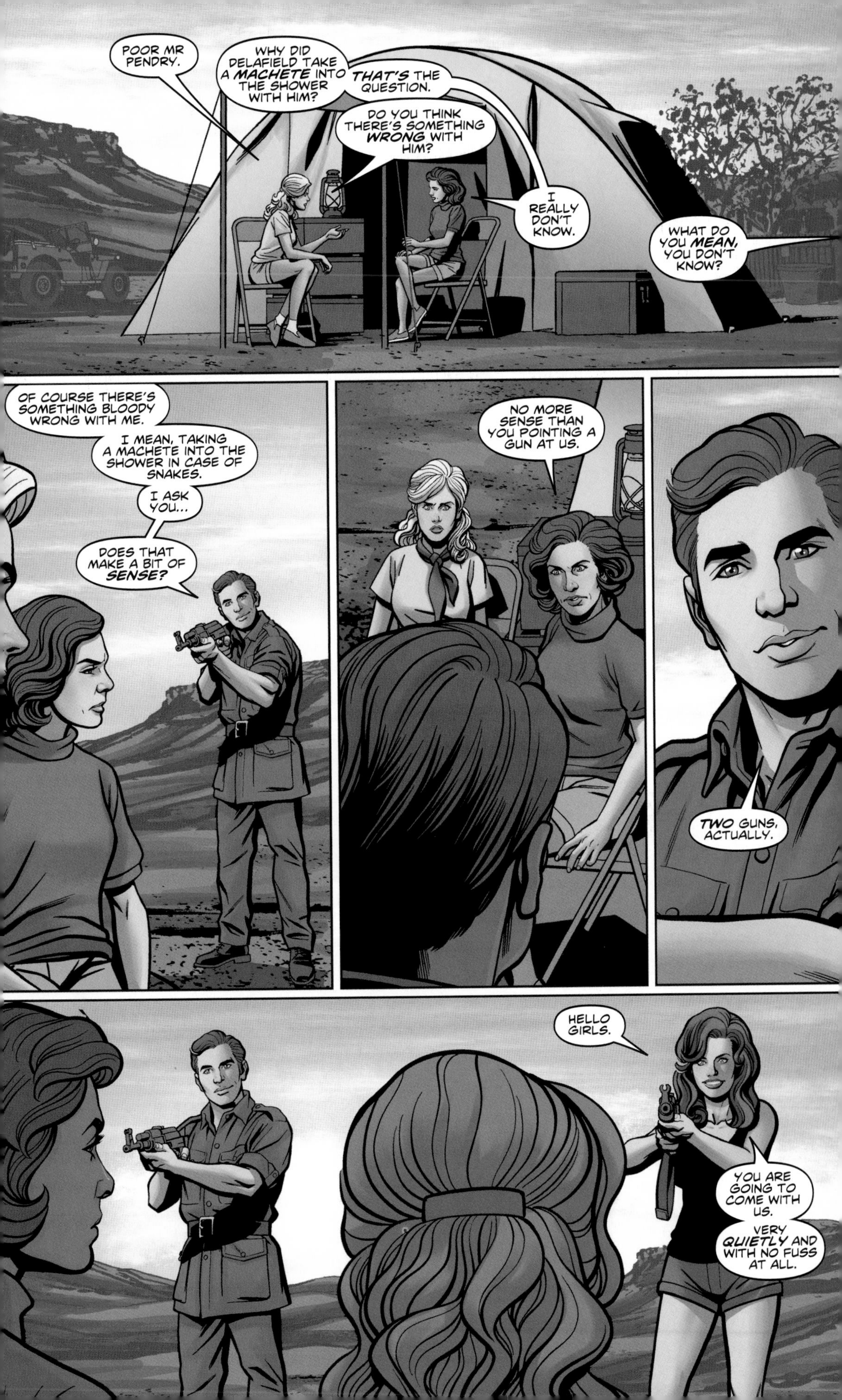
POOR MR PENDRY.
WHY DID DELAFIELD TAKE A MACHETE INTO THE SHOWER WITH HIM?
THAT'S THE QUESTION.
DO YOU THINK THERE'S SOMETHING WRONG WITH HIM?
I REALLY DON'T KNOW.
WHAT DO YOU MEAN, YOU DON'T KNOW?
OF COURSE THERE'S SOMETHING BLOODY WRONG WITH ME.
I MEAN, TAKING A MACHETE INTO THE SHOWER IN CASE OF SNAKES.
I ASK YOU...
DOES THAT MAKE A BIT OF SENSE?
NO MORE SENSE THAN YOU POINTING A GUN AT US.
TWO GUNS, ACTUALLY.
HELLO GIRLS.
YOU ARE GOING TO COME WITH US.
VERY QUIETLY AND WITH NO FUSS AT ALL.

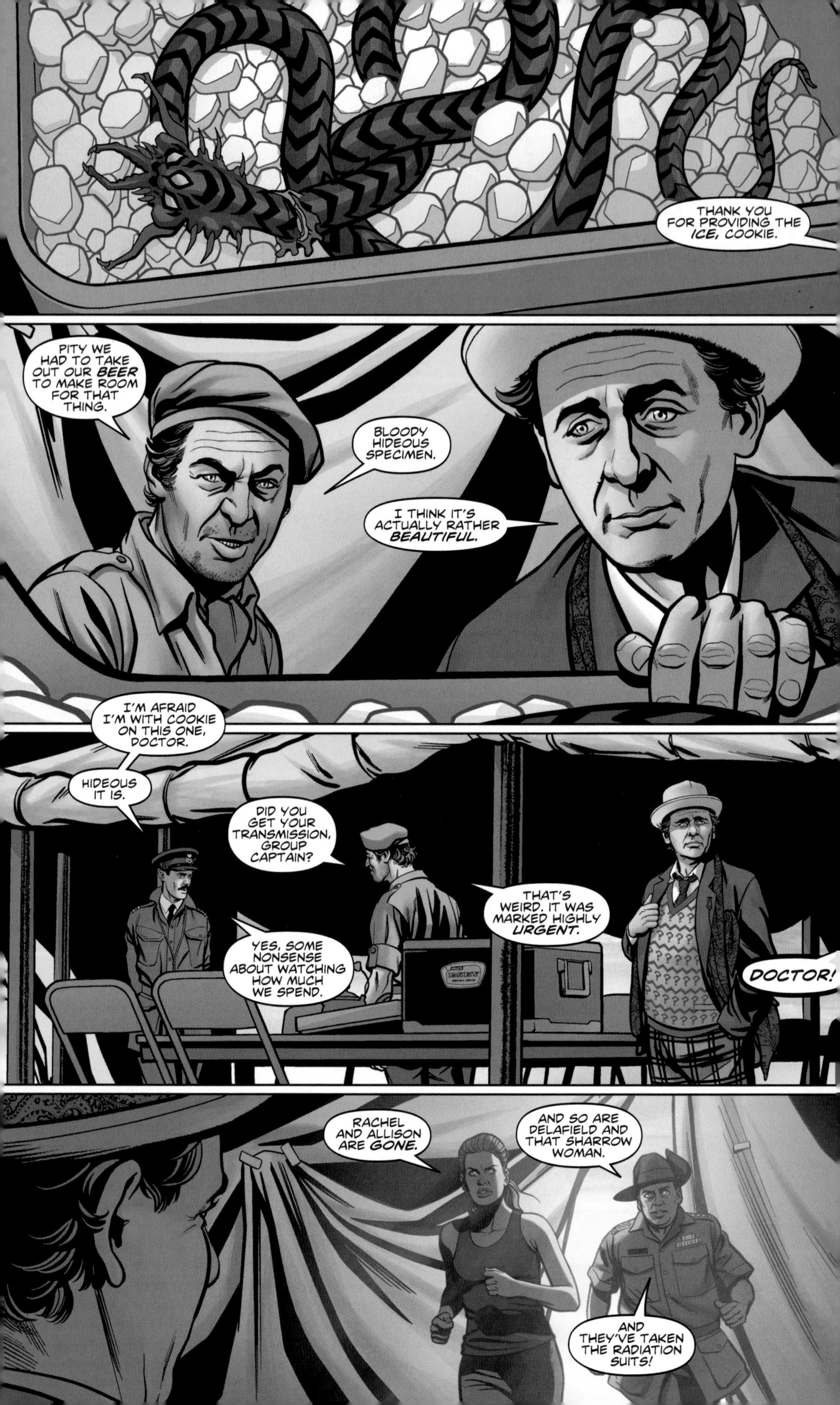
THANK YOU FOR PROVIDING THE ICE, COOKIE.
PITY WE HAD TO TAKE OUT OUR BEER TO MAKE ROOM FOR THAT THING.
BLOODY HIDEOUS SPECIMEN.
I THINK IT'S ACTUALLY RATHER BEAUTIFUL.
I'M AFRAID I'M WITH COOKIE ON THIS ONE, DOCTOR.
HIDEOUS IT IS.
DID YOU GET YOUR TRANSMISSION, GROUP CAPTAIN?
YES, SOME NONSENSE ABOUT WATCHING HOW MUCH WE SPEND.
THAT'S WEIRD. IT WAS MARKED HIGHLY URGENT.
DOCTOR!
RACHEL AND ALLISON ARE GONE.
AND SO ARE DELAFIELD AND THAT SHARROW WOMAN.
AND THEY'VE TAKEN THE RADIATION SUITS!

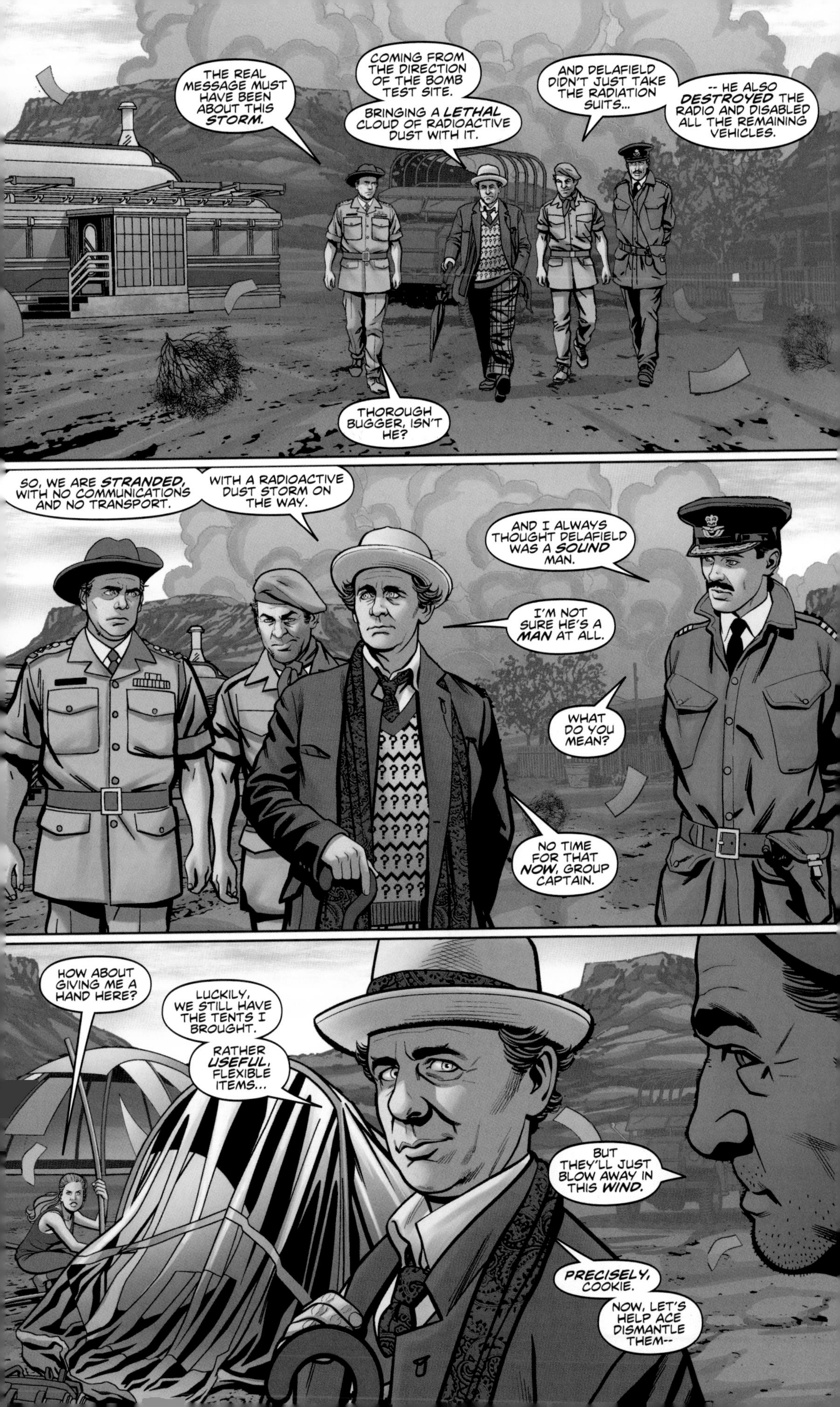
THE REAL MESSAGE MUST HAVE BEEN ABOUT THIS STORM.
COMING FROM THE DIRECTION OF THE BOMB TEST SITE.
BRINGING A LETHAL CLOUD OF RADIOACTIVE DUST WITH IT.
AND DELAFIELD DIDN'T JUST TAKE THE RADIATION SUITS...
-- HE ALSO DESTROYED THE RADIO AND DISABLED ALL THE REMAINING VEHICLES.
THOROUGH BUGGER, ISN'T HE?
SO, WE ARE STRANDED, WITH NO COMMUNICATIONS AND NO TRANSPORT.
WITH A RADIOACTIVE DUST STORM ON THE WAY.
AND I ALWAYS THOUGHT DELAFIELD WAS A SOUND MAN.
I'M NOT SURE HE'S A MAN AT ALL.
WHAT DO YOU MEAN?
NO TIME FOR THAT NOW, GROUP CAPTAIN.
HOW ABOUT GIVING ME A HAND HERE?
LUCKILY, WE STILL HAVE THE TENTS I BROUGHT.
RATHER USEFUL, FLEXIBLE ITEMS...
BUT THEY'LL JUST BLOW AWAY IN THIS WIND.
PRECISELY, COOKIE.
NOW, LET'S HELP ACE DISMANTLE THEM--

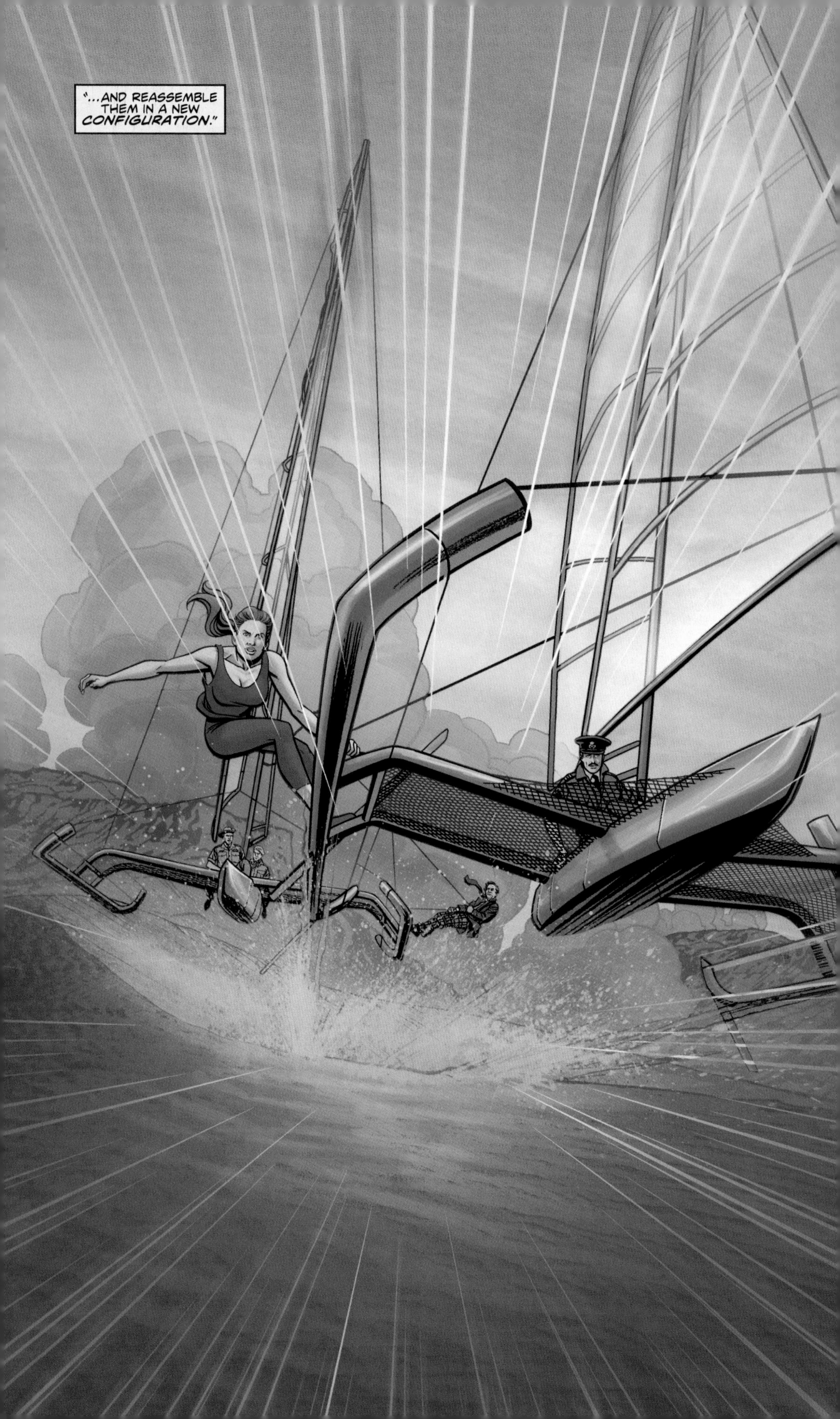
"...AND REASSEMBLE THEM IN A NEW CONFIGURATION."

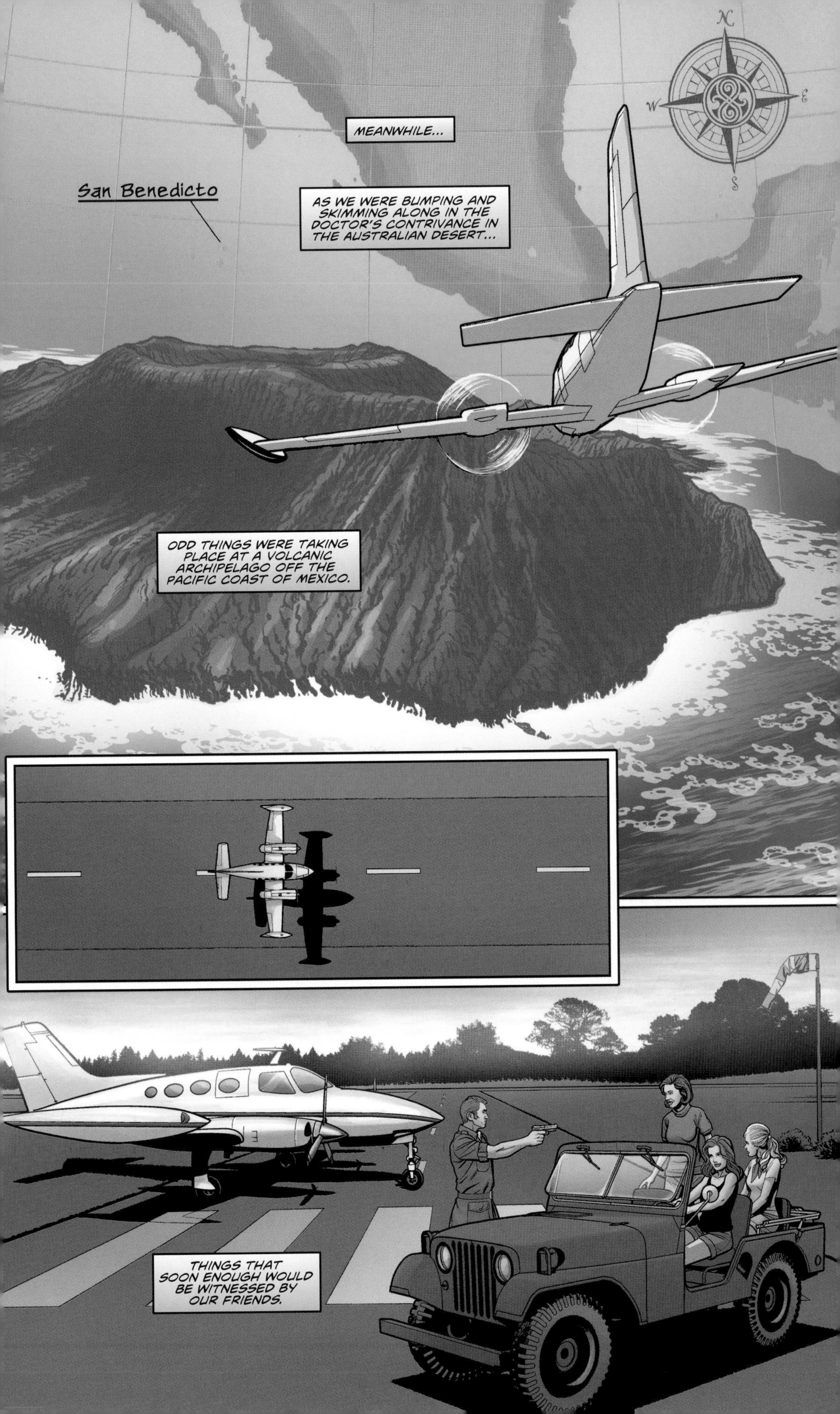
MEANWHILE...
San Benedicto
AS WE WERE BUMPING AND SKIMMING ALONG IN THE DOCTOR'S CONTRIVANCE IN THE AUSTRALIAN DESERT...
ODD THINGS WERE TAKING PLACE AT A VOLCANIC ARCHIPELAGO OFF THE PACIFIC COAST OF MEXICO.
THINGS THAT SOON ENOUGH WOULD BE WITNESSED BY OUR FRIENDS.

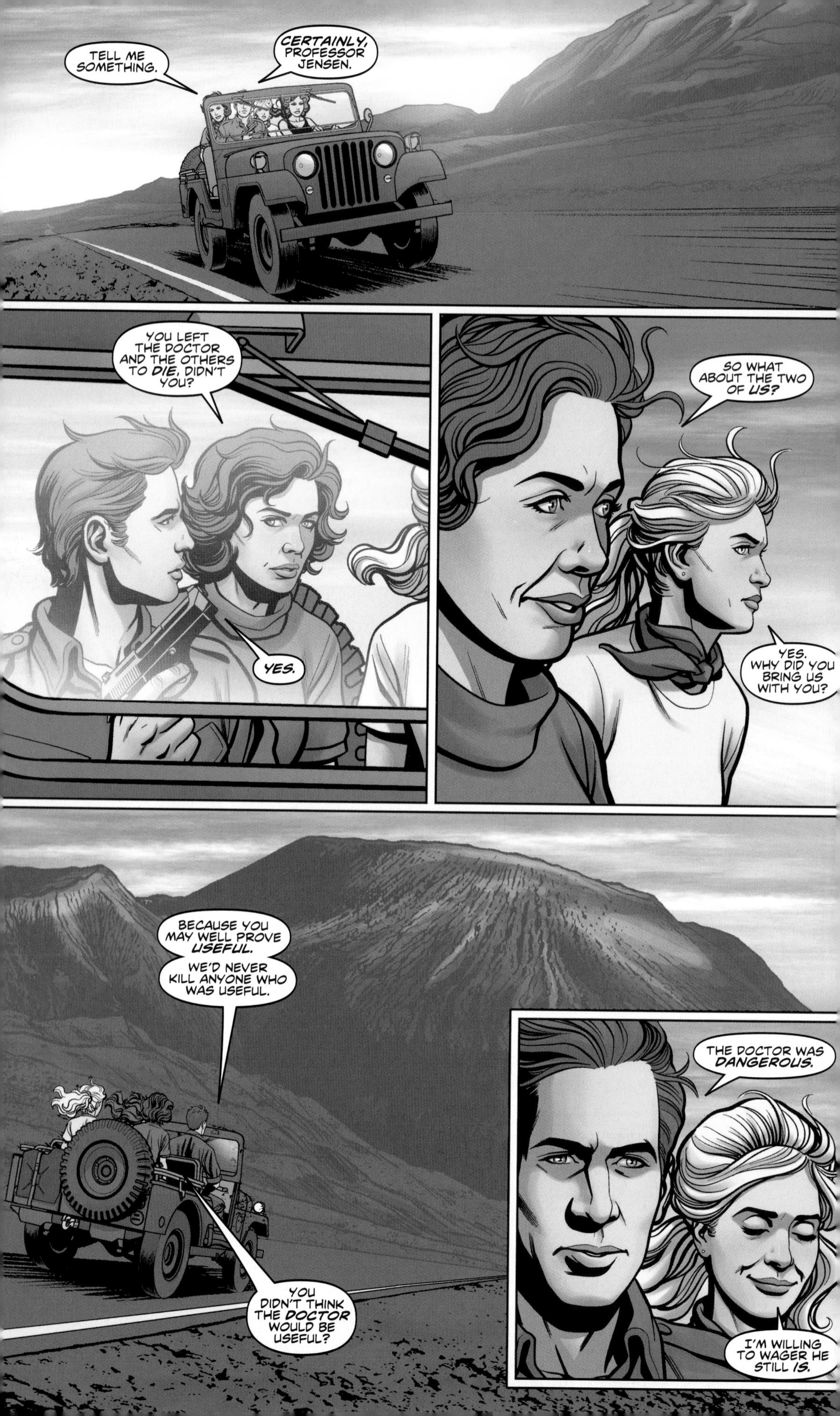
TELL ME SOMETHING.
CERTAINLY, PROFESSOR JENSEN.
YOU LEFT THE DOCTOR AND THE OTHERS TO DIE, DIDN'T YOU?
YES.
SO WHAT ABOUT THE TWO OF US?
YES. WHY DID YOU BRING US WITH YOU?
BECAUSE YOU MAY WELL PROVE USEFUL.
WE'D NEVER KILL ANYONE WHO WAS USEFUL.
YOU DIDN'T THINK THE DOCTOR WOULD BE USEFUL?
THE DOCTOR WAS DANGEROUS.
I'M WILLING TO WAGER HE STILL IS.

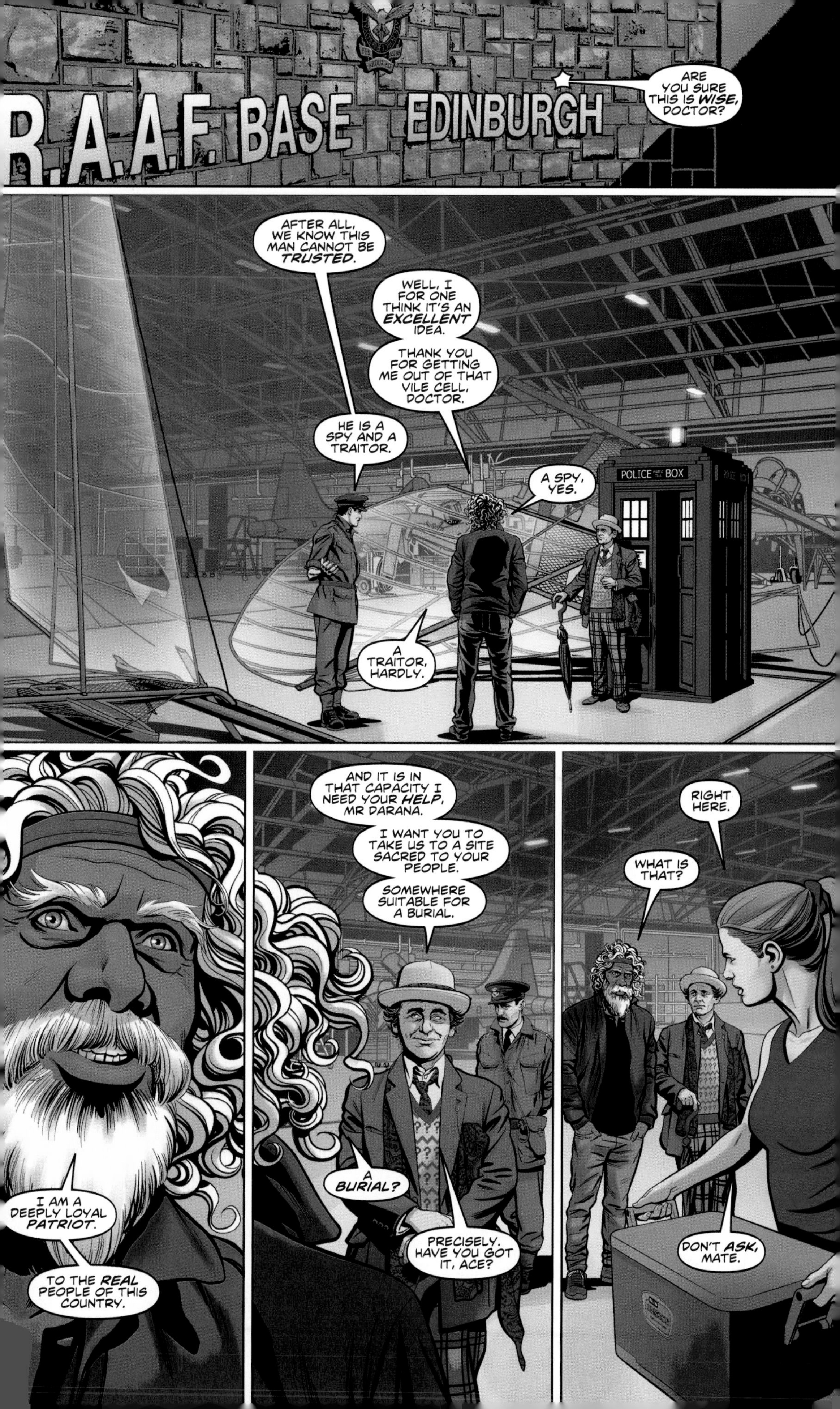
R.A.A.F. BASE EDINBURGH
ARE YOU SURE THIS IS WISE, DOCTOR?
AFTER ALL, WE KNOW THIS MAN CANNOT BE TRUSTED.
WELL, I FOR ONE THINK IT'S AN EXCELLENT IDEA.
THANK YOU FOR GETTING ME OUT OF THAT VILE CELL, DOCTOR.
HE IS A SPY AND A TRAITOR.
A SPY, YES.
POLICE BOX
A TRAITOR, HARDLY.
I AM A DEEPLY LOYAL PATRIOT.
TO THE REAL PEOPLE OF THIS COUNTRY.
AND IT IS IN THAT CAPACITY I NEED YOUR HELP, MR DARANA.
I WANT YOU TO TAKE US TO A SITE SACRED TO YOUR PEOPLE.
SOMEWHERE SUITABLE FOR A BURIAL.
A BURIAL?
PRECISELY. HAVE YOU GOT IT, ACE?
RIGHT HERE.
WHAT IS THAT?
DON'T ASK, MATE.

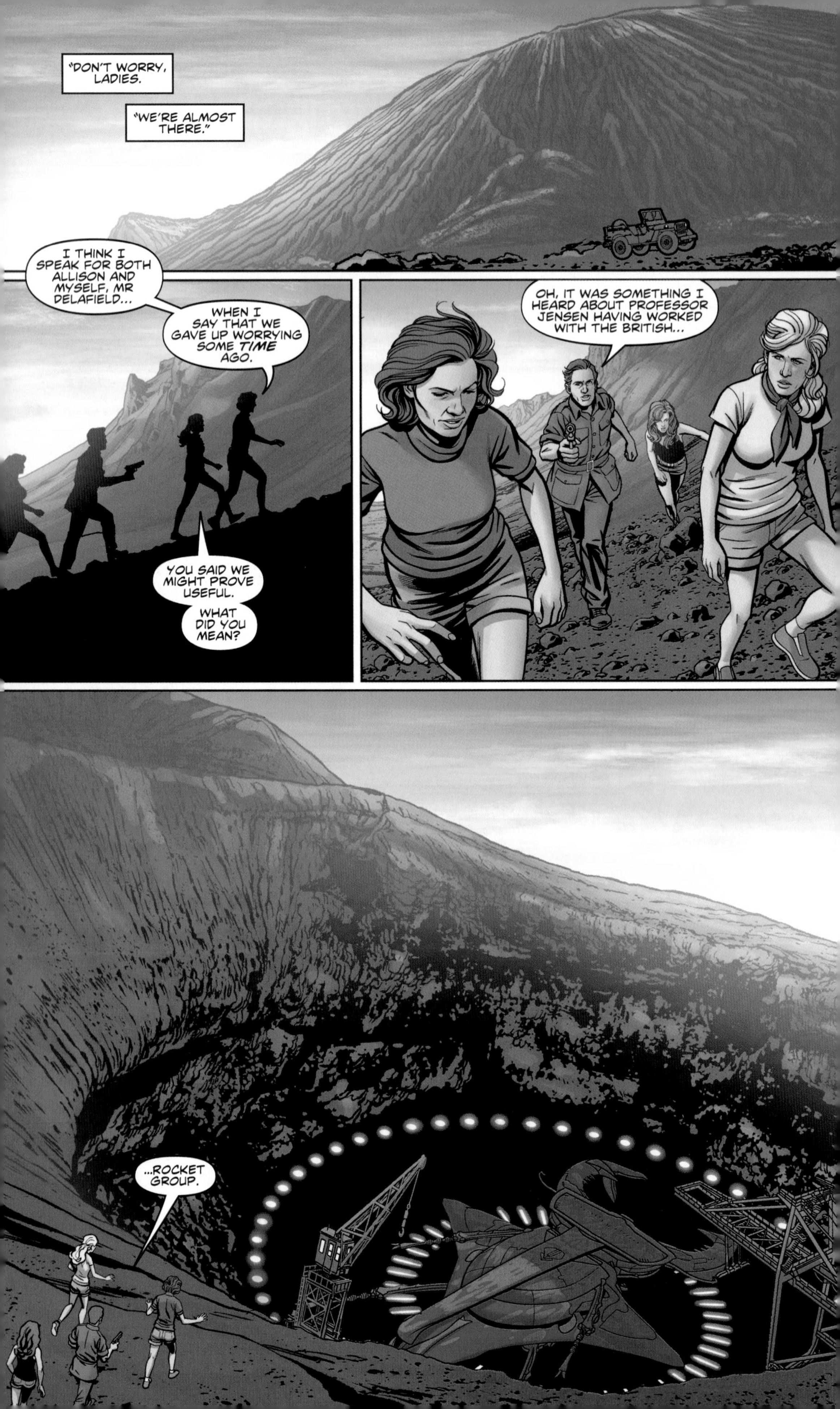
"DON'T WORRY, LADIES.
"WE'RE ALMOST THERE."
I THINK I SPEAK FOR BOTH ALLISON AND MYSELF, MR DELAFIELD...
WHEN I SAY THAT WE GAVE UP WORRYING SOME *TIME* AGO.
YOU SAID WE MIGHT PROVE USEFUL.
WHAT DID YOU MEAN?
OH, IT WAS SOMETHING I HEARD ABOUT PROFESSOR JENSEN HAVING WORKED WITH THE BRITISH...
...ROCKET GROUP.

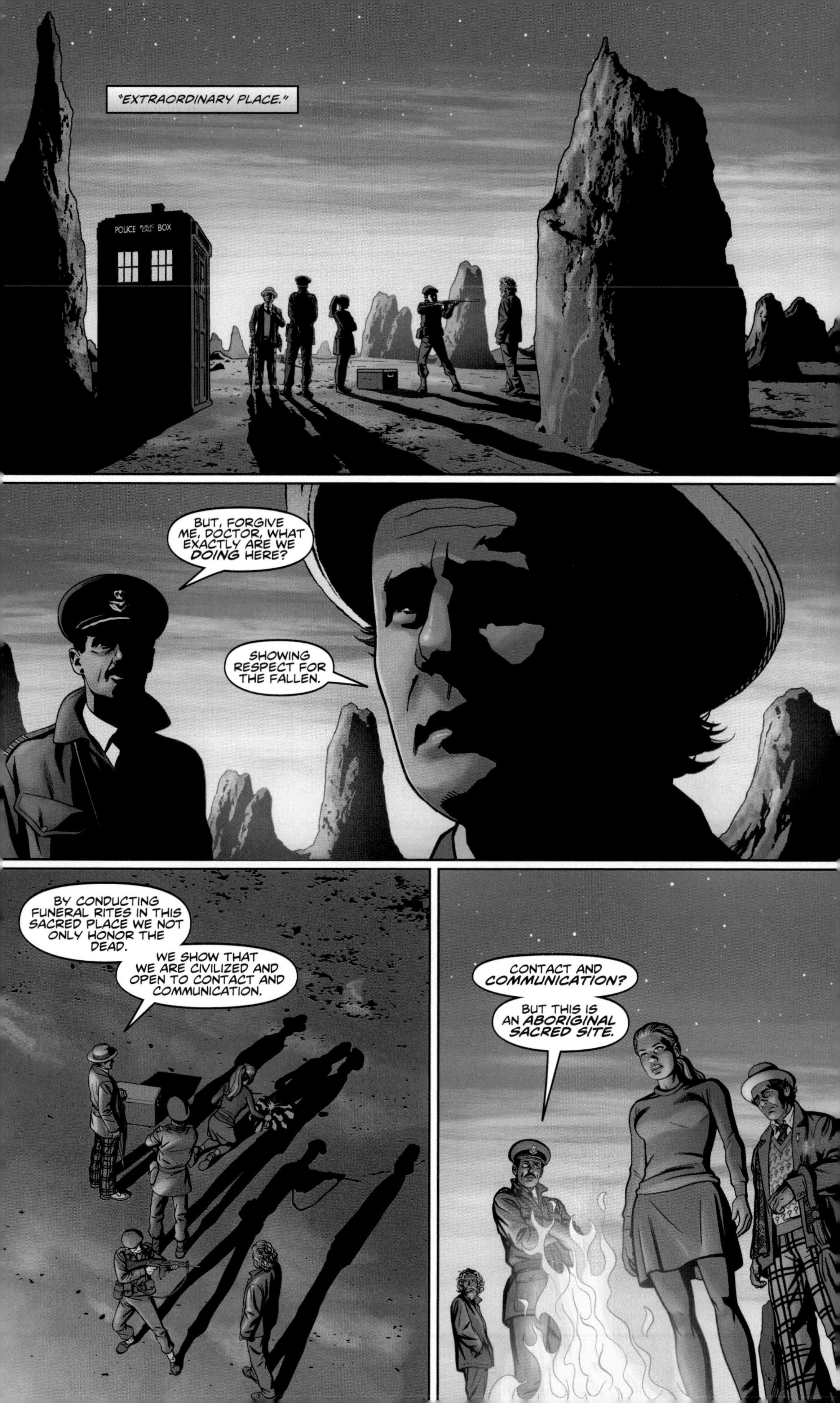
"EXTRAORDINARY PLACE."
POLICE PUBLIC CALL BOX
BUT, FORGIVE ME, DOCTOR, WHAT EXACTLY ARE WE DOING HERE?
SHOWING RESPECT FOR THE FALLEN.
BY CONDUCTING FUNERAL RITES IN THIS SACRED PLACE WE NOT ONLY HONOR THE DEAD.
WE SHOW THAT WE ARE CIVILIZED AND OPEN TO CONTACT AND COMMUNICATION.
CONTACT AND COMMUNICATION?
BUT THIS IS AN ABORIGINAL SACRED SITE.

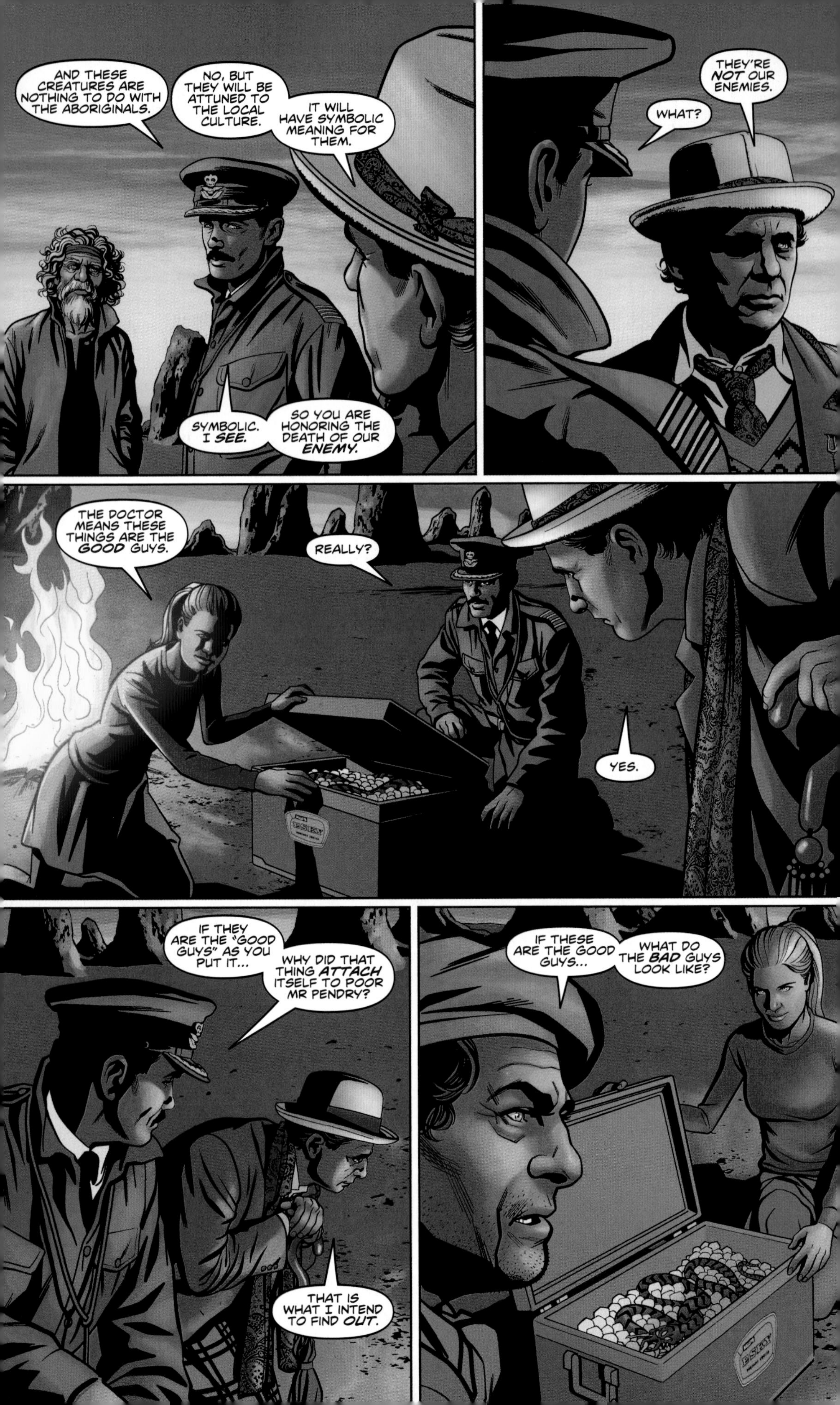
AND THESE CREATURES ARE NOTHING TO DO WITH THE ABORIGINALS.
NO, BUT THEY WILL BE ATTUNED TO THE LOCAL CULTURE.
IT WILL HAVE SYMBOLIC MEANING FOR THEM.
SYMBOLIC. I SEE.
SO YOU ARE HONORING THE DEATH OF OUR ENEMY.
WHAT?
THEY'RE NOT OUR ENEMIES.
THE DOCTOR MEANS THESE THINGS ARE THE GOOD GUYS.
REALLY?
YES.
IF THEY ARE THE "GOOD GUYS" AS YOU PUT IT...
WHY DID THAT THING ATTACH ITSELF TO POOR MR PENDRY?
THAT IS WHAT I INTEND TO FIND OUT.
IF THESE ARE THE GOOD GUYS...
WHAT DO THE BAD GUYS LOOK LIKE?

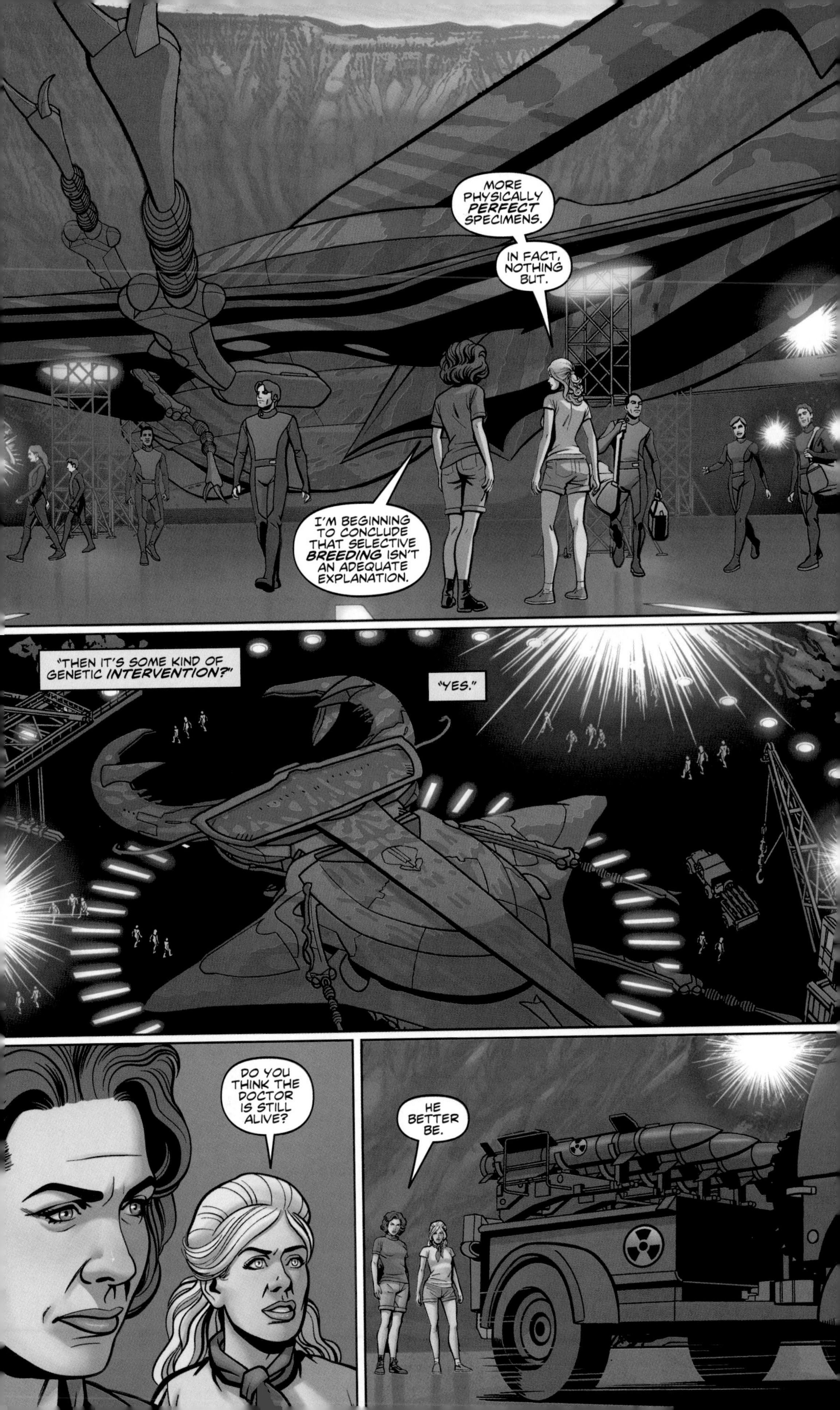
MORE PHYSICALLY PERFECT SPECIMENS.
IN FACT, NOTHING BUT.
I'M BEGINNING TO CONCLUDE THAT SELECTIVE BREEDING ISN'T AN ADEQUATE EXPLANATION.
"THEN IT'S SOME KIND OF GENETIC INTERVENTION?"
"YES."
DO YOU THINK THE DOCTOR IS STILL ALIVE?
HE BETTER BE.

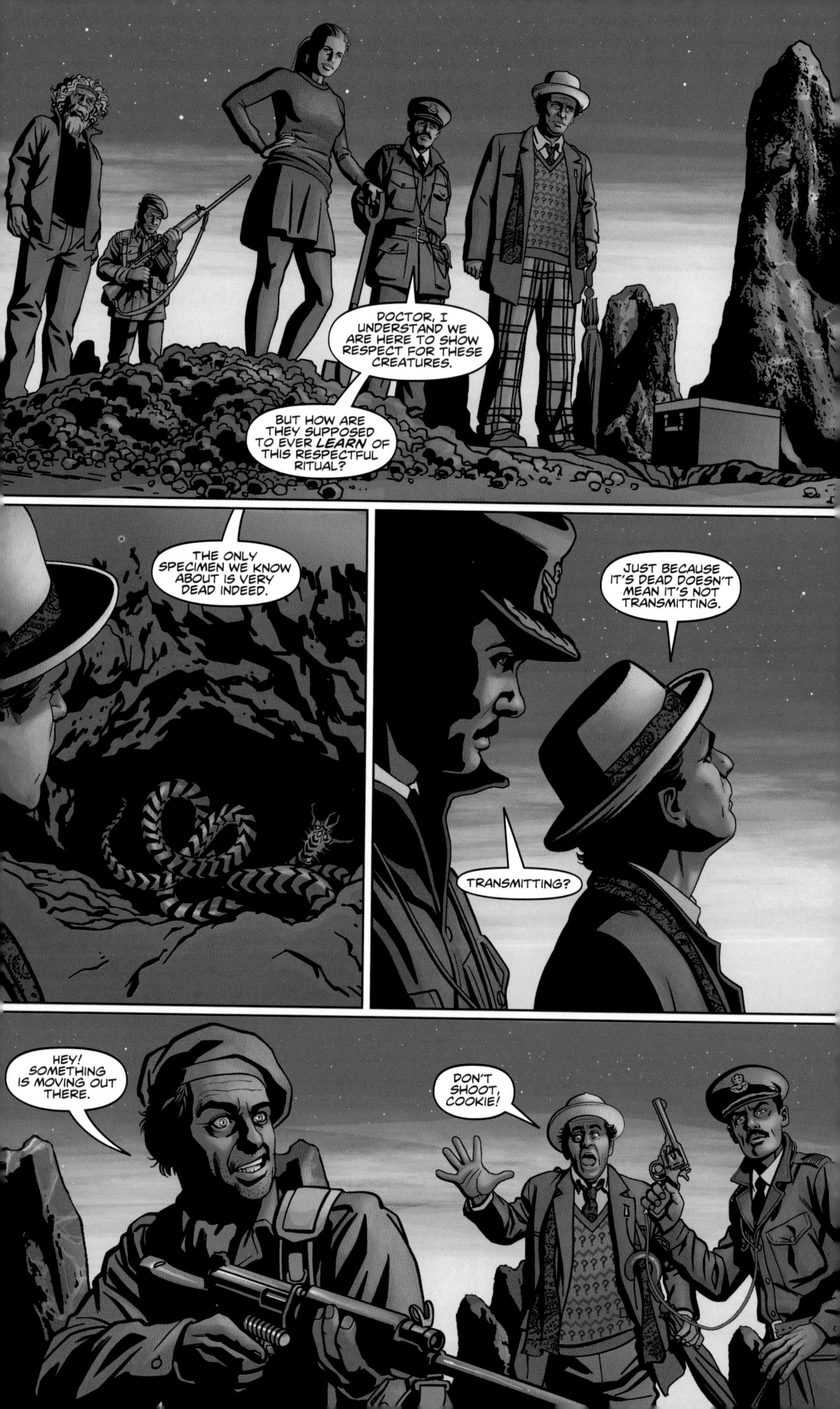
DOCTOR, I UNDERSTAND WE ARE HERE TO SHOW RESPECT FOR THESE CREATURES.
BUT HOW ARE THEY SUPPOSED TO EVER LEARN OF THIS RESPECTFUL RITUAL?
THE ONLY SPECIMEN WE KNOW ABOUT IS VERY DEAD INDEED.
JUST BECAUSE IT'S DEAD DOESN'T MEAN IT'S NOT TRANSMITTING.
TRANSMITTING?
HEY! SOMETHING IS MOVING OUT THERE.
DON'T SHOOT, COOKIE!

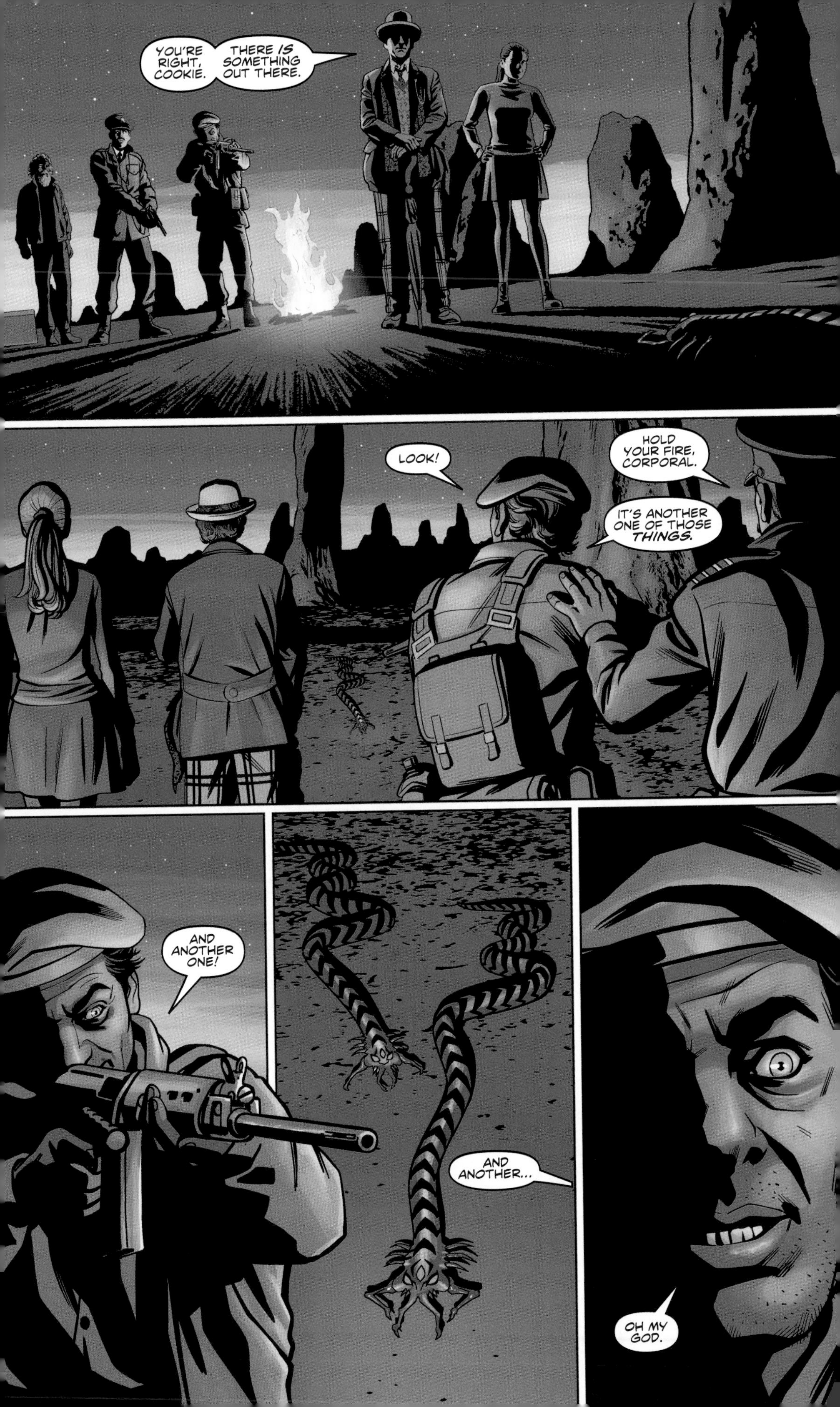
YOU'RE RIGHT, COOKIE.
THERE IS SOMETHING OUT THERE.
LOOK!
HOLD YOUR FIRE, CORPORAL.
IT'S ANOTHER ONE OF THOSE THINGS.
AND ANOTHER ONE!
AND ANOTHER...
OH MY GOD.

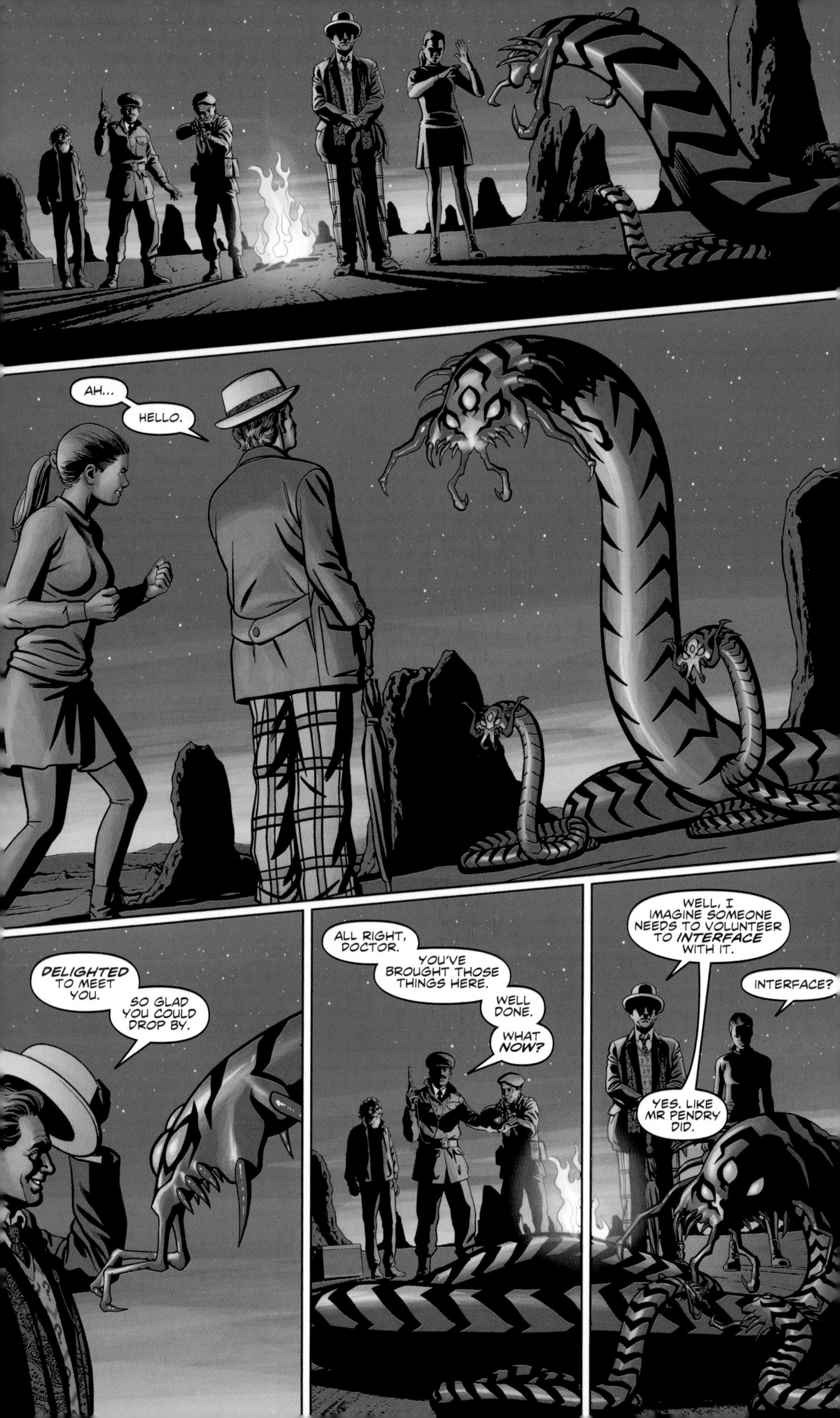

AH...
HELLO.
DELIGHTED TO MEET YOU.
SO GLAD YOU COULD DROP BY.
ALL RIGHT, DOCTOR.
YOU'VE BROUGHT THOSE THINGS HERE.
WELL DONE.
WHAT NOW?
WELL, I IMAGINE SOMEONE NEEDS TO VOLUNTEER TO INTERFACE WITH IT.
INTERFACE?
YES. LIKE MR PENDRY DID.

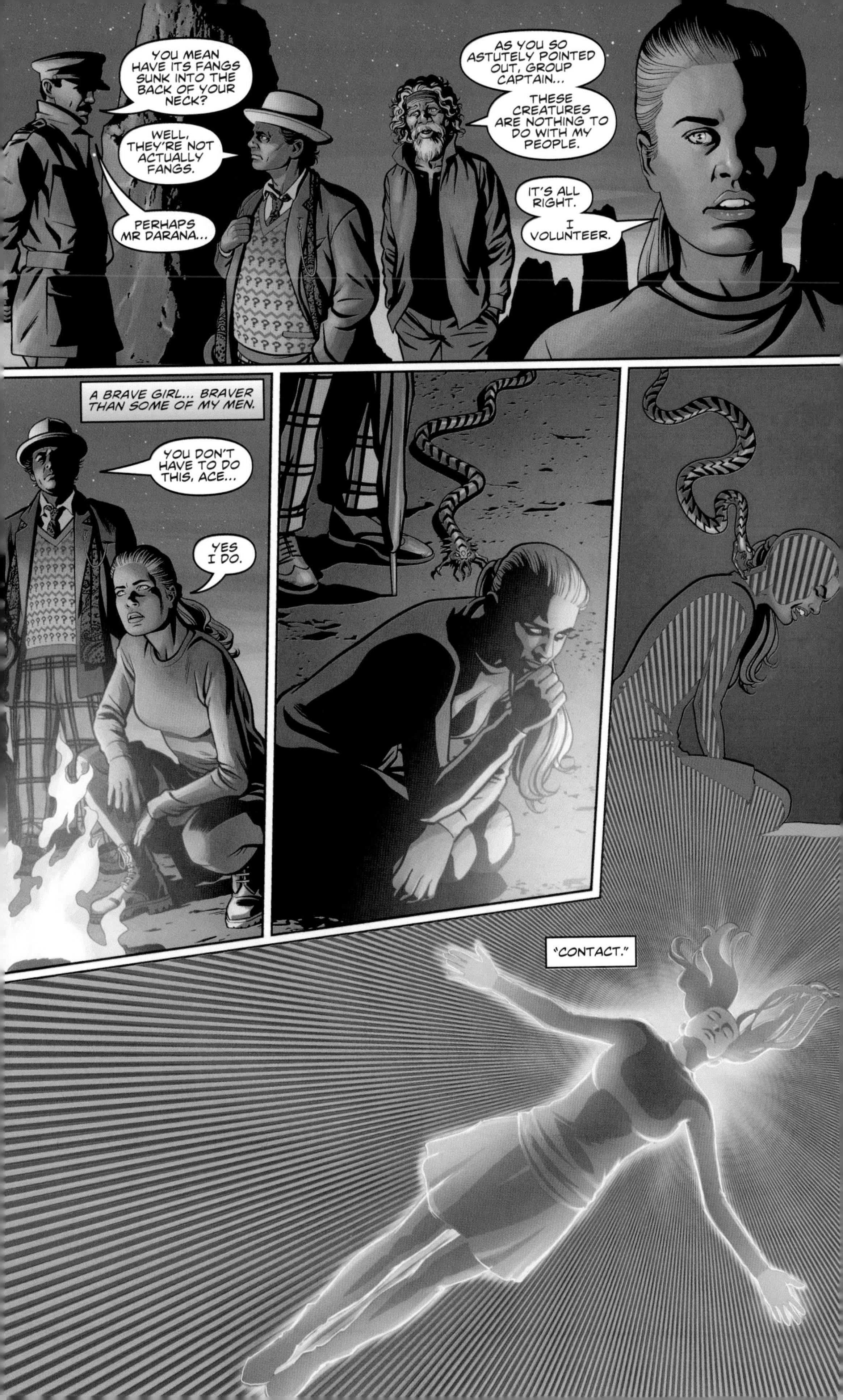
YOU MEAN HAVE ITS FANGS SUNK INTO THE BACK OF YOUR NECK?
WELL, THEY'RE NOT ACTUALLY FANGS.
PERHAPS MR DARANA...
AS YOU SO ASTUTELY POINTED OUT, GROUP CAPTAIN...
THESE CREATURES ARE NOTHING TO DO WITH MY PEOPLE.
IT'S ALL RIGHT.
I VOLUNTEER.
A BRAVE GIRL... BRAVER THAN SOME OF MY MEN.
YOU DON'T HAVE TO DO THIS, ACE...
YES I DO.
"CONTACT."

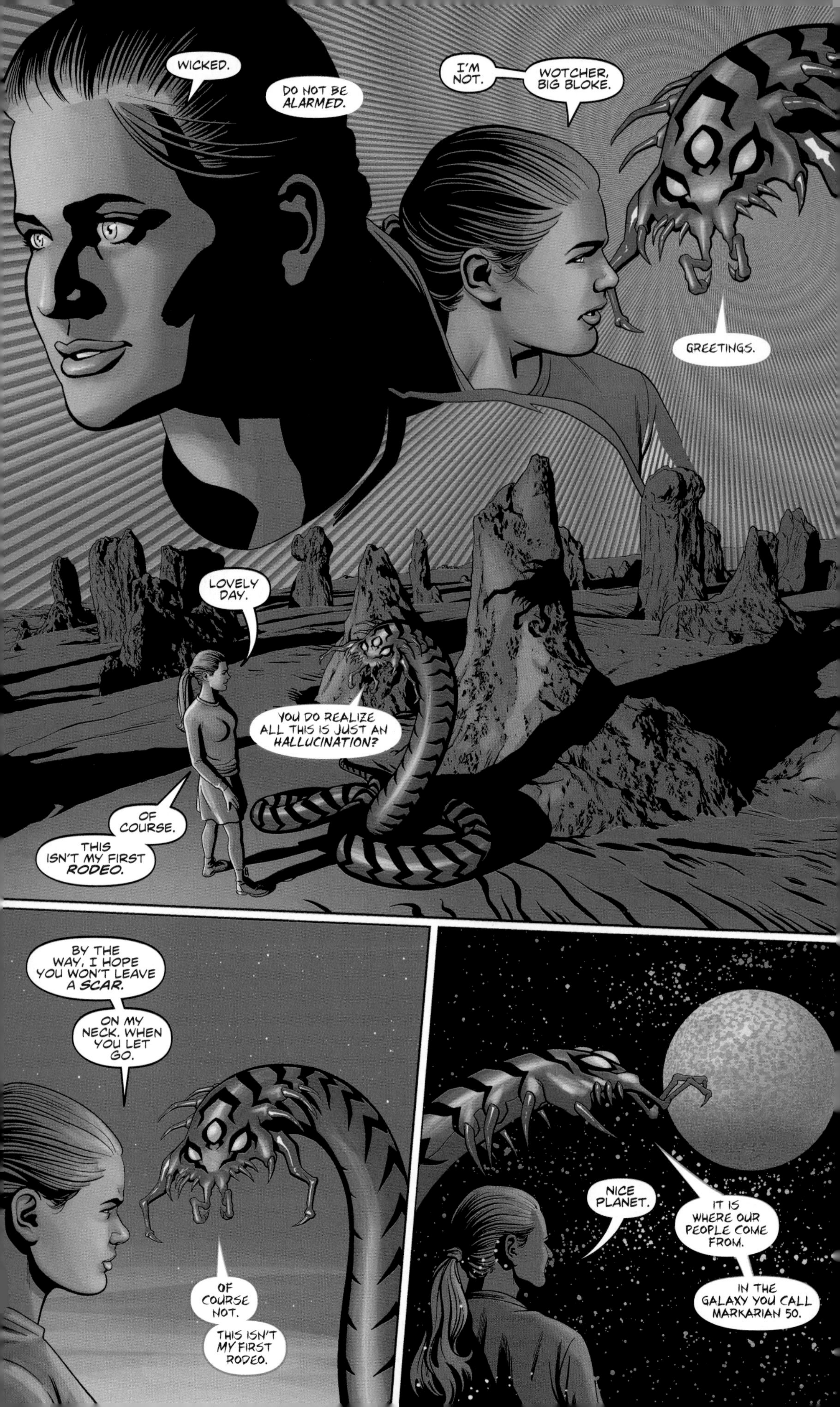
WICKED.
DO NOT BE ALARMED.
I'M NOT.
WOTCHER, BIG BLOKE.
GREETINGS.
LOVELY DAY.
YOU DO REALIZE ALL THIS IS JUST AN HALLUCINATION?
OF COURSE.
THIS ISN'T MY FIRST RODEO.
BY THE WAY, I HOPE YOU WON'T LEAVE A SCAR.
ON MY NECK. WHEN YOU LET GO.
OF COURSE NOT.
THIS ISN'T MY FIRST RODEO.
NICE PLANET.
IT IS WHERE OUR PEOPLE COME FROM.
IN THE GALAXY YOU CALL MARKARIAN 50.

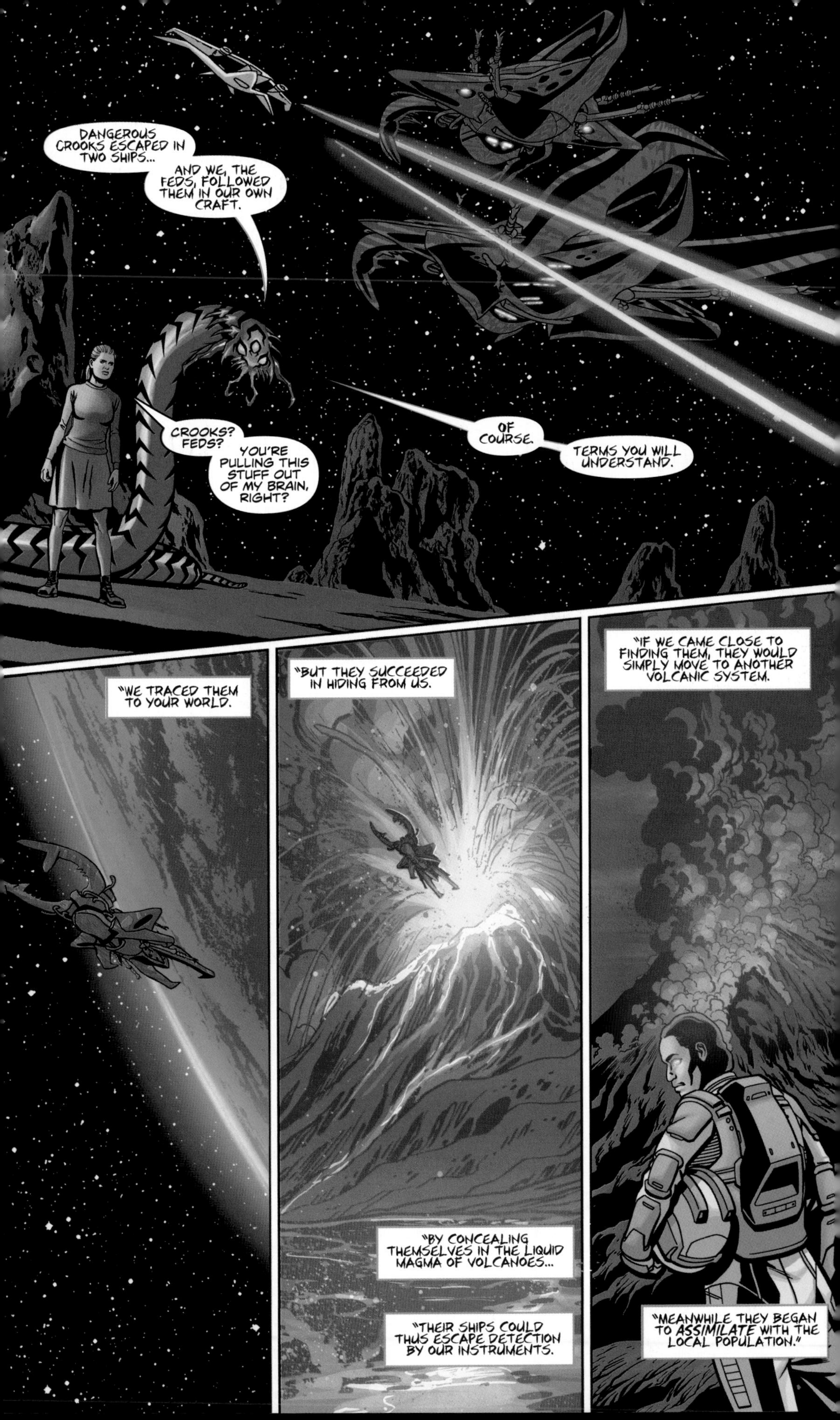
DANGEROUS CROOKS ESCAPED IN TWO SHIPS...
AND WE, THE FEDS, FOLLOWED THEM IN OUR OWN CRAFT.
CROOKS? FEDS?
YOU'RE PULLING THIS STUFF OUT OF MY BRAIN, RIGHT?
OF COURSE.
TERMS YOU WILL UNDERSTAND.
"WE TRACED THEM TO YOUR WORLD.
"BUT THEY SUCCEEDED IN HIDING FROM US.
"BY CONCEALING THEMSELVES IN THE LIQUID MAGMA OF VOLCANOES...
"THEIR SHIPS COULD THUS ESCAPE DETECTION BY OUR INSTRUMENTS.
"IF WE CAME CLOSE TO FINDING THEM, THEY WOULD SIMPLY MOVE TO ANOTHER VOLCANIC SYSTEM.
"MEANWHILE THEY BEGAN TO ASSIMILATE WITH THE LOCAL POPULATION."

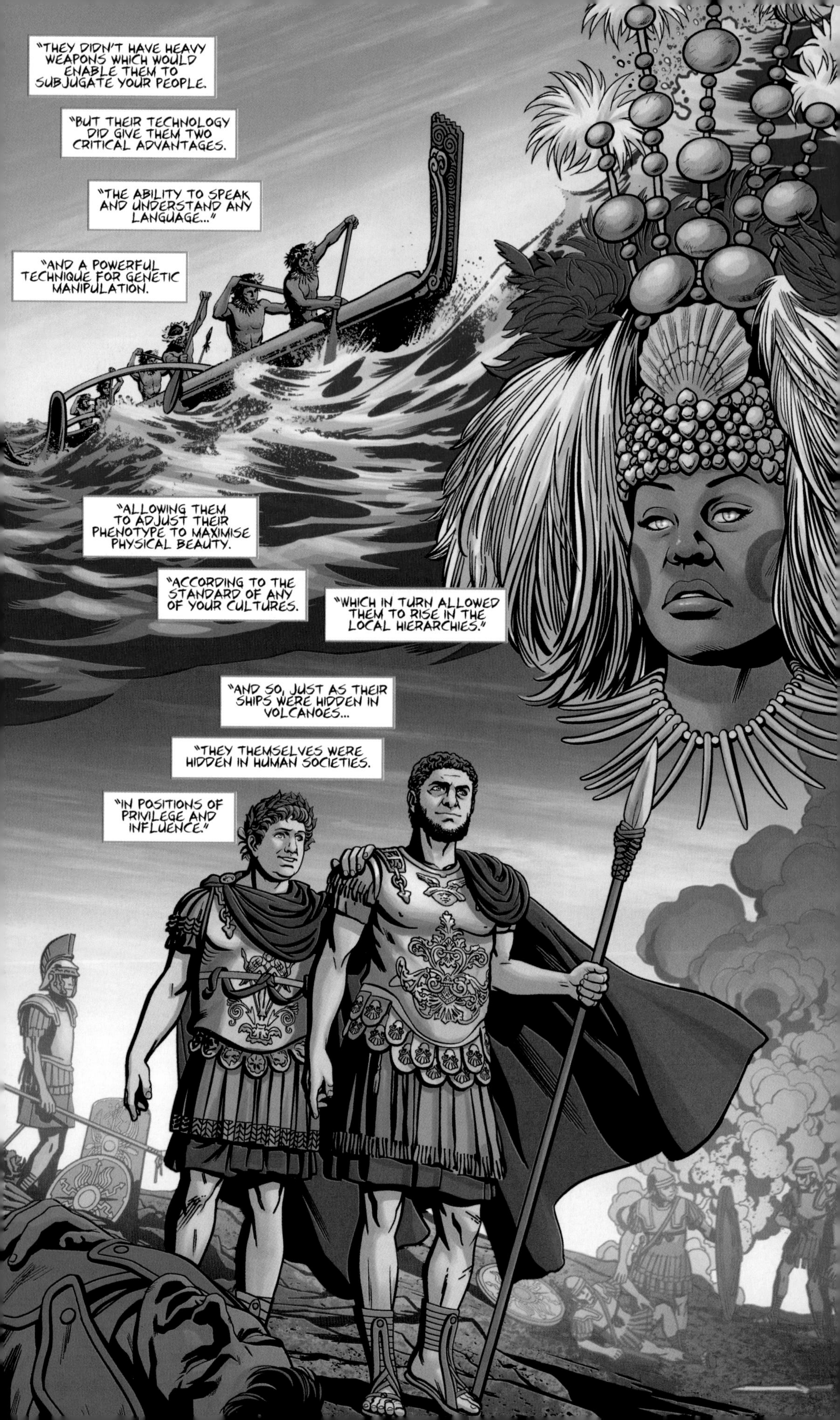
"THEY DIDN'T HAVE HEAVY WEAPONS WHICH WOULD ENABLE THEM TO SUBJUGATE YOUR PEOPLE.
"BUT THEIR TECHNOLOGY DID GIVE THEM TWO CRITICAL ADVANTAGES.
"THE ABILITY TO SPEAK AND UNDERSTAND ANY LANGUAGE..."
"AND A POWERFUL TECHNIQUE FOR GENETIC MANIPULATION.
"ALLOWING THEM TO ADJUST THEIR PHENOTYPE TO MAXIMISE PHYSICAL BEAUTY.
"ACCORDING TO THE STANDARD OF ANY OF YOUR CULTURES.
"WHICH IN TURN ALLOWED THEM TO RISE IN THE LOCAL HIERARCHIES."
"AND SO, JUST AS THEIR SHIPS WERE HIDDEN IN VOLCANOES...
"THEY THEMSELVES WERE HIDDEN IN HUMAN SOCIETIES.
"IN POSITIONS OF PRIVILEGE AND INFLUENCE."

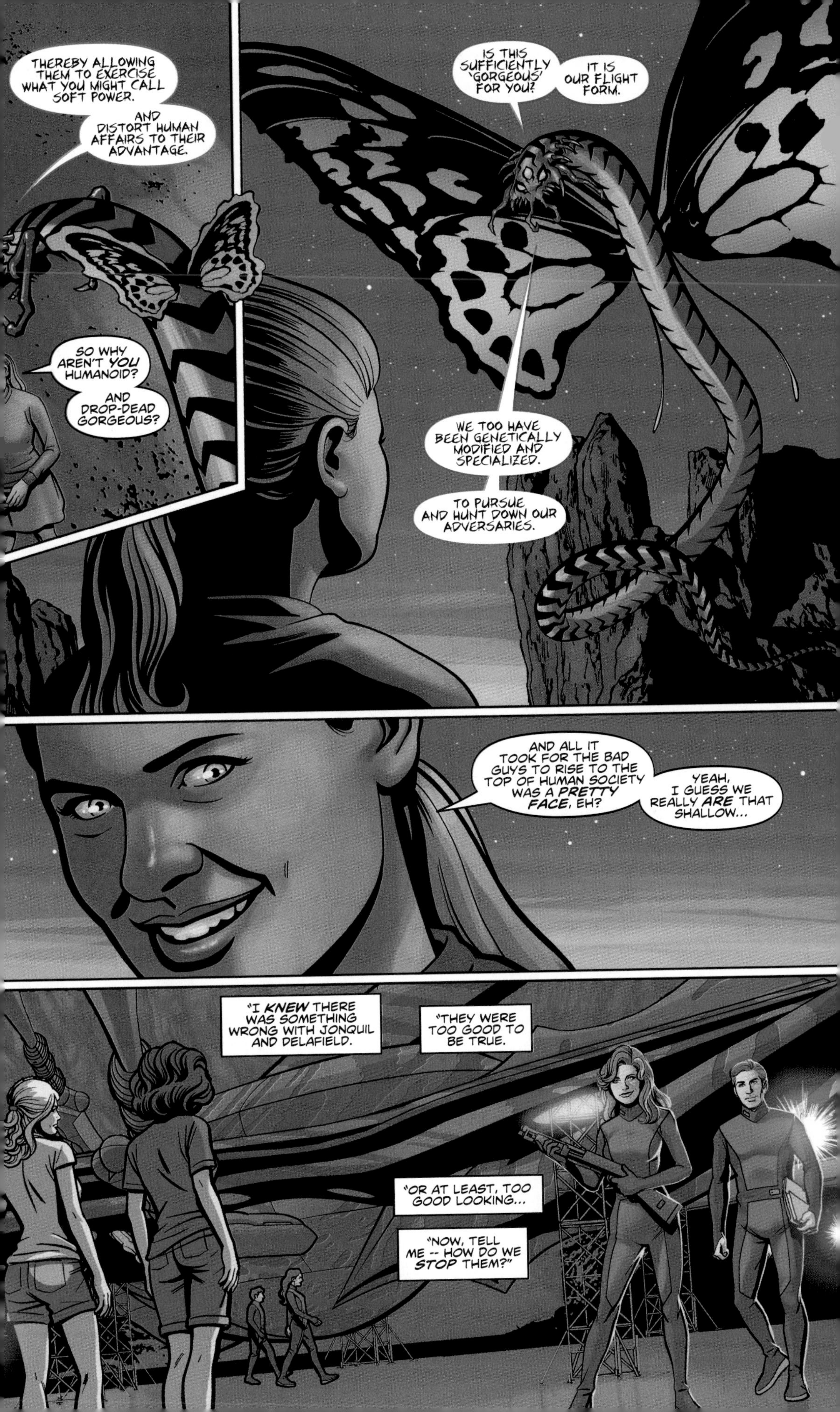
THEREBY ALLOWING THEM TO EXERCISE WHAT YOU MIGHT CALL SOFT POWER.
AND DISTORT HUMAN AFFAIRS TO THEIR ADVANTAGE.
SO WHY AREN'T *YOU* HUMANOID?
AND DROP-DEAD GORGEOUS?
IS THIS SUFFICIENTLY 'GORGEOUS' FOR YOU?
IT IS OUR FLIGHT FORM.
WE TOO HAVE BEEN GENETICALLY MODIFIED AND SPECIALIZED.
TO PURSUE AND HUNT DOWN OUR ADVERSARIES.
AND ALL IT TOOK FOR THE BAD GUYS TO RISE TO THE TOP OF HUMAN SOCIETY WAS A *PRETTY FACE*, EH?
YEAH, I GUESS WE REALLY *ARE* THAT SHALLOW...
"I *KNEW* THERE WAS SOMETHING WRONG WITH JONQUIL AND DELAFIELD.
"THEY WERE TOO GOOD TO BE TRUE.
"OR AT LEAST, TOO GOOD LOOKING...
"NOW, TELL ME -- HOW DO WE *STOP* THEM?"

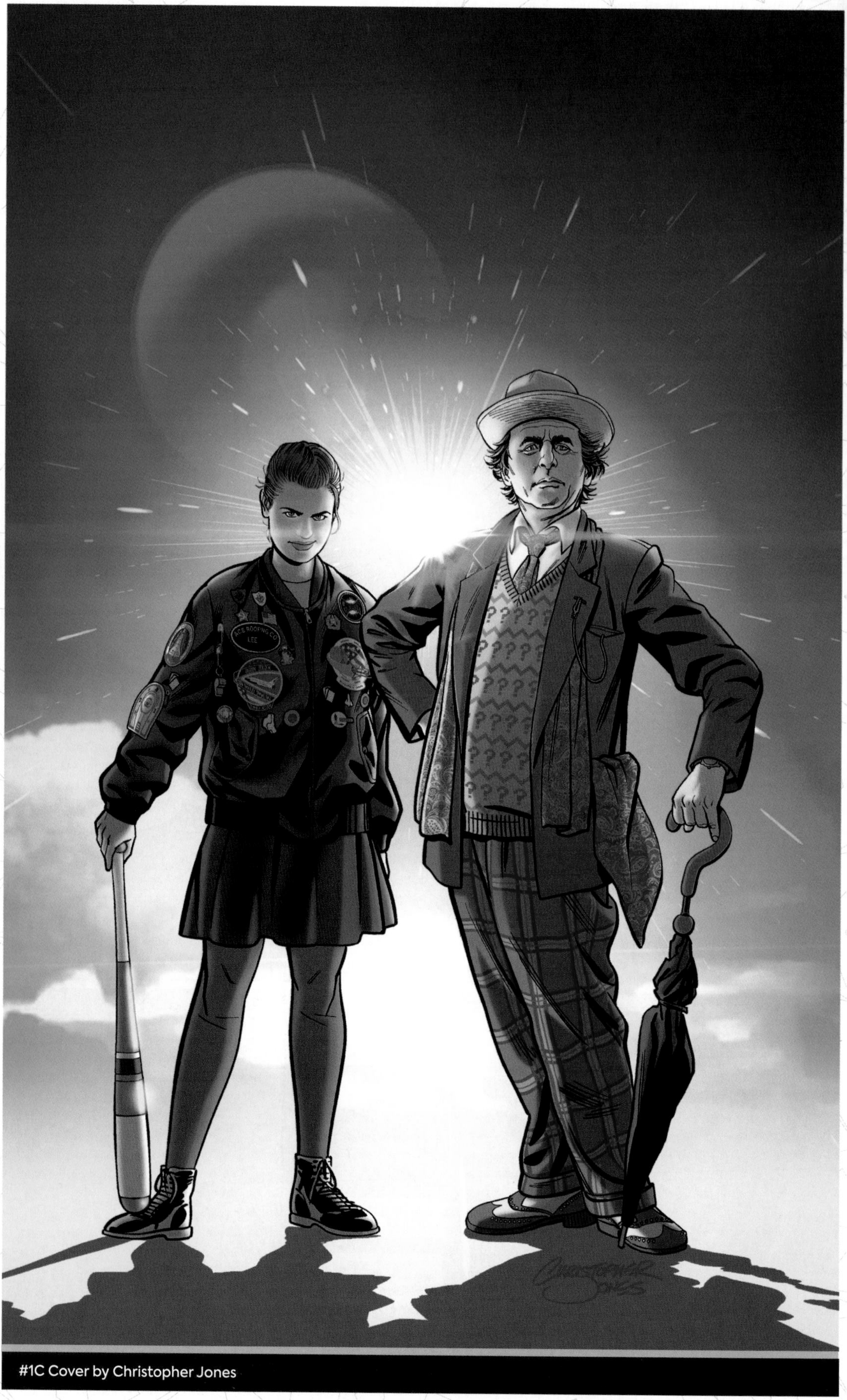
ACE ROOFING CO
LEE

#1C Cover by Christopher Jones

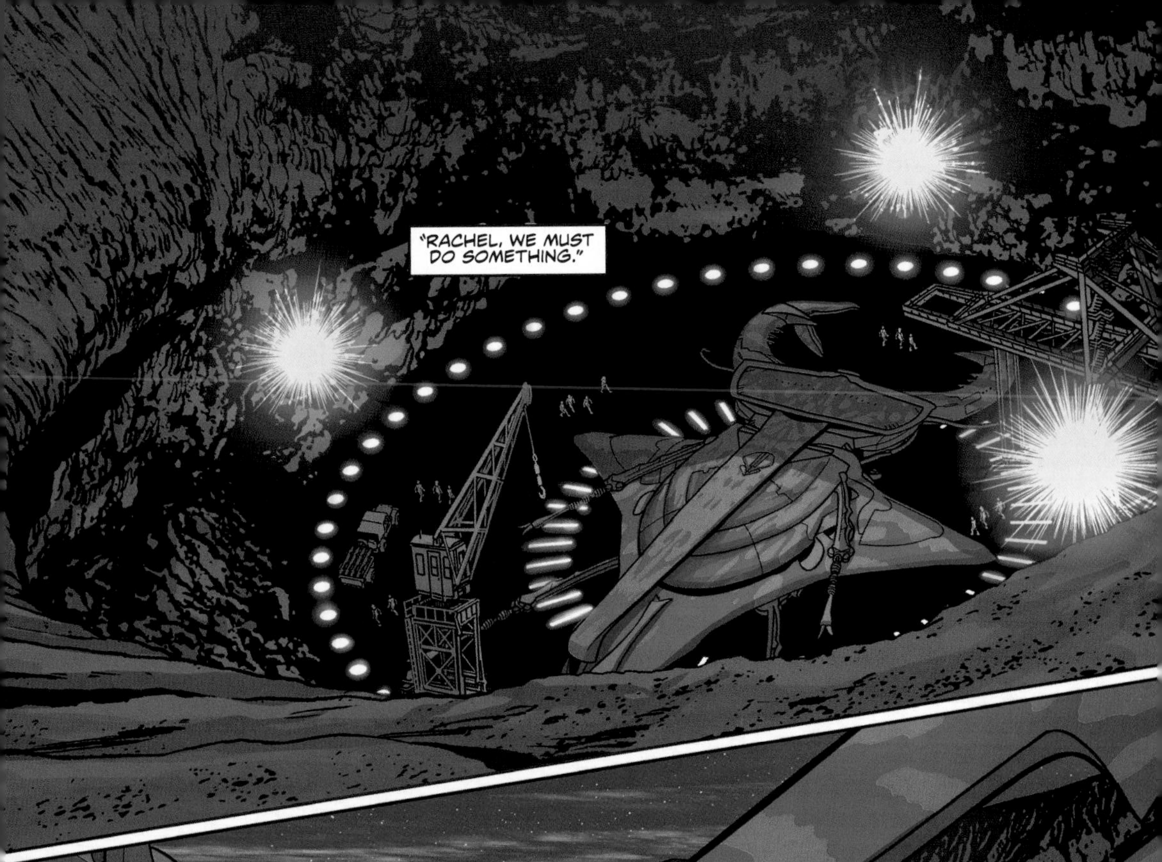
"RACHEL, WE MUST DO SOMETHING."

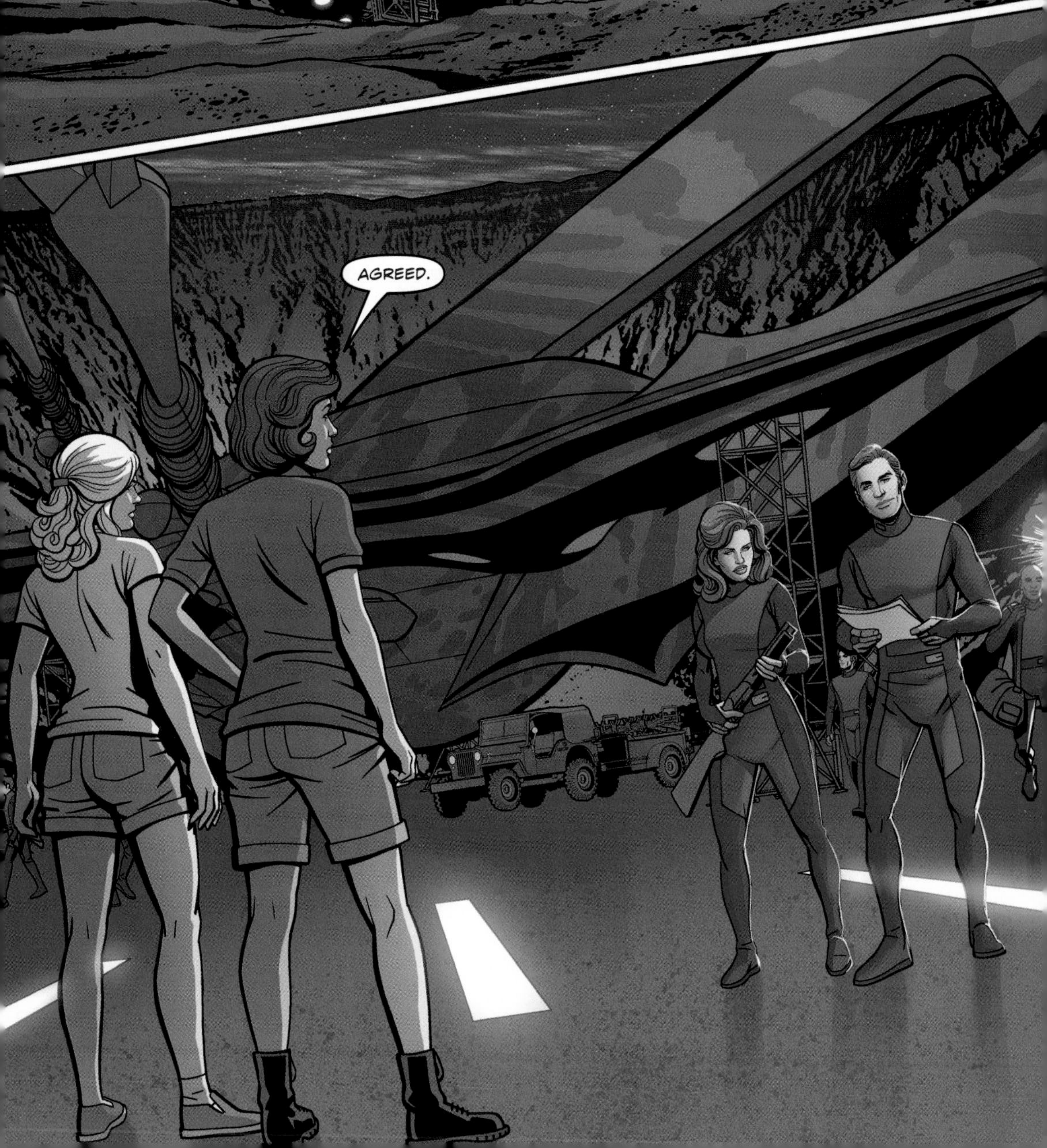
AGREED.

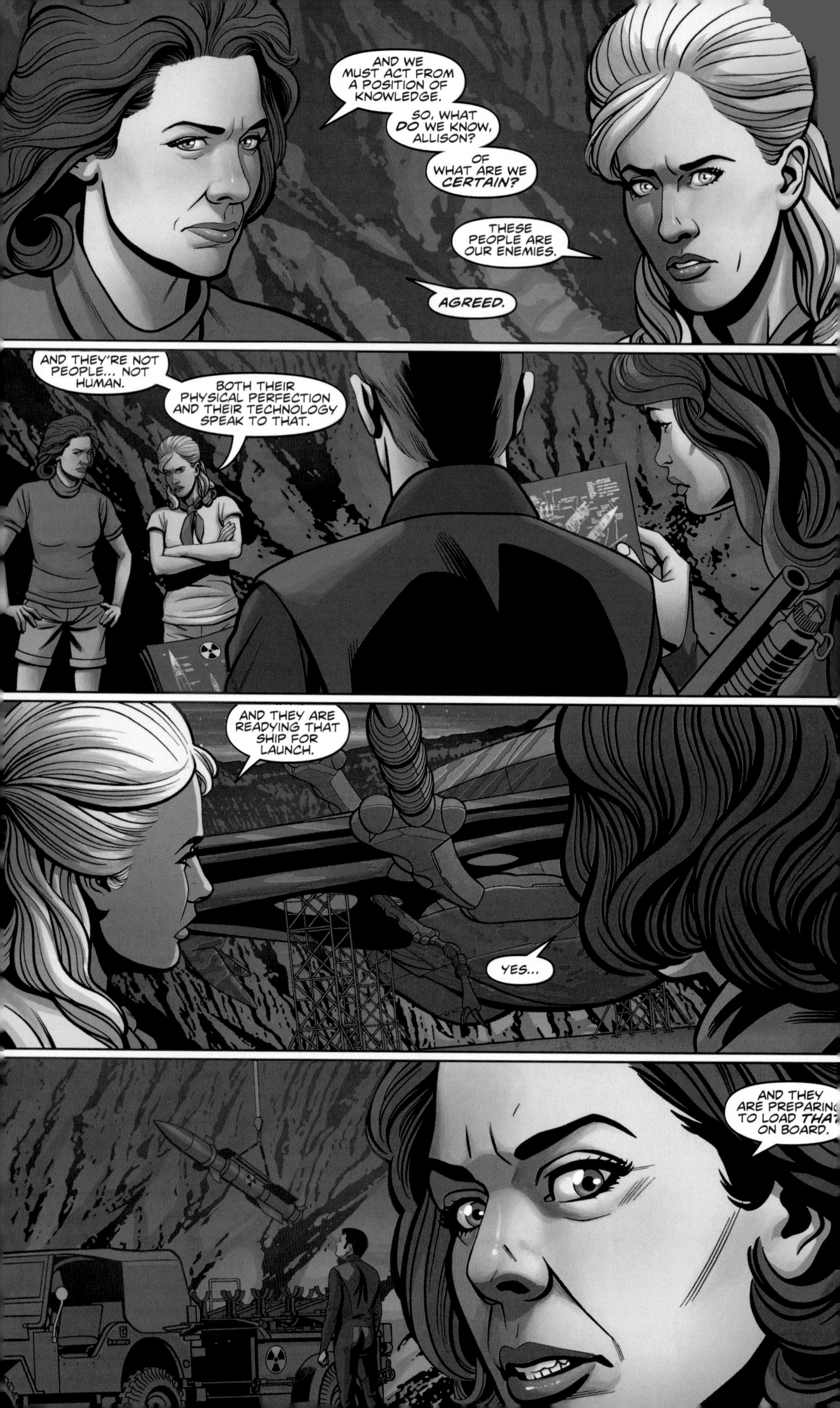

AND WE MUST ACT FROM A POSITION OF KNOWLEDGE.
SO, WHAT *DO* WE KNOW, ALLISON?
OF WHAT ARE WE *CERTAIN?*
THESE PEOPLE ARE OUR ENEMIES.
AGREED.
AND THEY'RE NOT PEOPLE... NOT HUMAN.
BOTH THEIR PHYSICAL PERFECTION AND THEIR TECHNOLOGY SPEAK TO THAT.
AND THEY ARE READYING THAT SHIP FOR LAUNCH.
YES...
AND THEY ARE PREPARING TO LOAD *THAT* ON BOARD.

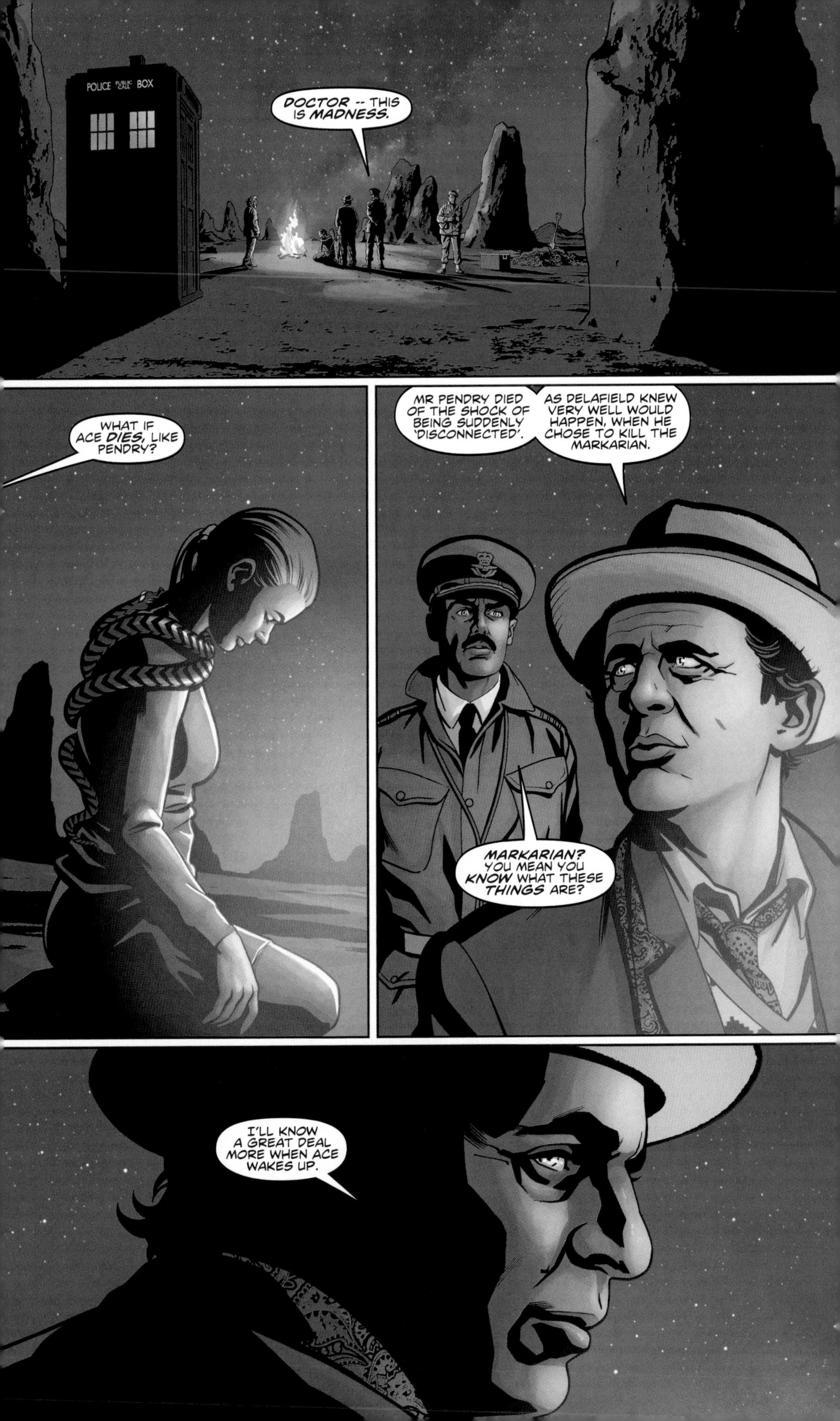
POLICE PUBLIC CALL BOX
DOCTOR -- THIS IS MADNESS.
WHAT IF ACE DIES, LIKE PENDRY?
MR PENDRY DIED OF THE SHOCK OF BEING SUDDENLY 'DISCONNECTED'.
AS DELAFIELD KNEW VERY WELL WOULD HAPPEN, WHEN HE CHOSE TO KILL THE MARKARIAN.
MARKARIAN? YOU MEAN YOU KNOW WHAT THESE THINGS ARE?
I'LL KNOW A GREAT DEAL MORE WHEN ACE WAKES UP.

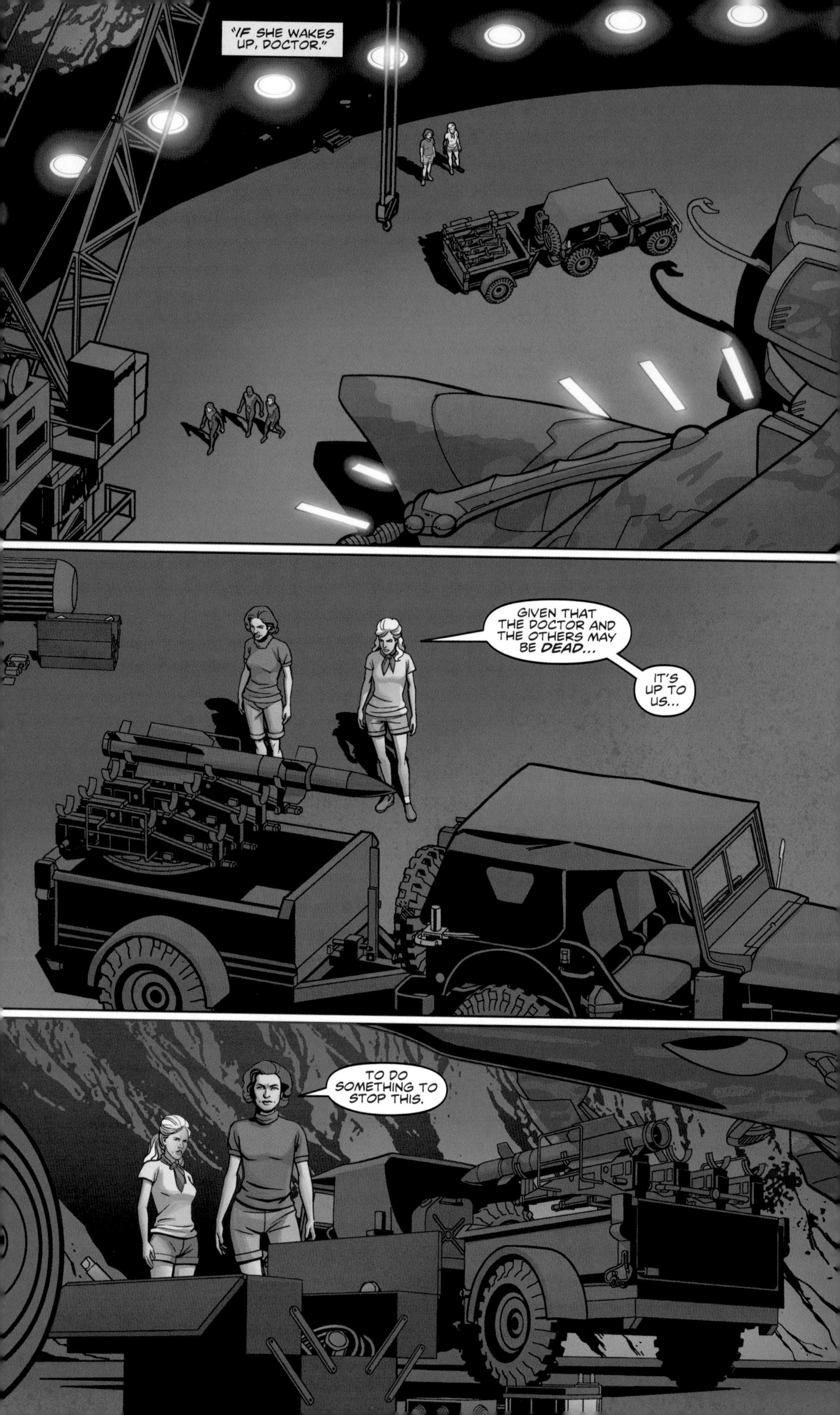
"IF SHE WAKES UP, DOCTOR."
GIVEN THAT THE DOCTOR AND THE OTHERS MAY BE DEAD...
IT'S UP TO US...
TO DO SOMETHING TO STOP THIS.

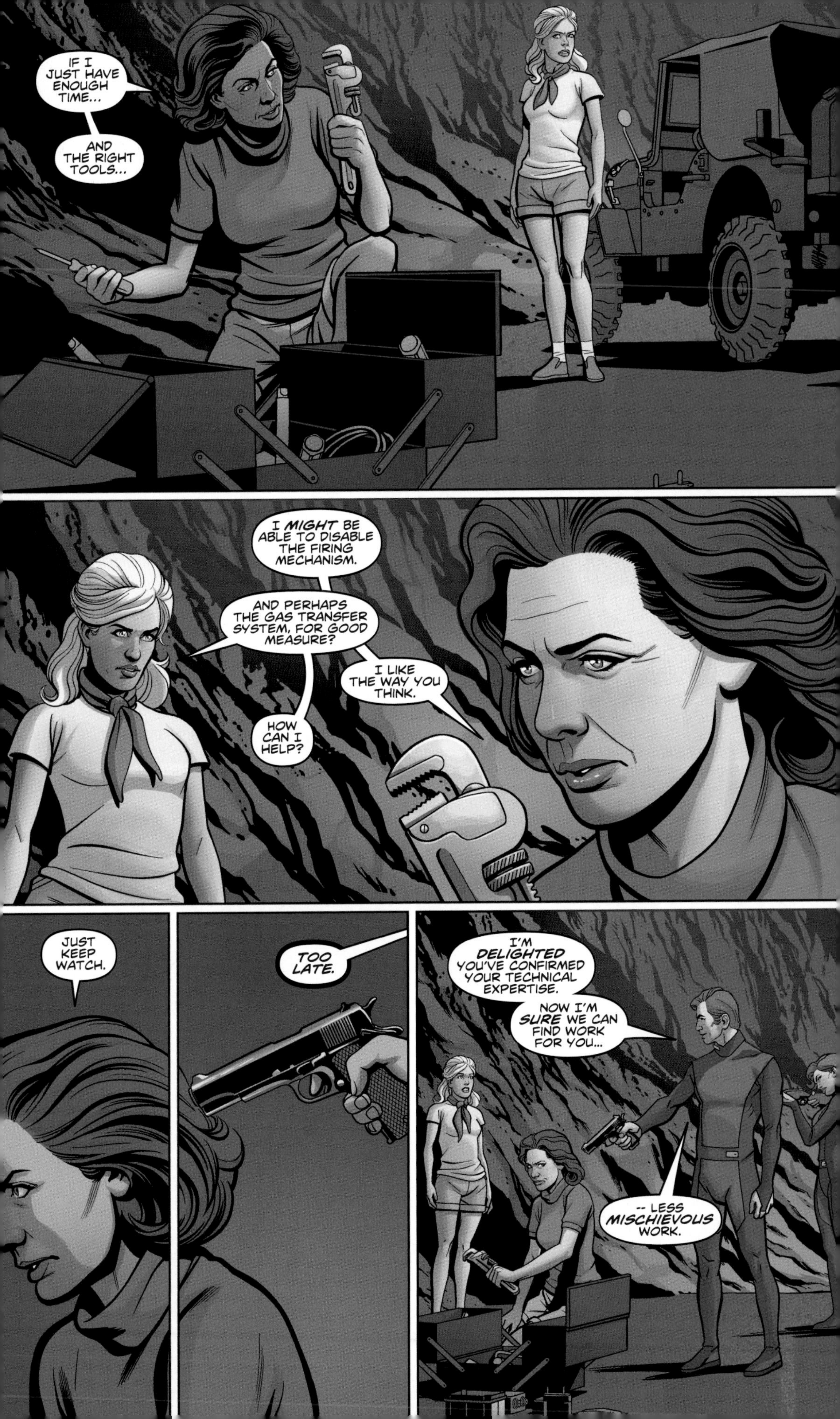
IF I JUST HAVE ENOUGH TIME...
AND THE RIGHT TOOLS...
I *MIGHT* BE ABLE TO DISABLE THE FIRING MECHANISM.
AND PERHAPS THE GAS TRANSFER SYSTEM, FOR GOOD MEASURE?
I LIKE THE WAY YOU THINK.
HOW CAN I HELP?
JUST KEEP WATCH.
TOO LATE.
I'M *DELIGHTED* YOU'VE CONFIRMED YOUR TECHNICAL EXPERTISE.
NOW I'M *SURE* WE CAN FIND WORK FOR YOU...
-- LESS *MISCHIEVOUS* WORK.

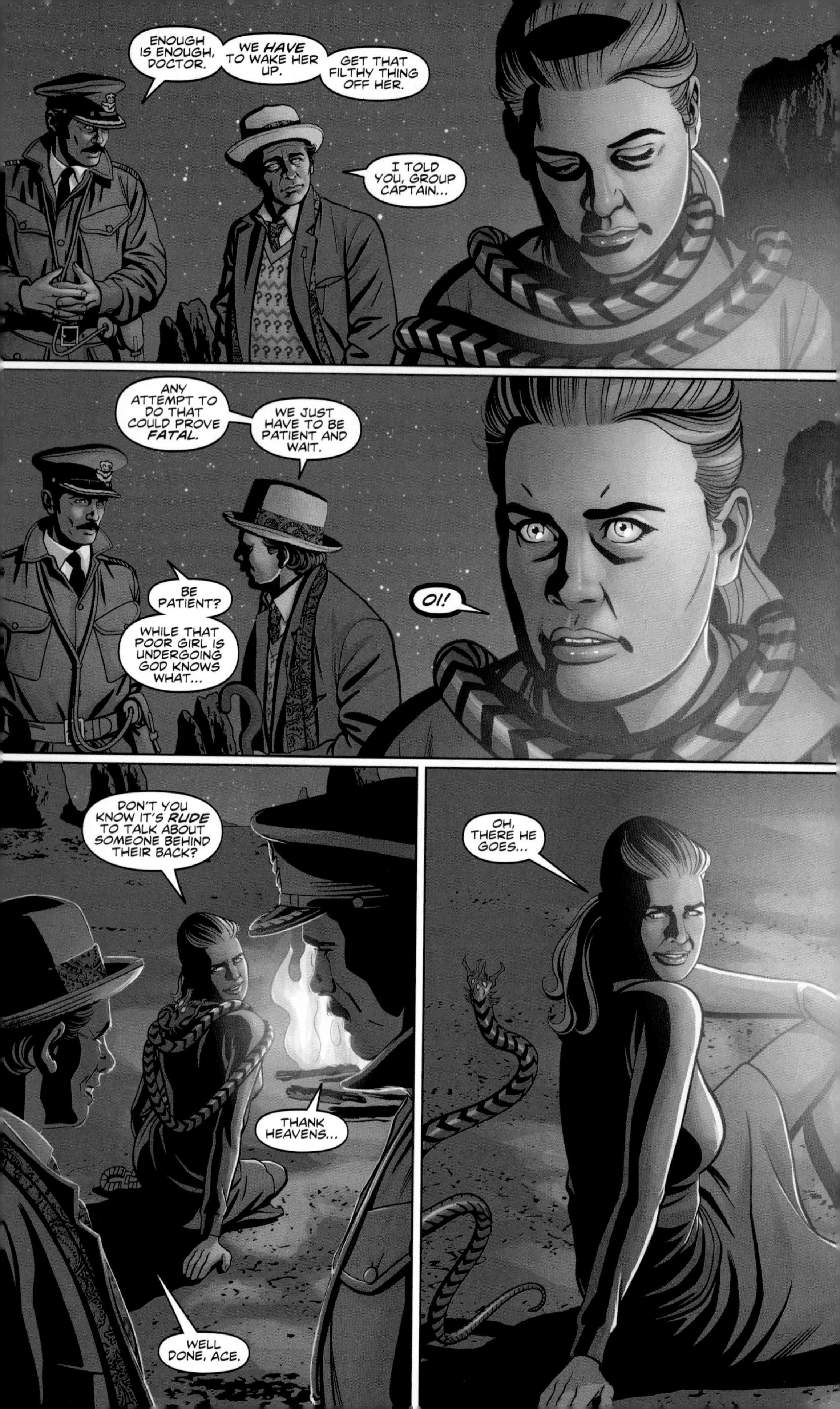
ENOUGH IS ENOUGH, DOCTOR.
WE HAVE TO WAKE HER UP.
GET THAT FILTHY THING OFF HER.
I TOLD YOU, GROUP CAPTAIN...
ANY ATTEMPT TO DO THAT COULD PROVE FATAL.
WE JUST HAVE TO BE PATIENT AND WAIT.
BE PATIENT?
WHILE THAT POOR GIRL IS UNDERGOING GOD KNOWS WHAT...
OI!
DON'T YOU KNOW IT'S RUDE TO TALK ABOUT SOMEONE BEHIND THEIR BACK?
THANK HEAVENS...
WELL DONE, ACE.
OH, THERE HE GOES...

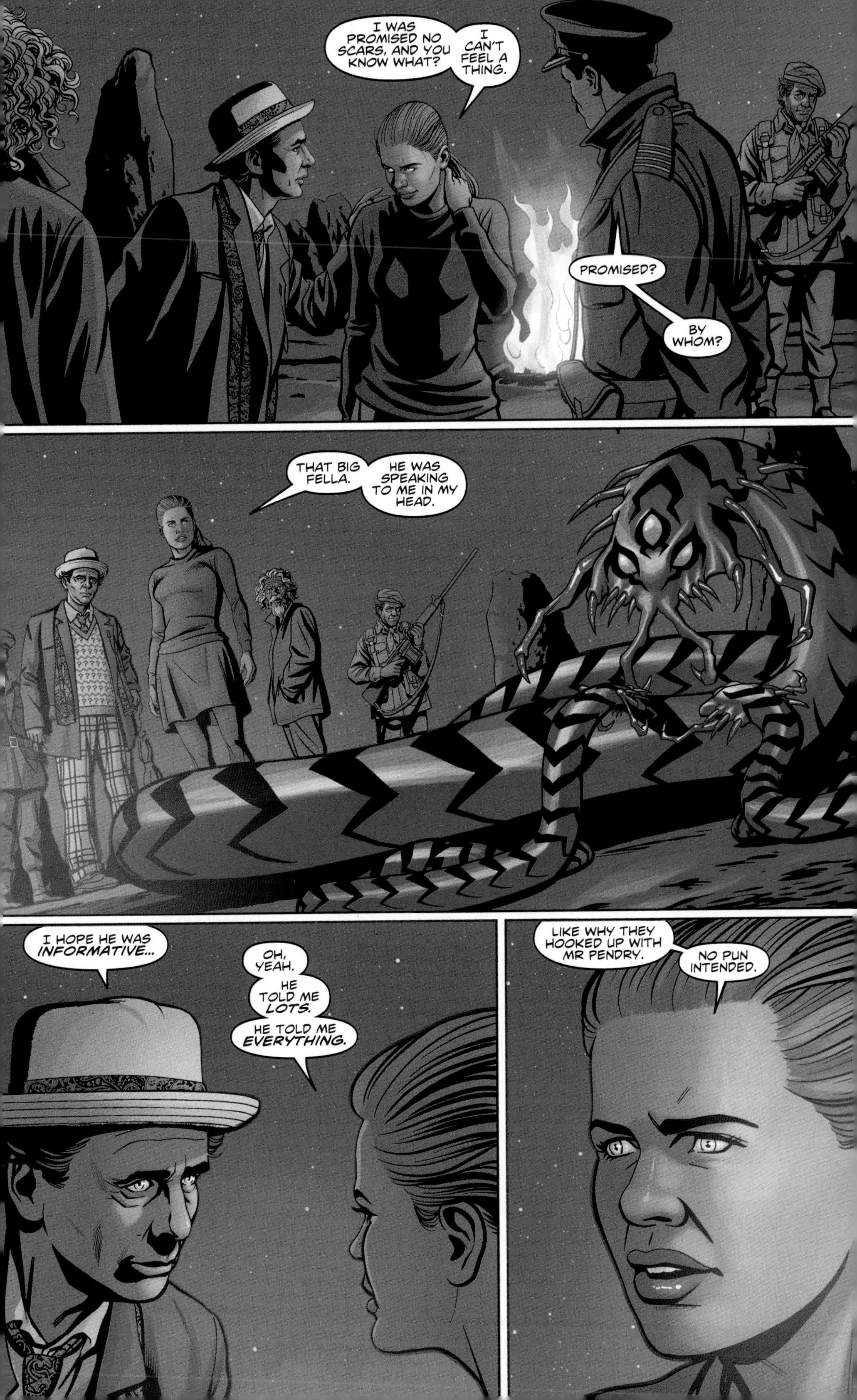
I WAS PROMISED NO SCARS, AND YOU KNOW WHAT?
I CAN'T FEEL A THING.
PROMISED?
BY WHOM?
THAT BIG FELLA.
HE WAS SPEAKING TO ME IN MY HEAD.
I HOPE HE WAS *INFORMATIVE*...
OH, YEAH.
HE TOLD ME *LOTS.*
HE TOLD ME *EVERYTHING.*
LIKE WHY THEY HOOKED UP WITH MR PENDRY.
NO PUN INTENDED.

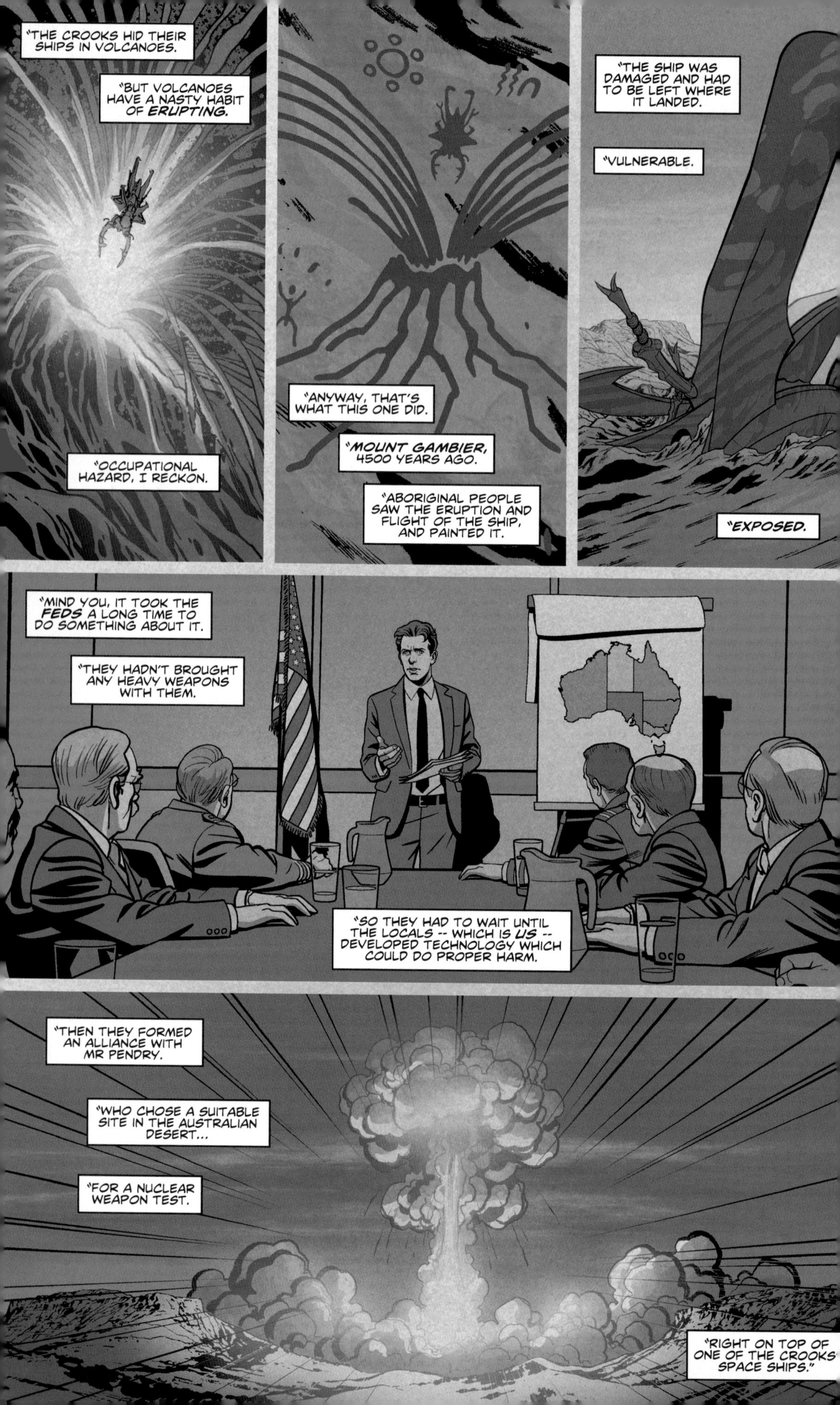

"THE CROOKS HID THEIR SHIPS IN VOLCANOES.
"BUT VOLCANOES HAVE A NASTY HABIT OF ERUPTING.
"OCCUPATIONAL HAZARD, I RECKON.
"ANYWAY, THAT'S WHAT THIS ONE DID.
"MOUNT GAMBIER, 4500 YEARS AGO.
"ABORIGINAL PEOPLE SAW THE ERUPTION AND FLIGHT OF THE SHIP, AND PAINTED IT.
"THE SHIP WAS DAMAGED AND HAD TO BE LEFT WHERE IT LANDED.
"VULNERABLE.
"EXPOSED.
"MIND YOU, IT TOOK THE FEDS A LONG TIME TO DO SOMETHING ABOUT IT.
"THEY HADN'T BROUGHT ANY HEAVY WEAPONS WITH THEM.
"SO THEY HAD TO WAIT UNTIL THE LOCALS -- WHICH IS US -- DEVELOPED TECHNOLOGY WHICH COULD DO PROPER HARM.
"THEN THEY FORMED AN ALLIANCE WITH MR PENDRY.
"WHO CHOSE A SUITABLE SITE IN THE AUSTRALIAN DESERT...
"FOR A NUCLEAR WEAPON TEST.
"RIGHT ON TOP OF ONE OF THE CROOKS SPACE SHIPS."

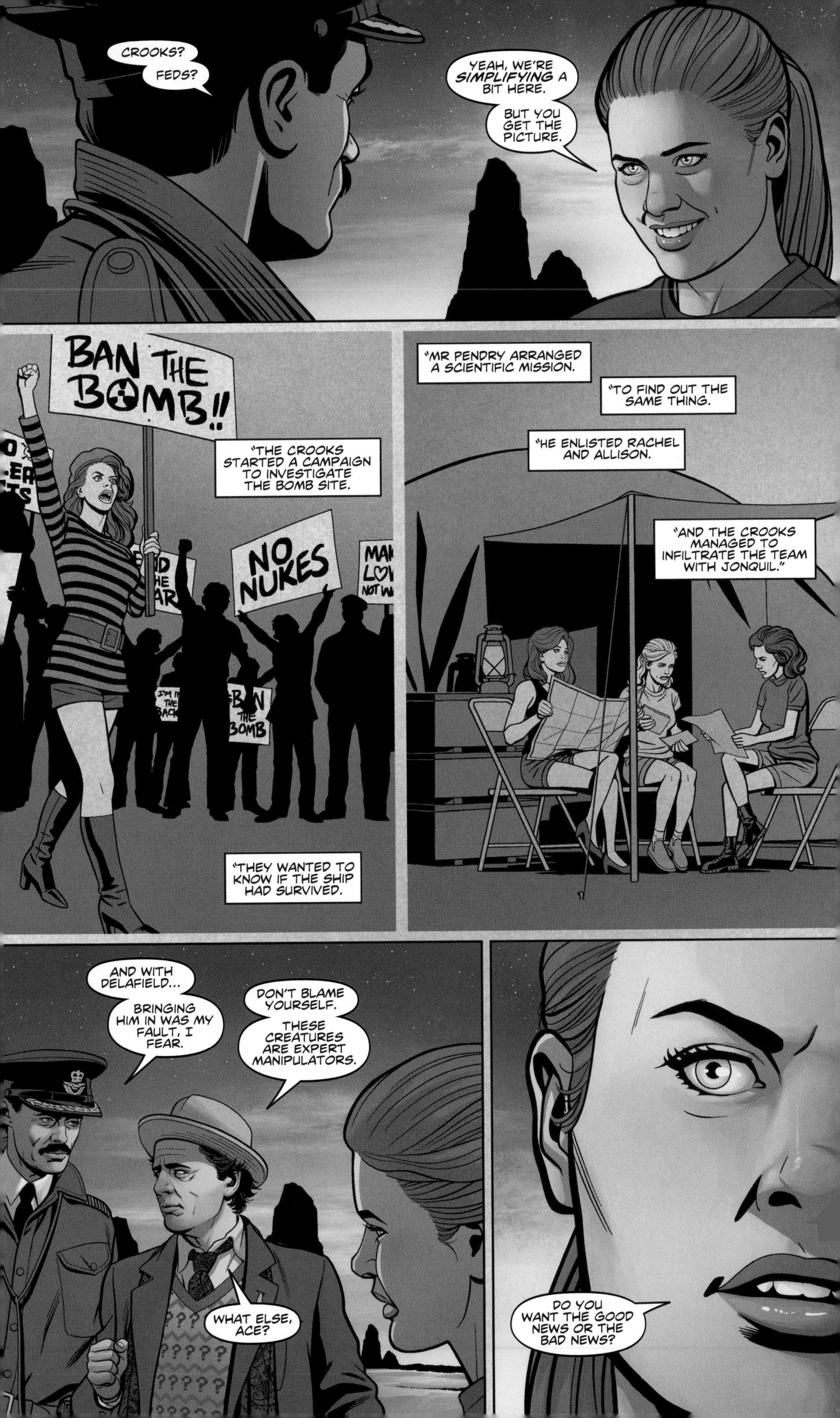
CROOKS?
FEDS?
YEAH, WE'RE SIMPLIFYING A BIT HERE.
BUT YOU GET THE PICTURE.
BAN THE BOMB!!
"THE CROOKS STARTED A CAMPAIGN TO INVESTIGATE THE BOMB SITE.
NO NUKES
BAN THE BOMB
"THEY WANTED TO KNOW IF THE SHIP HAD SURVIVED.
"MR PENDRY ARRANGED A SCIENTIFIC MISSION.
"TO FIND OUT THE SAME THING.
"HE ENLISTED RACHEL AND ALLISON.
"AND THE CROOKS MANAGED TO INFILTRATE THE TEAM WITH JONQUIL."
AND WITH DELAFIELD...
BRINGING HIM IN WAS MY FAULT, I FEAR.
DON'T BLAME YOURSELF.
THESE CREATURES ARE EXPERT MANIPULATORS.
WHAT ELSE, ACE?
DO YOU WANT THE GOOD NEWS OR THE BAD NEWS?

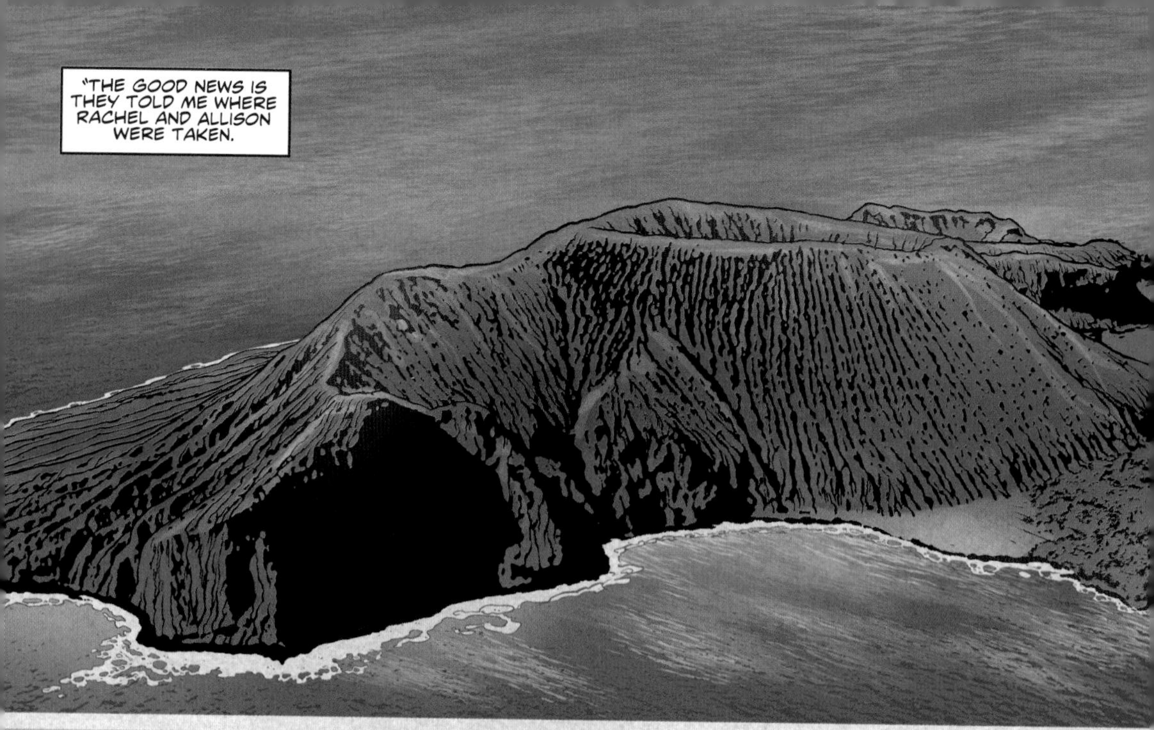
"THE GOOD NEWS IS THEY TOLD ME WHERE RACHEL AND ALLISON WERE TAKEN.

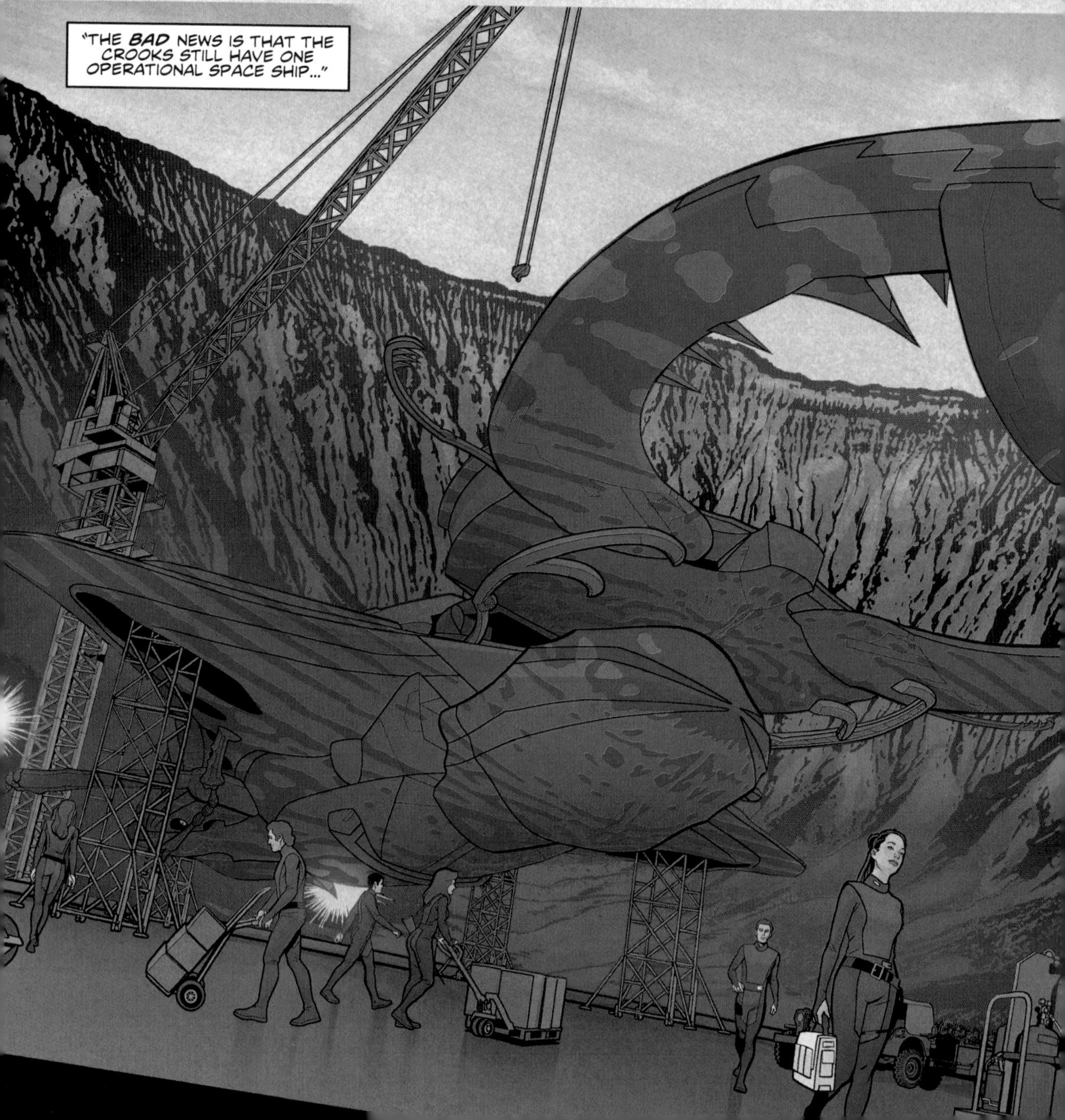
"THE BAD NEWS IS THAT THE CROOKS STILL HAVE ONE OPERATIONAL SPACE SHIP..."

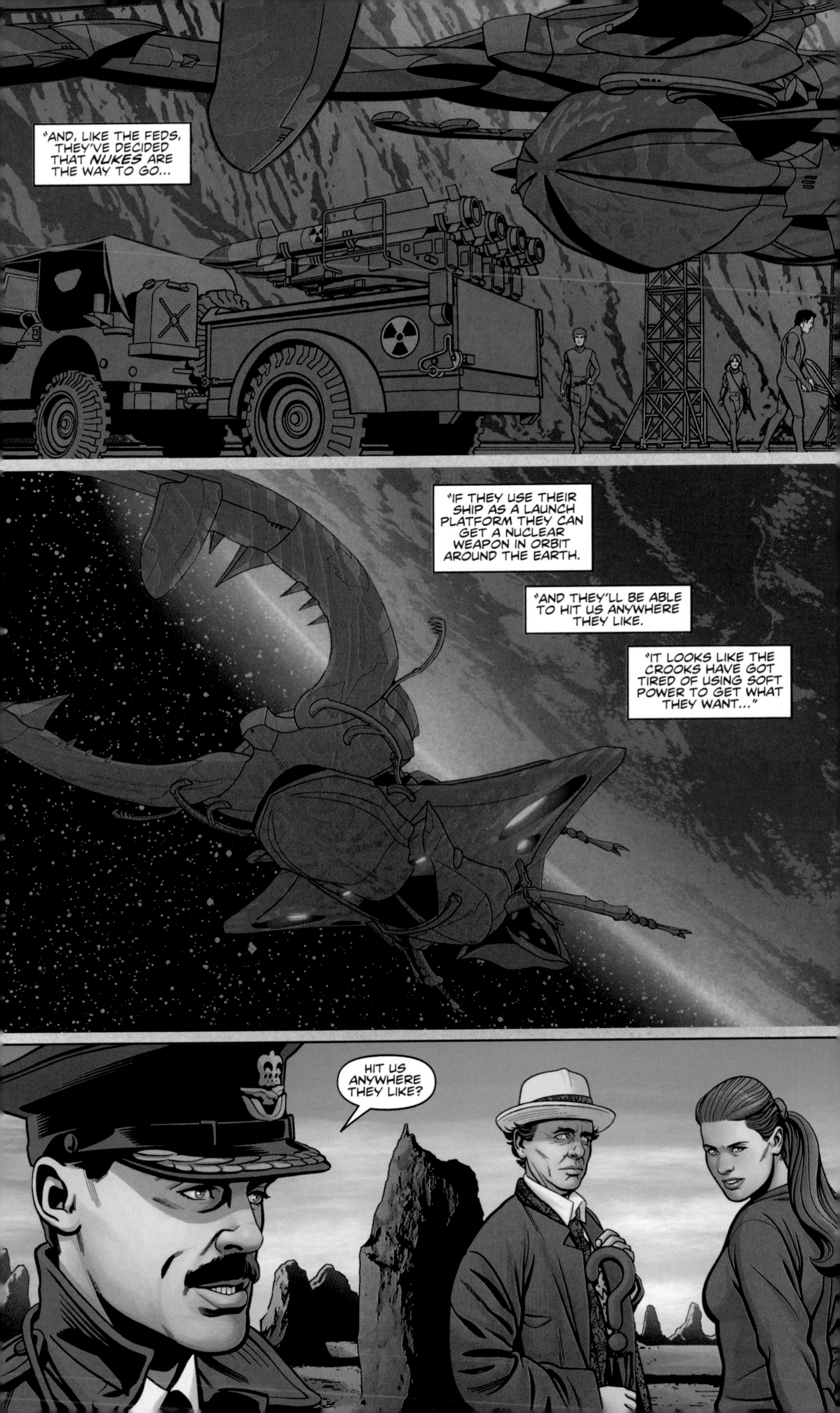
"AND, LIKE THE FEDS, THEY'VE DECIDED THAT NUKES ARE THE WAY TO GO...
"IF THEY USE THEIR SHIP AS A LAUNCH PLATFORM THEY CAN GET A NUCLEAR WEAPON IN ORBIT AROUND THE EARTH.
"AND THEY'LL BE ABLE TO HIT US ANYWHERE THEY LIKE.
"IT LOOKS LIKE THE CROOKS HAVE GOT TIRED OF USING SOFT POWER TO GET WHAT THEY WANT..."
HIT US ANYWHERE THEY LIKE?

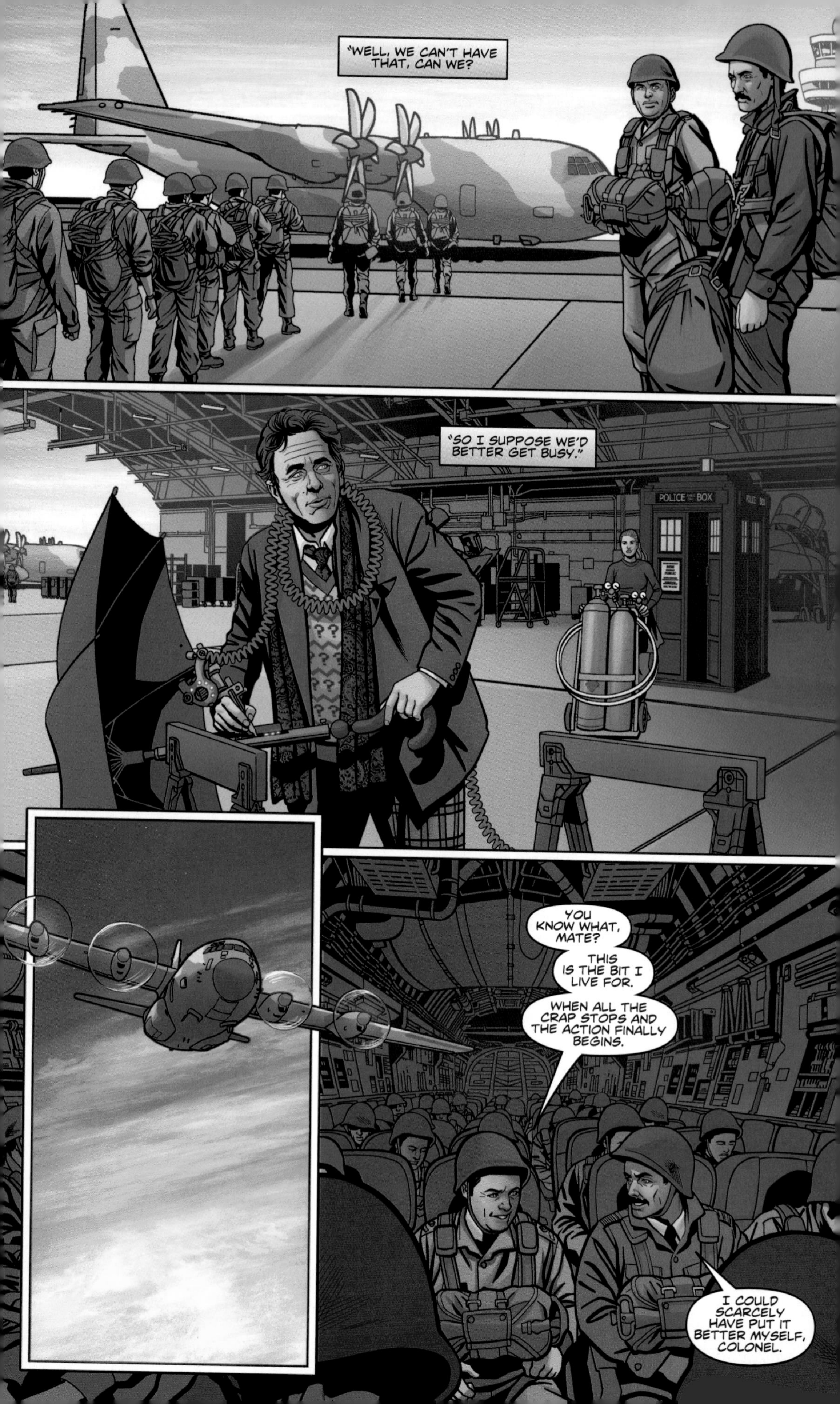
"WELL, WE CAN'T HAVE THAT, CAN WE?
"SO I SUPPOSE WE'D BETTER GET BUSY."
POLICE BOX
YOU KNOW WHAT, MATE?
THIS IS THE BIT I LIVE FOR.
WHEN ALL THE CRAP STOPS AND THE ACTION FINALLY BEGINS.
I COULD SCARCELY HAVE PUT IT BETTER MYSELF, COLONEL.

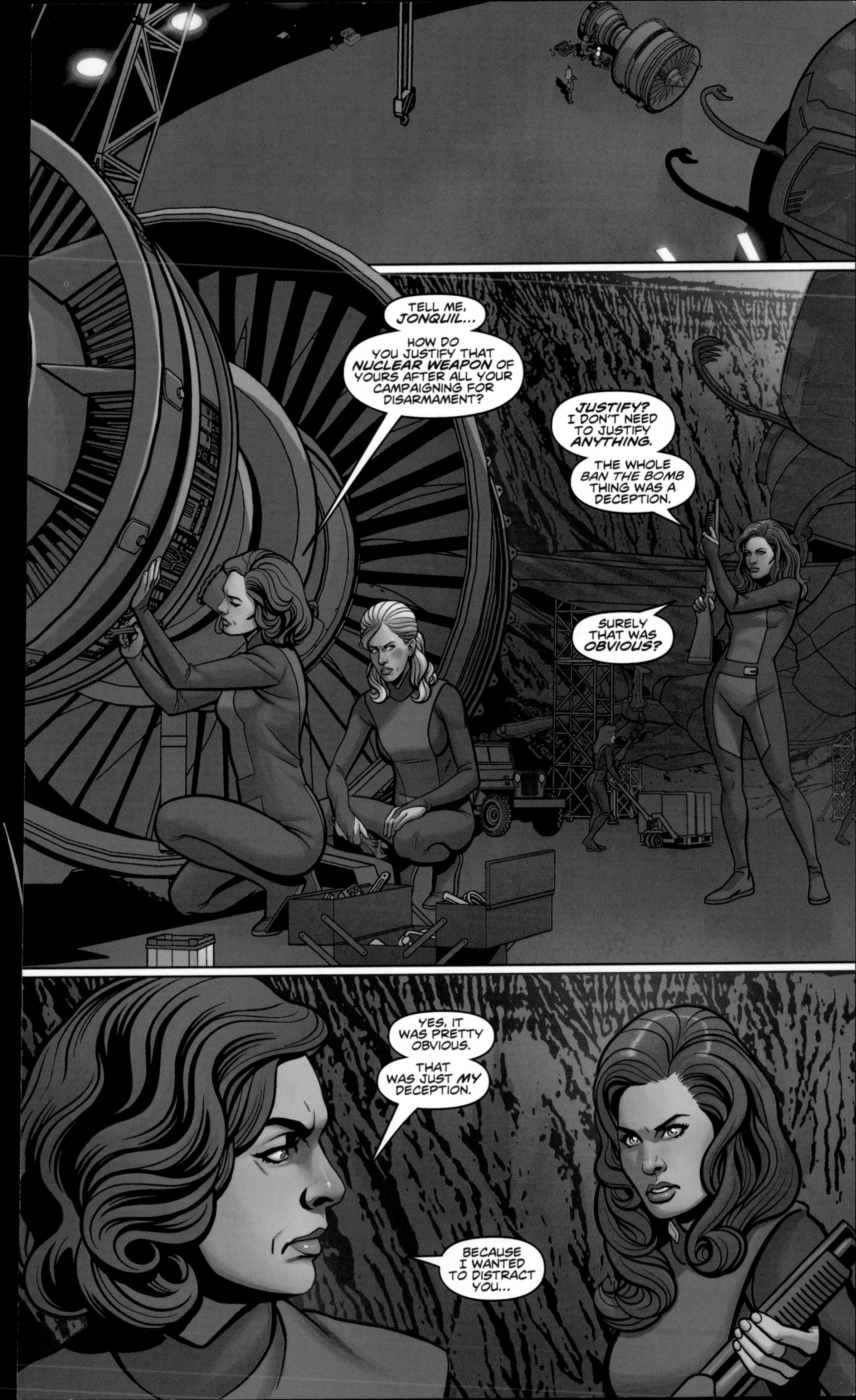

TELL ME, JONQUIL...
HOW DO YOU JUSTIFY THAT NUCLEAR WEAPON OF YOURS AFTER ALL YOUR CAMPAIGNING FOR DISARMAMENT?
JUSTIFY? I DON'T NEED TO JUSTIFY ANYTHING.
THE WHOLE BAN THE BOMB THING WAS A DECEPTION.
SURELY THAT WAS OBVIOUS?
YES, IT WAS PRETTY OBVIOUS.
THAT WAS JUST MY DECEPTION.
BECAUSE I WANTED TO DISTRACT YOU...

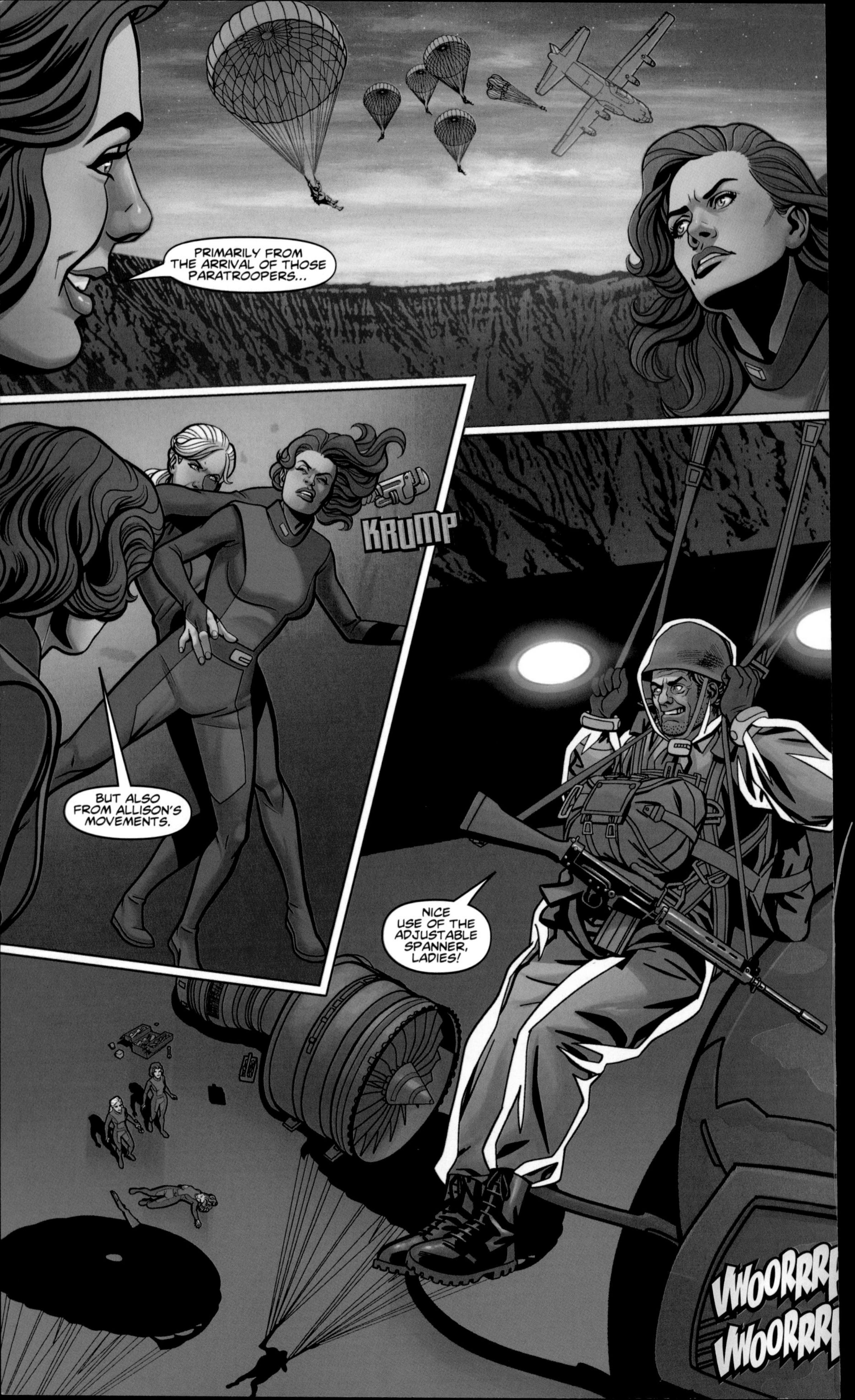
PRIMARILY FROM THE ARRIVAL OF THOSE PARATROOPERS...
BUT ALSO FROM ALLISON'S MOVEMENTS.
KRUMP
NICE USE OF THE ADJUSTABLE SPANNER, LADIES!
VWOORRRR
VWOORRRR

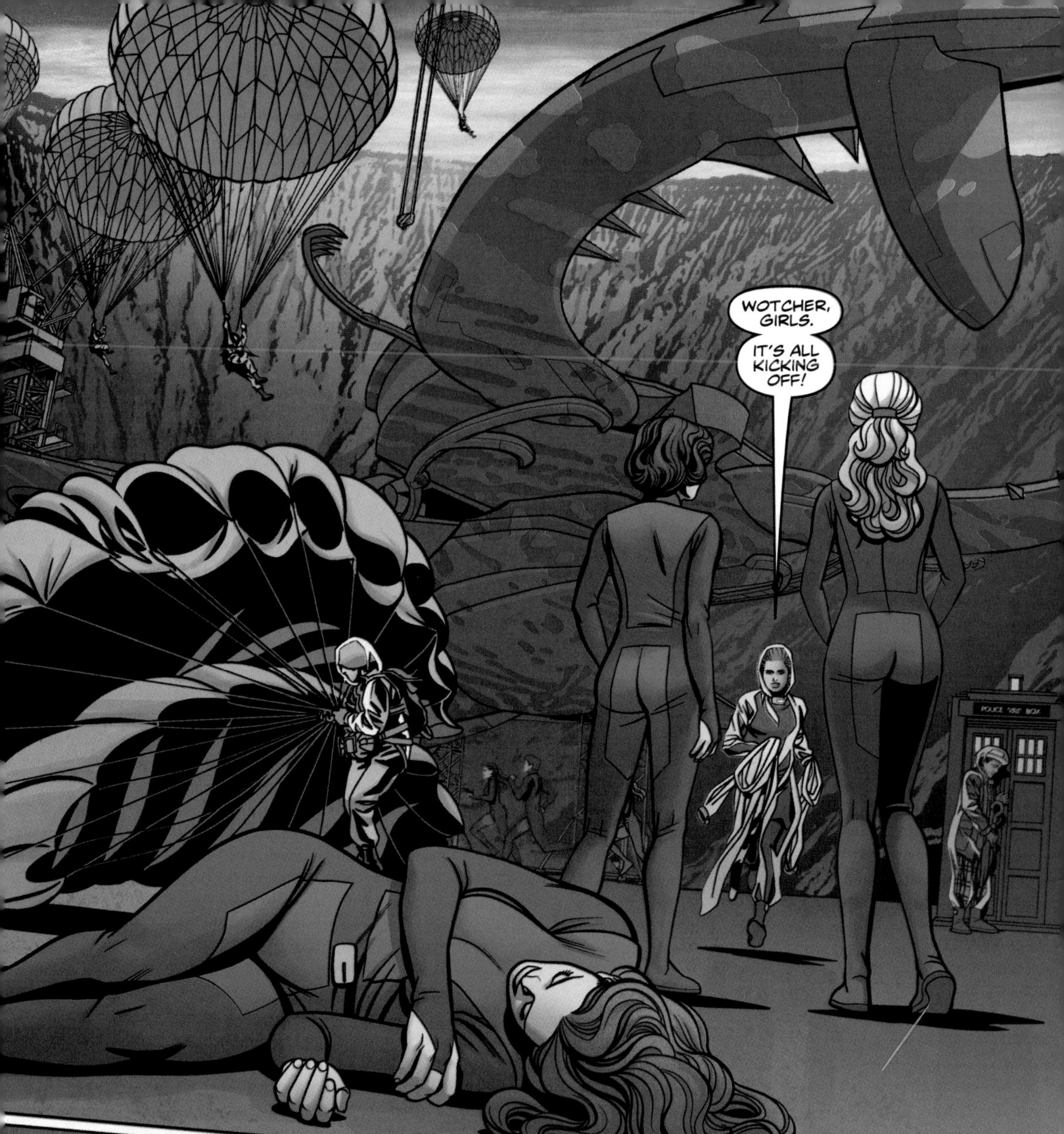
WOTCHER, GIRLS.
IT'S ALL KICKING OFF!
POLICE BOX

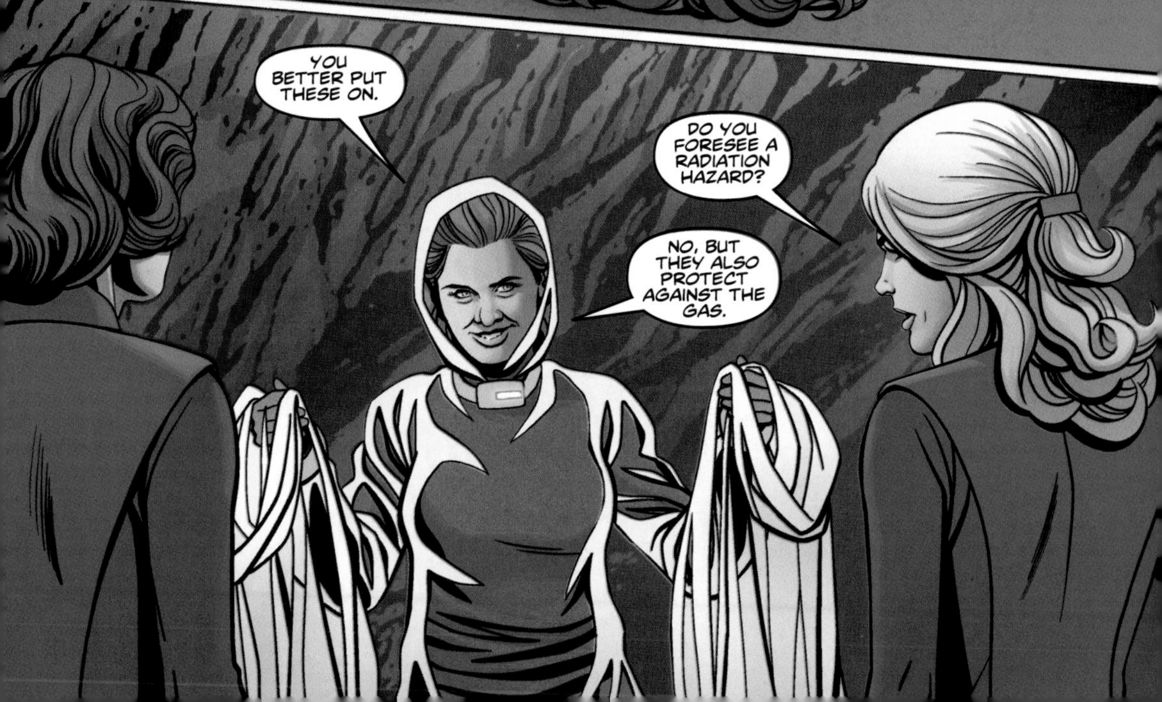
YOU BETTER PUT THESE ON.
DO YOU FORESEE A RADIATION HAZARD?
NO, BUT THEY ALSO PROTECT AGAINST THE GAS.

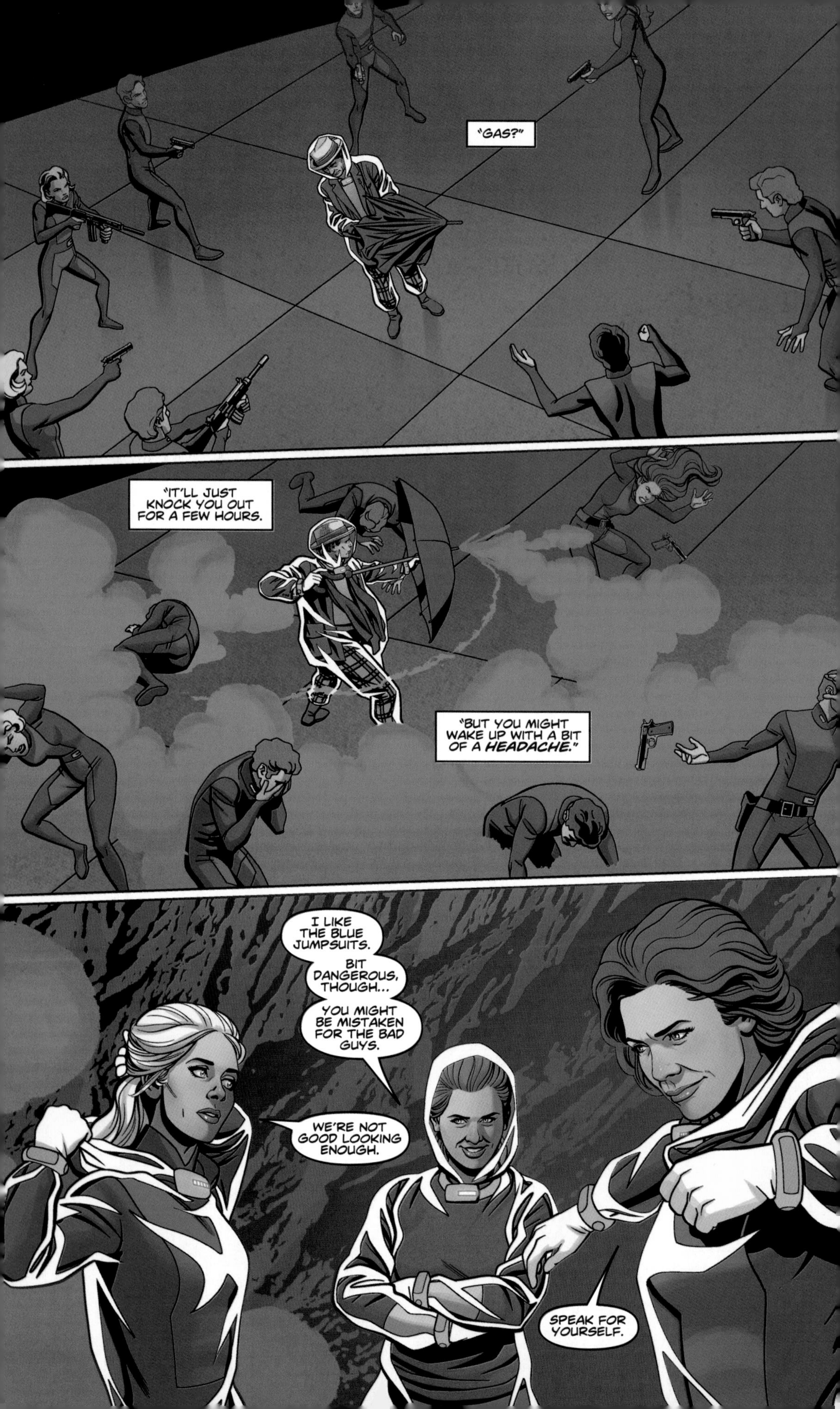
"GAS?"
"IT'LL JUST KNOCK YOU OUT FOR A FEW HOURS.
"BUT YOU MIGHT WAKE UP WITH A BIT OF A *HEADACHE.*"
I LIKE THE BLUE JUMPSUITS.
BIT DANGEROUS, THOUGH...
YOU MIGHT BE MISTAKEN FOR THE BAD GUYS.
WE'RE NOT GOOD LOOKING ENOUGH.
SPEAK FOR YOURSELF.

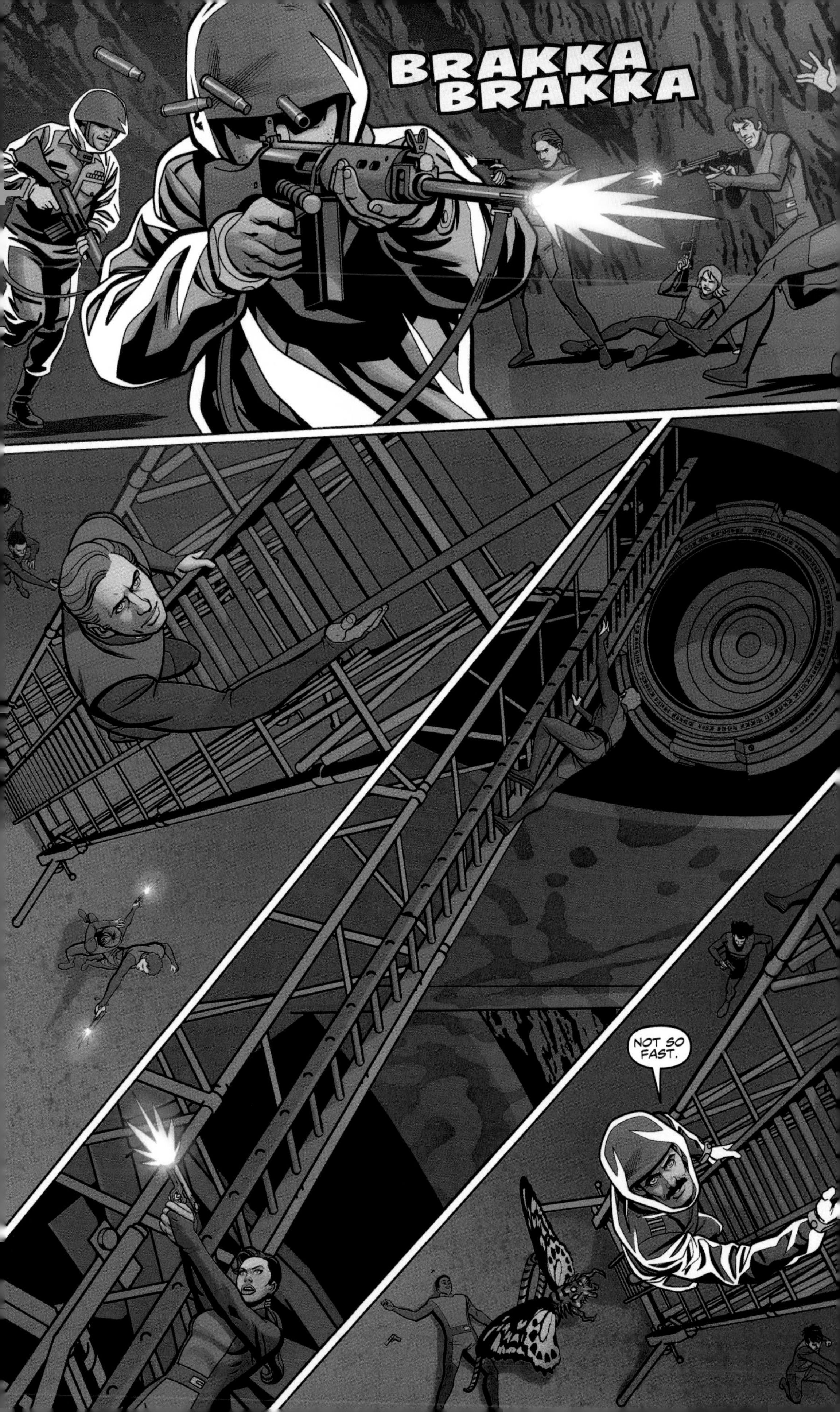
BRAKKA
BRAKKA
NOT SO FAST.

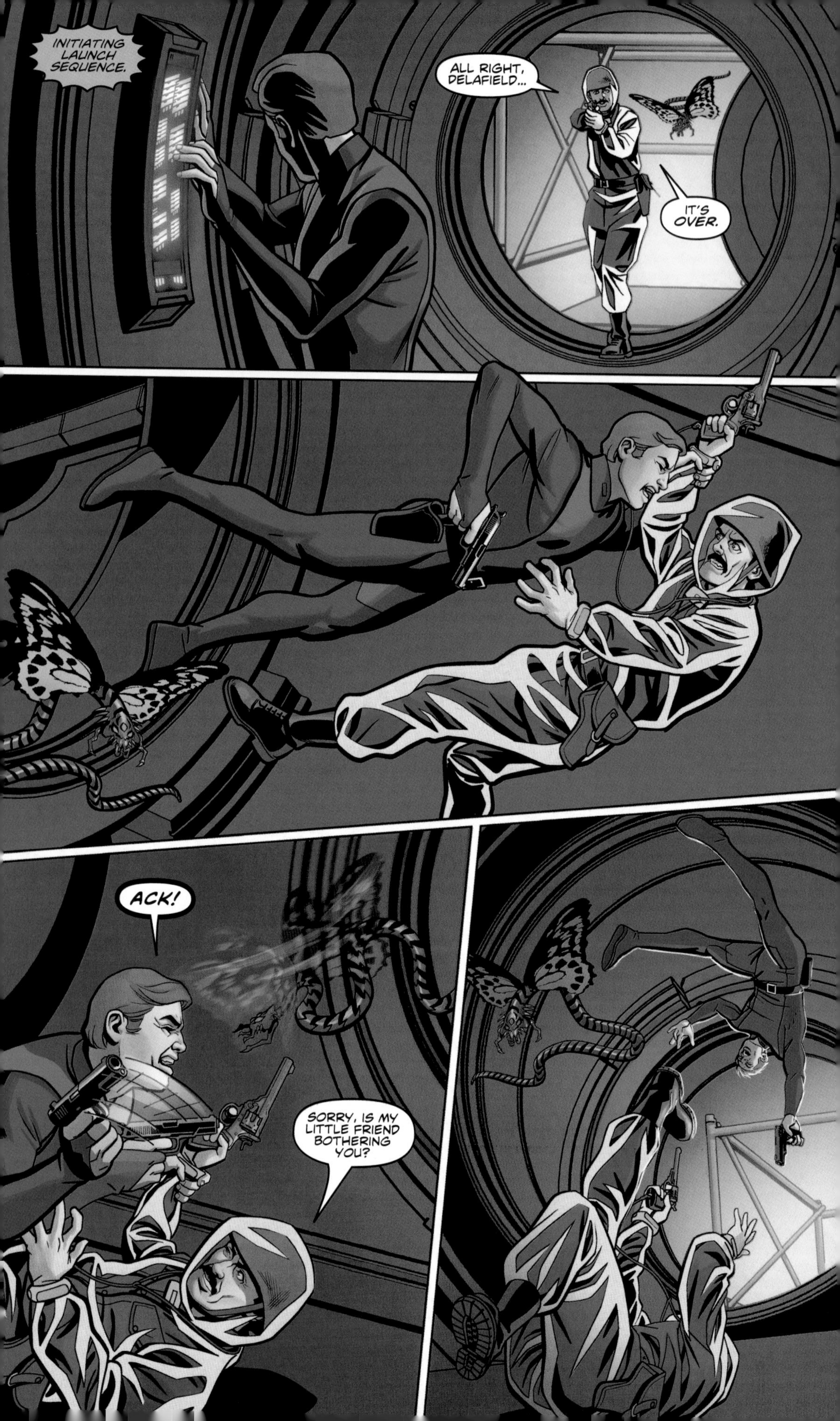
INITIATING LAUNCH SEQUENCE.
ALL RIGHT, DELAFIELD...
IT'S OVER.
ACK!
SORRY, IS MY LITTLE FRIEND BOTHERING YOU?

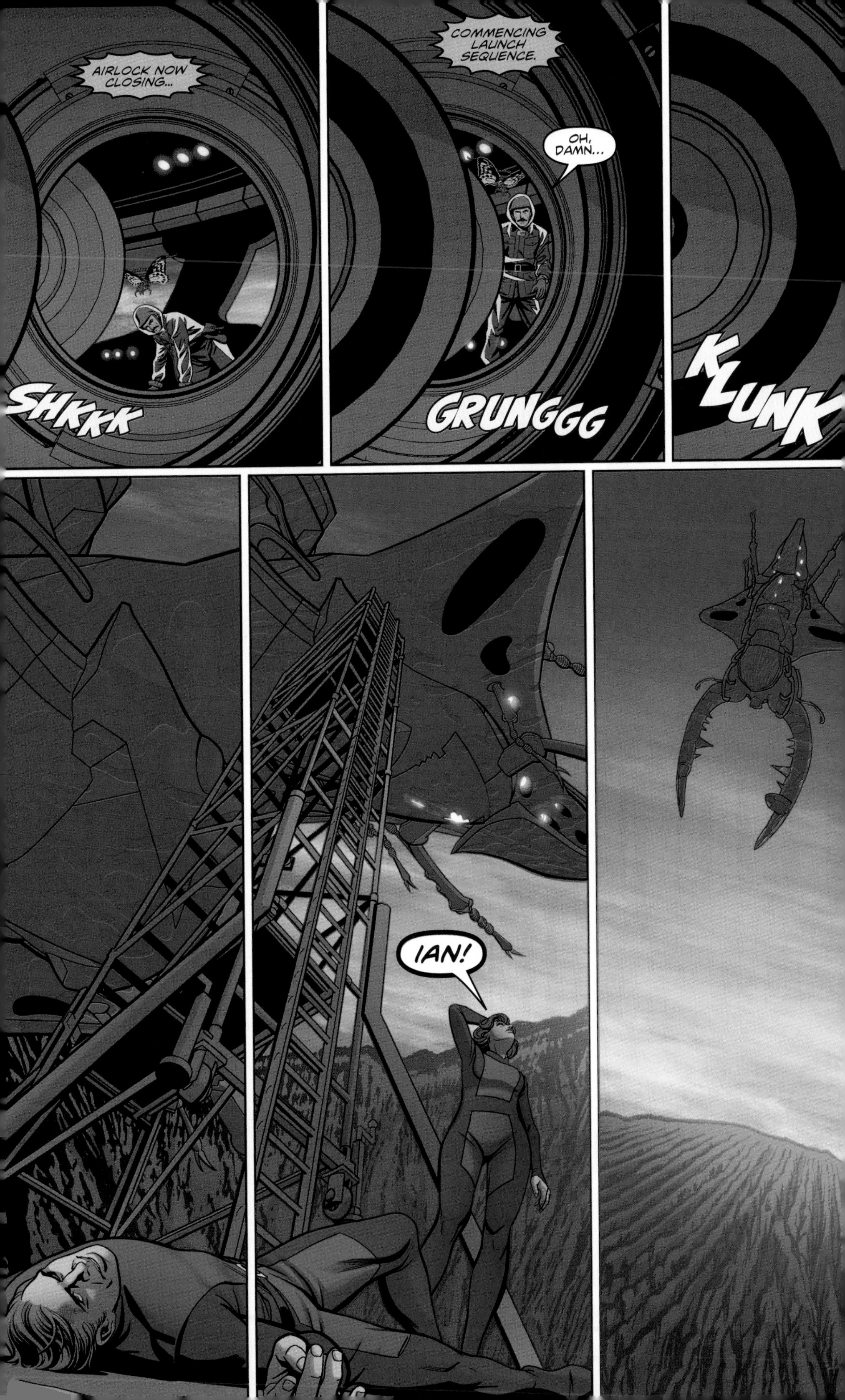
AIRLOCK NOW CLOSING...
SHKKK
COMMENCING LAUNCH SEQUENCE.
OH, DAMN...
GRUNGGG
KLUNK
IAN!

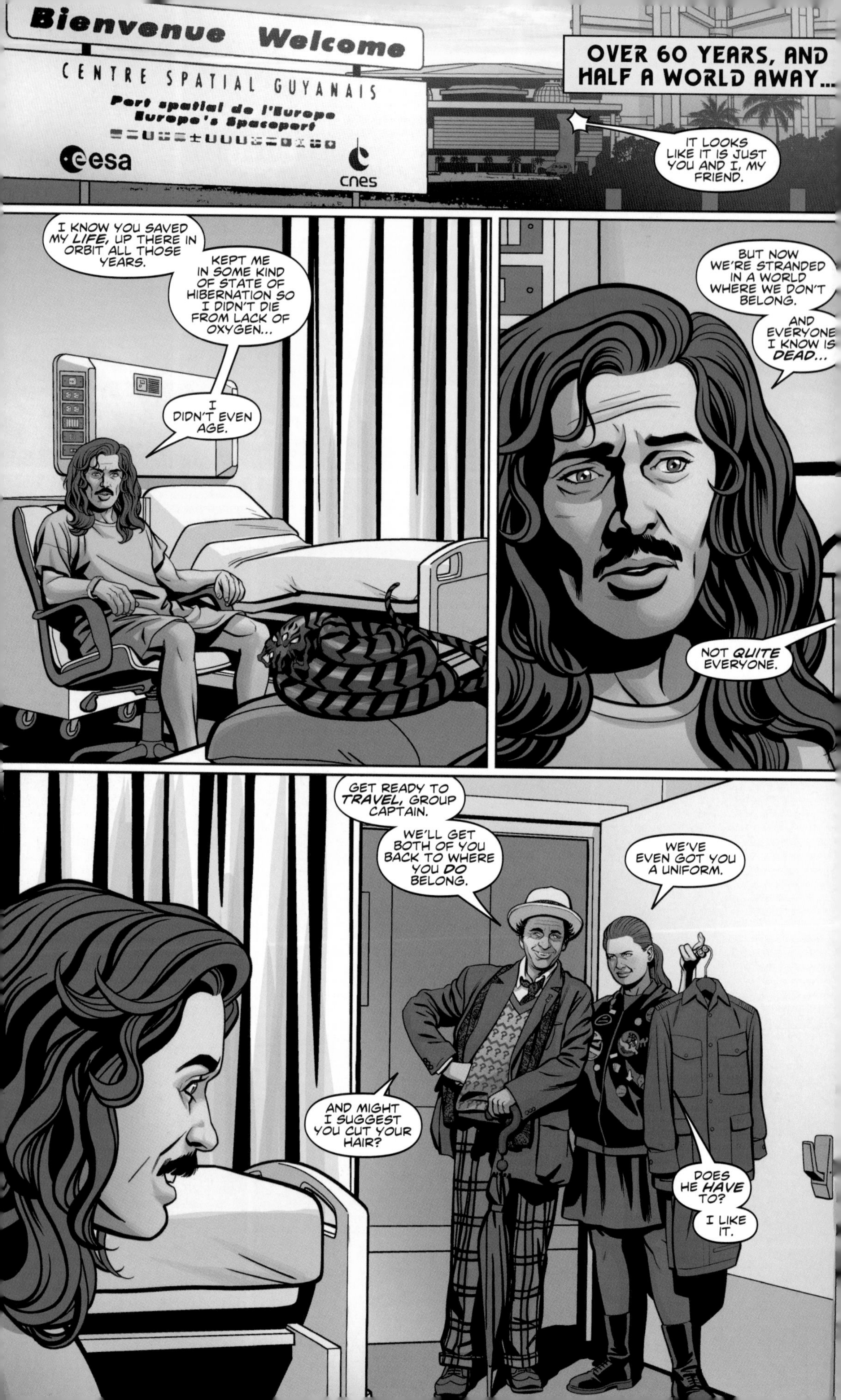
Bienvenue Welcome
CENTRE SPATIAL GUYANAIS
Port spatial de l'Europe
Europe's Spaceport
esa
cnes
OVER 60 YEARS, AND HALF A WORLD AWAY...
IT LOOKS LIKE IT IS JUST YOU AND I, MY FRIEND.
I KNOW YOU SAVED MY LIFE, UP THERE IN ORBIT ALL THOSE YEARS.
KEPT ME IN SOME KIND OF STATE OF HIBERNATION SO I DIDN'T DIE FROM LACK OF OXYGEN...
I DIDN'T EVEN AGE.
BUT NOW WE'RE STRANDED IN A WORLD WHERE WE DON'T BELONG.
AND EVERYONE I KNOW IS DEAD...
NOT QUITE EVERYONE.
GET READY TO TRAVEL, GROUP CAPTAIN.
WE'LL GET BOTH OF YOU BACK TO WHERE YOU DO BELONG.
WE'VE EVEN GOT YOU A UNIFORM.
AND MIGHT I SUGGEST YOU CUT YOUR HAIR?
DOES HE HAVE TO?
I LIKE IT.

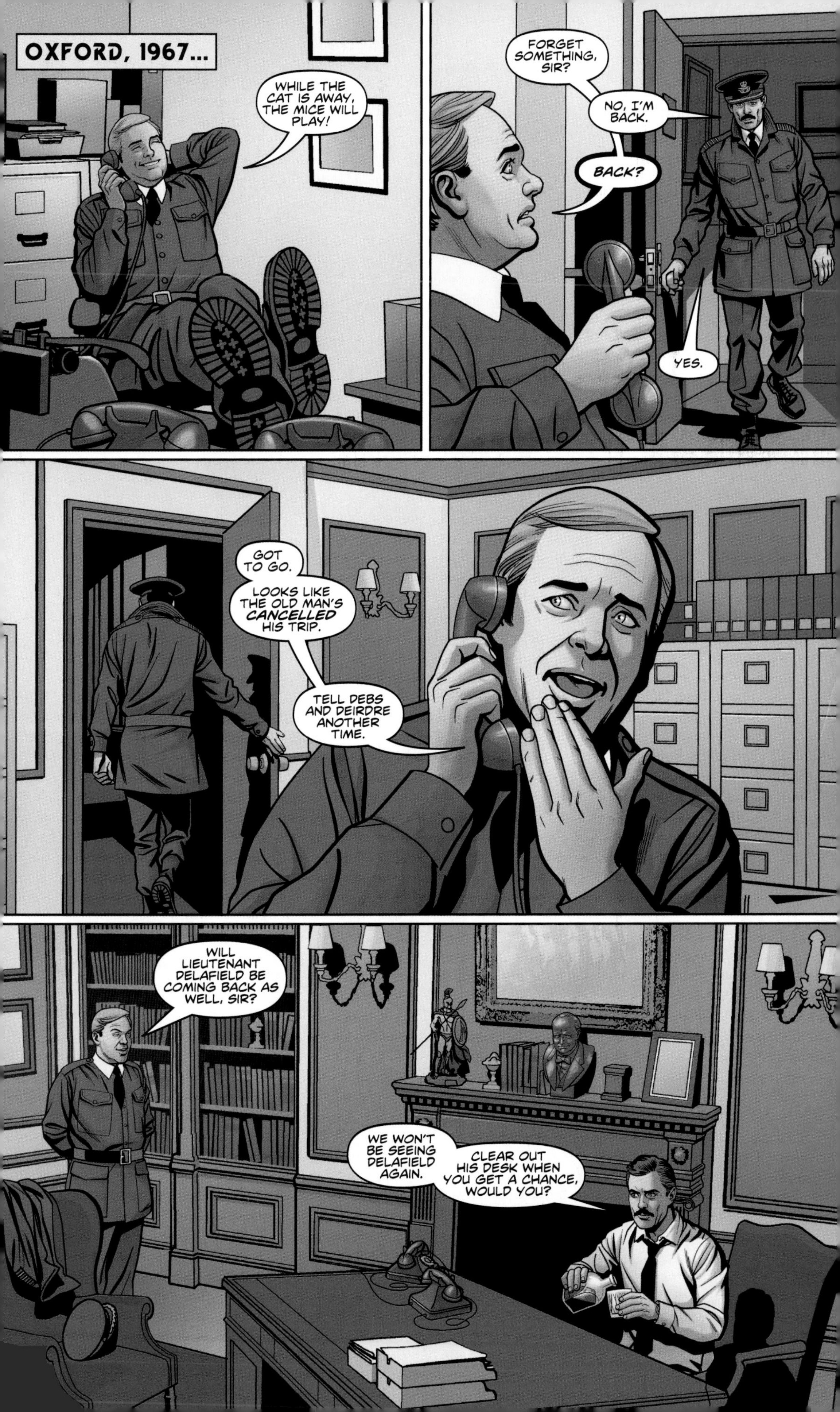
OXFORD, 1967...
WHILE THE CAT IS AWAY, THE MICE WILL PLAY!
FORGET SOMETHING, SIR?
NO, I'M BACK.
BACK?
YES.
GOT TO GO.
LOOKS LIKE THE OLD MAN'S CANCELLED HIS TRIP.
TELL DEBS AND DEIRDRE ANOTHER TIME.
WILL LIEUTENANT DELAFIELD BE COMING BACK AS WELL, SIR?
WE WON'T BE SEEING DELAFIELD AGAIN.
CLEAR OUT HIS DESK WHEN YOU GET A CHANCE, WOULD YOU?

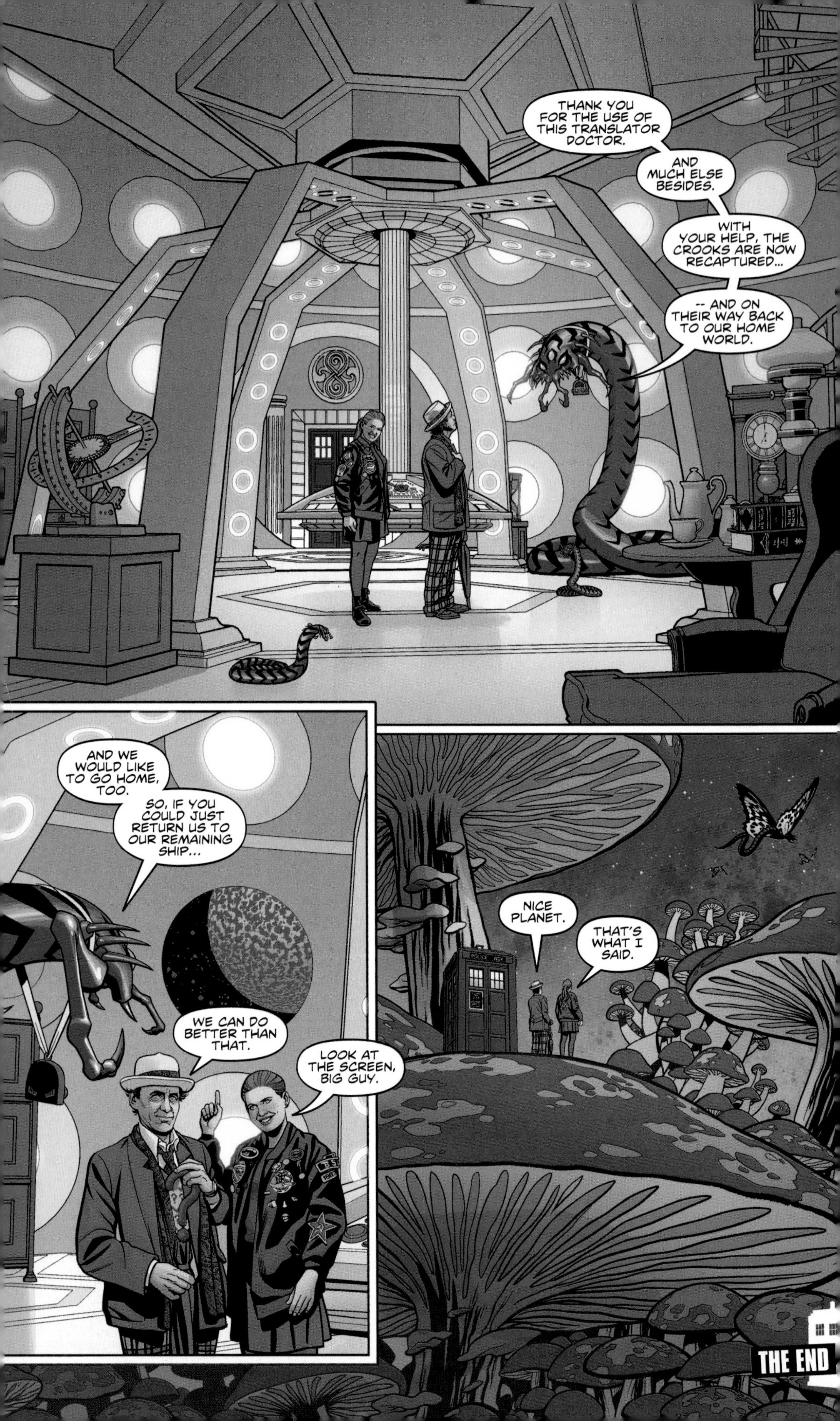

THANK YOU FOR THE USE OF THIS TRANSLATOR DOCTOR.
AND MUCH ELSE BESIDES.
WITH YOUR HELP, THE CROOKS ARE NOW RECAPTURED...
-- AND ON THEIR WAY BACK TO OUR HOME WORLD.
AND WE WOULD LIKE TO GO HOME, TOO.
SO, IF YOU COULD JUST RETURN US TO OUR REMAINING SHIP...
WE CAN DO BETTER THAN THAT.
LOOK AT THE SCREEN, BIG GUY.
NICE PLANET.
THAT'S WHAT I SAID.
POLICE BOX
THE END

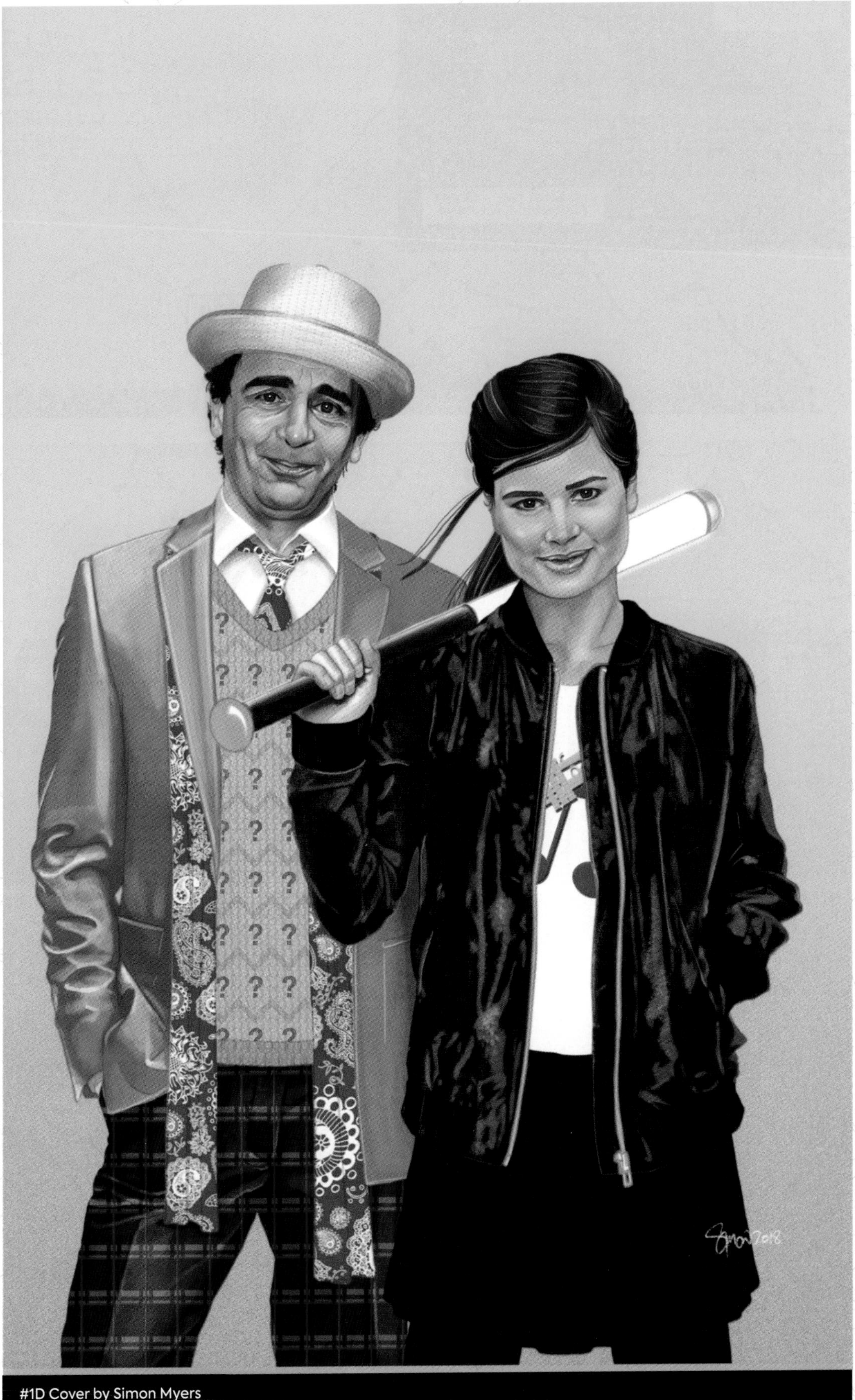
Simon 2018

#1D Cover by Simon Myers

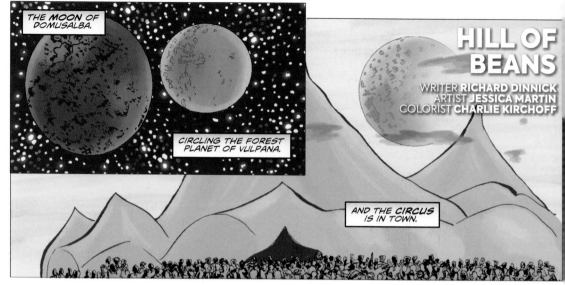

THE MOON OF DOMUSALBA.

CIRCLING THE FOREST PLANET OF VULPANA.

HILL OF BEANS

WRITER **RICHARD DINNICK**
ARTIST **JESSICA MARTIN**
COLORIST **CHARLIE KIRCHOFF**

AND THE *CIRCUS* IS IN TOWN.

BUT IT WILL TAKE A *SPECIAL* TYPE OF CIRCUS TO CHEER UP THE PEOPLE HERE.

WHY ARE THEY ALL SO *SAD*, TAYLOR?

WOW, QUIANA. NEWS IS SOMETHING THAT HAPPENS TO *OTHER* PEOPLE, ISN'T IT?

VULPANAN FORCES HAVE JUST *ANNEXED* THE MOON.

AND THEY ARE *NOT* THE GOOD GUYS.

THEY'RE *FORCING* THE REFUGEES FROM THEIR OWN PLANET TO WEAR *ARMBANDS* TO MARK THEM OUT.

FORTUNATELY, THIS IS NO *ORDINARY* CIRCUS.

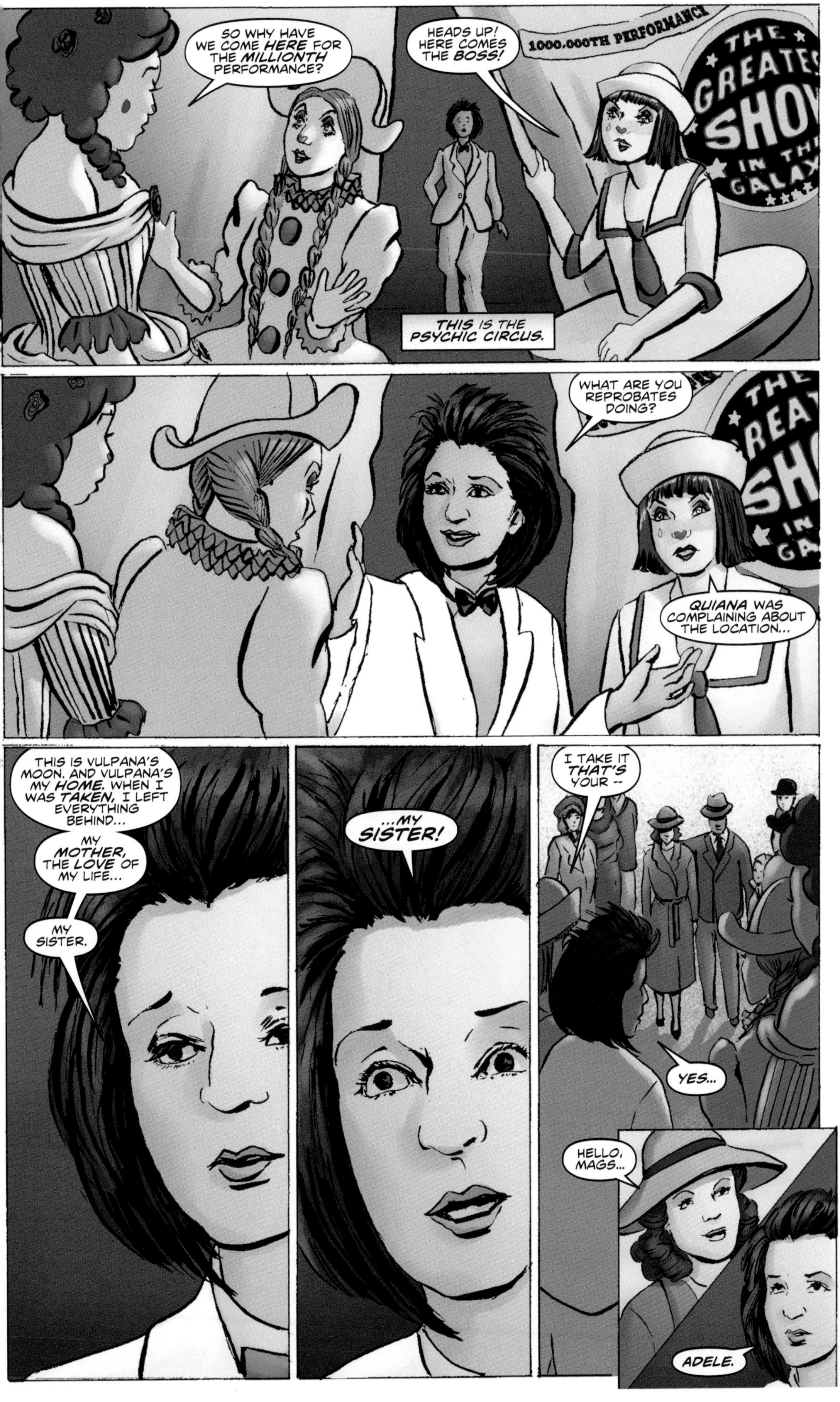

SO WHY HAVE WE COME HERE FOR THE MILLIONTH PERFORMANCE?
HEADS UP! HERE COMES THE BOSS!
1000,000TH PERFORMANCE
THE GREATEST SHOW IN THE GALAXY
THIS IS THE PSYCHIC CIRCUS.
WHAT ARE YOU REPROBATES DOING?
QUIANA WAS COMPLAINING ABOUT THE LOCATION...
THIS IS VULPANA'S MOON. AND VULPANA'S MY HOME. WHEN I WAS TAKEN, I LEFT EVERYTHING BEHIND...
MY MOTHER, THE LOVE OF MY LIFE...
MY SISTER.
...MY SISTER!
I TAKE IT THAT'S YOUR --
YES...
HELLO, MAGS...
ADELE.

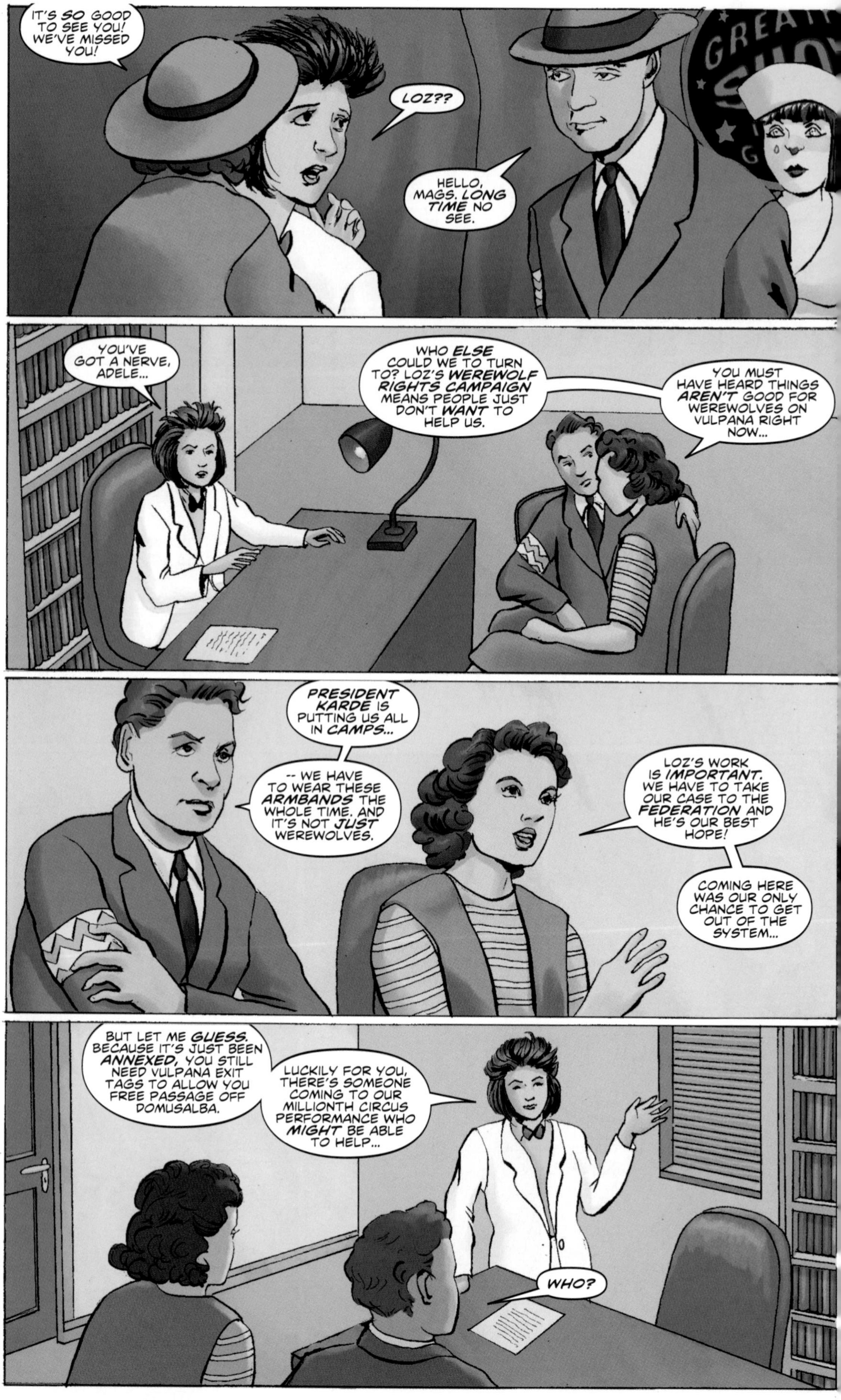
IT'S SO GOOD TO SEE YOU! WE'VE MISSED YOU!
LOZ??
HELLO, MAGS. LONG TIME NO SEE.
YOU'VE GOT A NERVE, ADELE...
WHO ELSE COULD WE TO TURN TO? LOZ'S WEREWOLF RIGHTS CAMPAIGN MEANS PEOPLE JUST DON'T WANT TO HELP US.
YOU MUST HAVE HEARD THINGS AREN'T GOOD FOR WEREWOLVES ON VULPANA RIGHT NOW...
PRESIDENT KARDE IS PUTTING US ALL IN CAMPS...
-- WE HAVE TO WEAR THESE ARMBANDS THE WHOLE TIME. AND IT'S NOT JUST WEREWOLVES.
LOZ'S WORK IS IMPORTANT. WE HAVE TO TAKE OUR CASE TO THE FEDERATION AND HE'S OUR BEST HOPE!
COMING HERE WAS OUR ONLY CHANCE TO GET OUT OF THE SYSTEM...
BUT LET ME GUESS. BECAUSE IT'S JUST BEEN ANNEXED, YOU STILL NEED VULPANA EXIT TAGS TO ALLOW YOU FREE PASSAGE OFF DOMUSALBA.
LUCKILY FOR YOU, THERE'S SOMEONE COMING TO OUR MILLIONTH CIRCUS PERFORMANCE WHO MIGHT BE ABLE TO HELP...
WHO?

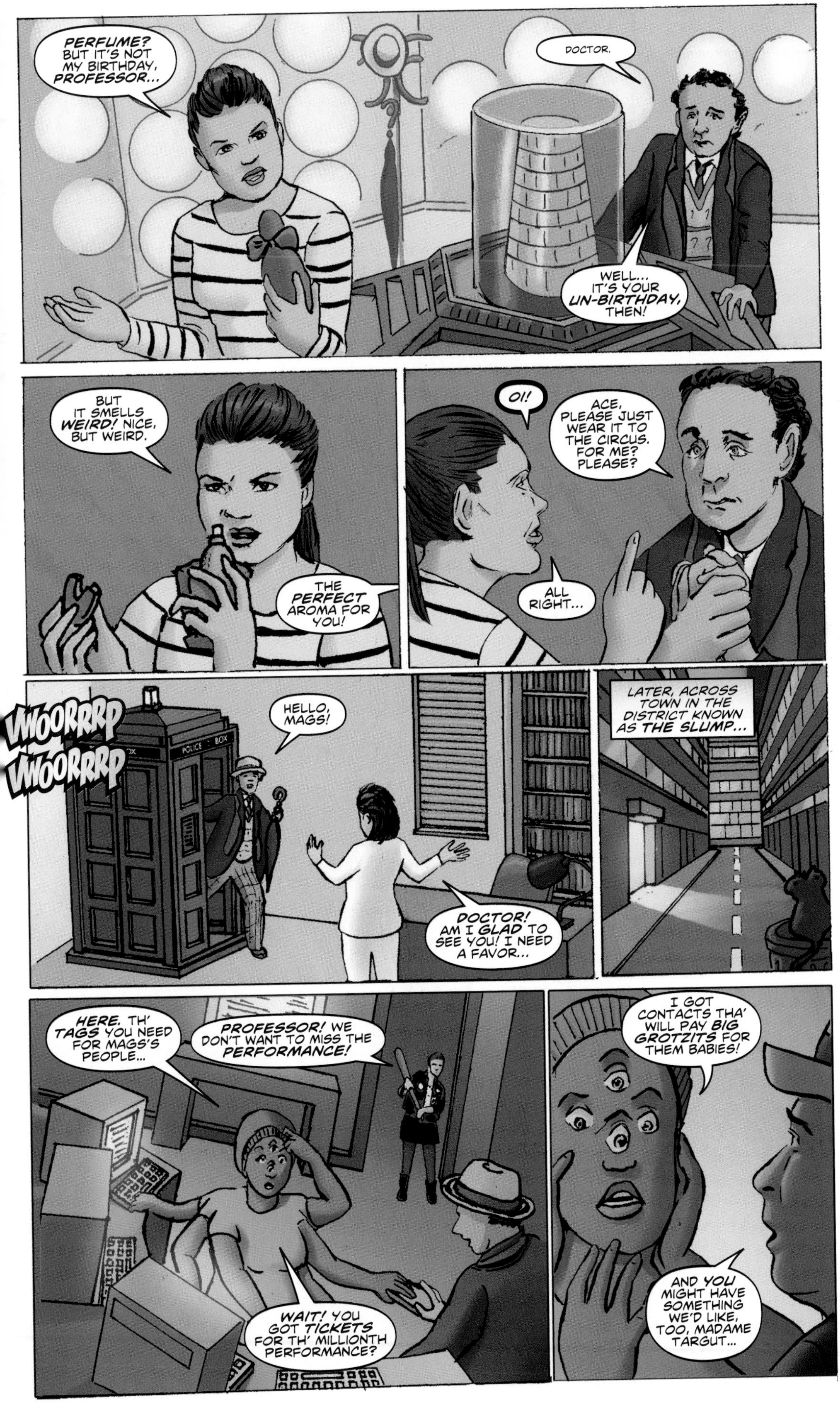
PERFUME? BUT IT'S NOT MY BIRTHDAY, PROFESSOR...
DOCTOR.
WELL... IT'S YOUR UN-BIRTHDAY, THEN!
BUT IT SMELLS WEIRD! NICE, BUT WEIRD.
THE PERFECT AROMA FOR YOU!
OI!
ACE, PLEASE JUST WEAR IT TO THE CIRCUS. FOR ME? PLEASE?
ALL RIGHT...
VWOORRRP
VWOORRRP
POLICE BOX
HELLO, MAGS!
DOCTOR! AM I GLAD TO SEE YOU! I NEED A FAVOR...
LATER, ACROSS TOWN IN THE DISTRICT KNOWN AS THE SLUMP...
HERE. TH' TAGS YOU NEED FOR MAGS'S PEOPLE...
PROFESSOR! WE DON'T WANT TO MISS THE PERFORMANCE!
WAIT! YOU GOT TICKETS FOR TH' MILLIONTH PERFORMANCE?
I GOT CONTACTS THA' WILL PAY BIG GROTZITS FOR THEM BABIES!
AND YOU MIGHT HAVE SOMETHING WE'D LIKE, TOO, MADAME TARGUT...

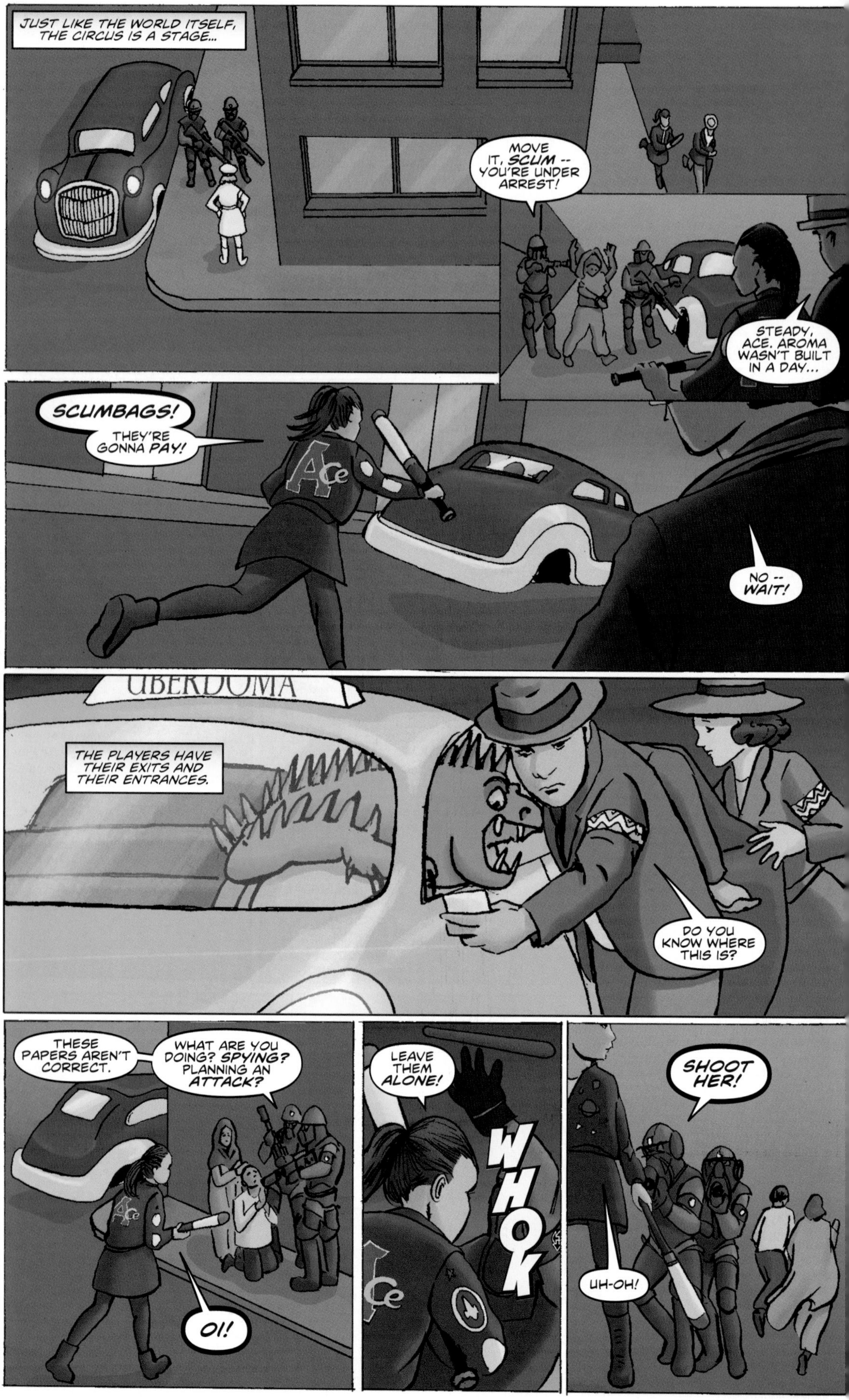
JUST LIKE THE WORLD ITSELF, THE CIRCUS IS A STAGE...
MOVE IT, SCUM -- YOU'RE UNDER ARREST!
STEADY, ACE. AROMA WASN'T BUILT IN A DAY...
SCUMBAGS!
THEY'RE GONNA PAY!
NO -- WAIT!
UBERDOMA
THE PLAYERS HAVE THEIR EXITS AND THEIR ENTRANCES.
DO YOU KNOW WHERE THIS IS?
THESE PAPERS AREN'T CORRECT.
WHAT ARE YOU DOING? SPYING? PLANNING AN ATTACK?
OI!
LEAVE THEM ALONE!
WHOK
SHOOT HER!
UH-OH!

FZZZZZT FZZZZZT
FZZZZZT FZZZZZT

FZZZZZT
FZZZZZT

~ PLEASE RECALL ONE THING ~

~ A FLING IS STILL A FLING ~

WHO'S THE *OWNER* HERE? WE'RE LOOKING FOR A *WOMAN*.

I'M *MAGNU SVALK*, I AM THE PROPRIETOR.

BUT THIS ISN'T THAT KINDA *PLACE*... YOU WANT *BARE NECESSITIES*, DOWN THE STREET.

SHE'S *NOT* HERE. LET'S GO...

'SPOSE WE CAN TRY THE PLACE *DOWN THE STREET*...

I KNOW *ALL* MY WAITRESSES. YOU AIN'T ONE OF THEM. EVEN THOUGH YOU SMELL... NICE!

TALK!

THEY TOOK A FRIEND OF MINE -- *TARGUT.* I WAS *TRYING* TO GET HER BACK.

THEY WERE TRYING TO *KILL* ME.

I KNOW MADAME TARGUT. YOU'LL FIND HER AT THE *DETENTION CENTER.* I'LL CLUE YOU IN HOW TO GET THERE.

THANKS. I THINK...

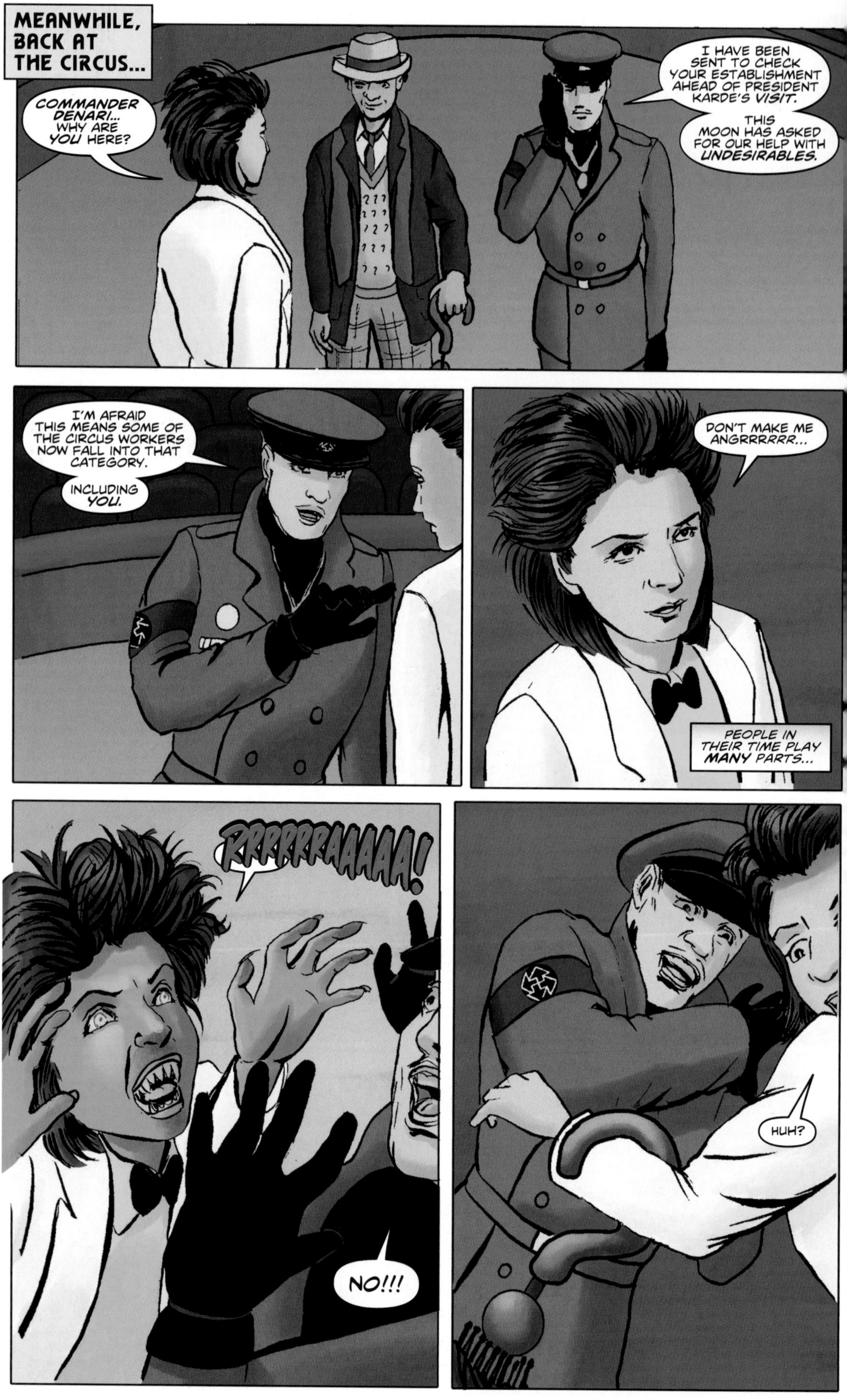
MEANWHILE, BACK AT THE CIRCUS...
COMMANDER DENARI... WHY ARE YOU HERE?
I HAVE BEEN SENT TO CHECK YOUR ESTABLISHMENT AHEAD OF PRESIDENT KARDE'S VISIT.
THIS MOON HAS ASKED FOR OUR HELP WITH UNDESIRABLES.
I'M AFRAID THIS MEANS SOME OF THE CIRCUS WORKERS NOW FALL INTO THAT CATEGORY.
INCLUDING YOU.
DON'T MAKE ME ANGRRRRRR...
PEOPLE IN THEIR TIME PLAY MANY PARTS...
RRRRRRAAAAA!
NO!!!
HUH?

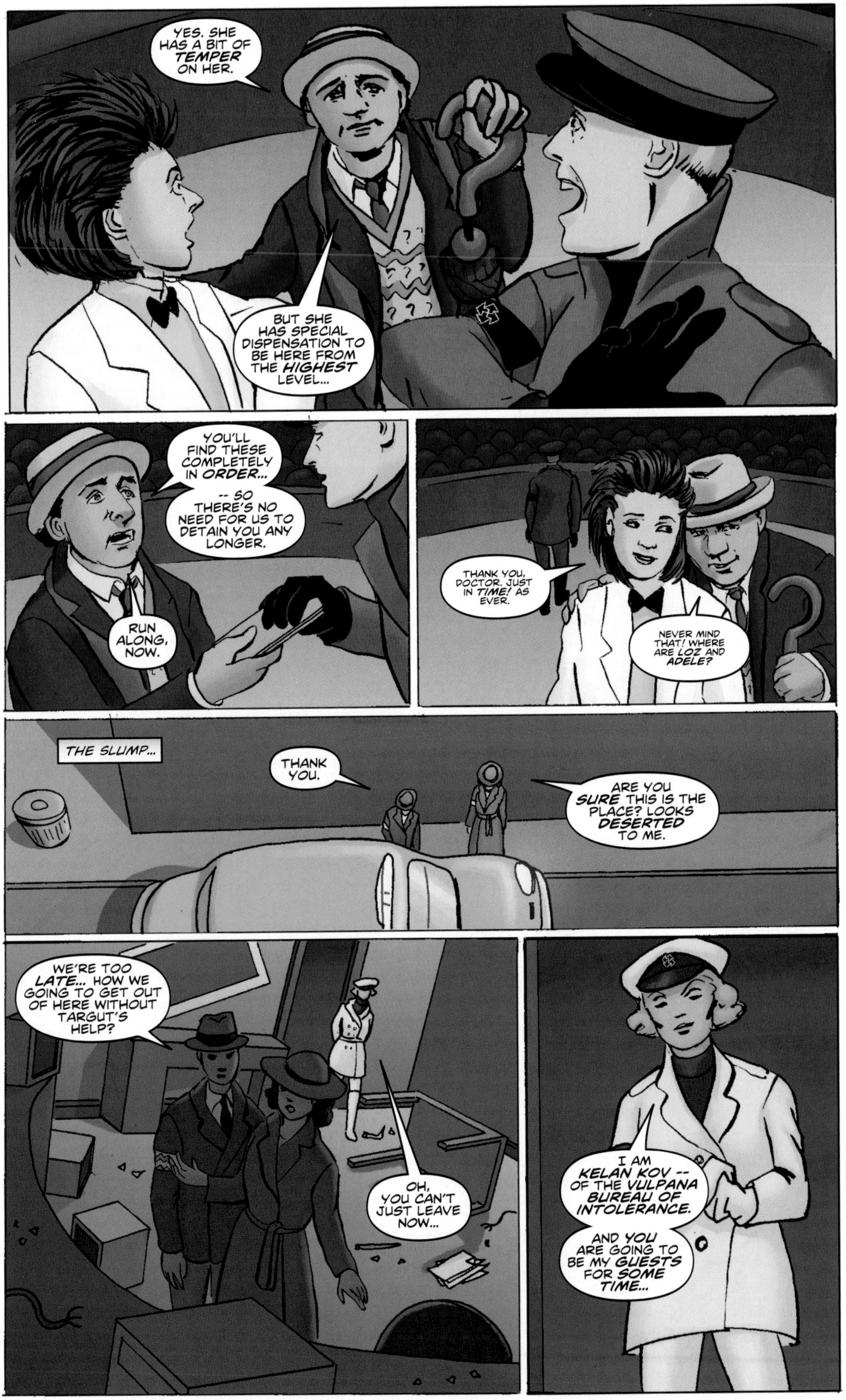
YES. SHE HAS A BIT OF TEMPER ON HER.
BUT SHE HAS SPECIAL DISPENSATION TO BE HERE FROM THE HIGHEST LEVEL...
YOU'LL FIND THESE COMPLETELY IN ORDER...
-- SO THERE'S NO NEED FOR US TO DETAIN YOU ANY LONGER.
RUN ALONG, NOW.
THANK YOU, DOCTOR. JUST IN TIME! AS EVER.
NEVER MIND THAT! WHERE ARE LOZ AND ADELE?
THE SLUMP...
THANK YOU.
ARE YOU SURE THIS IS THE PLACE? LOOKS DESERTED TO ME.
WE'RE TOO LATE... HOW WE GOING TO GET OUT OF HERE WITHOUT TARGUT'S HELP?
OH, YOU CAN'T JUST LEAVE NOW...
I AM KELAN KOV -- OF THE VULPANA BUREAU OF INTOLERANCE.
AND YOU ARE GOING TO BE MY GUESTS FOR SOME TIME...

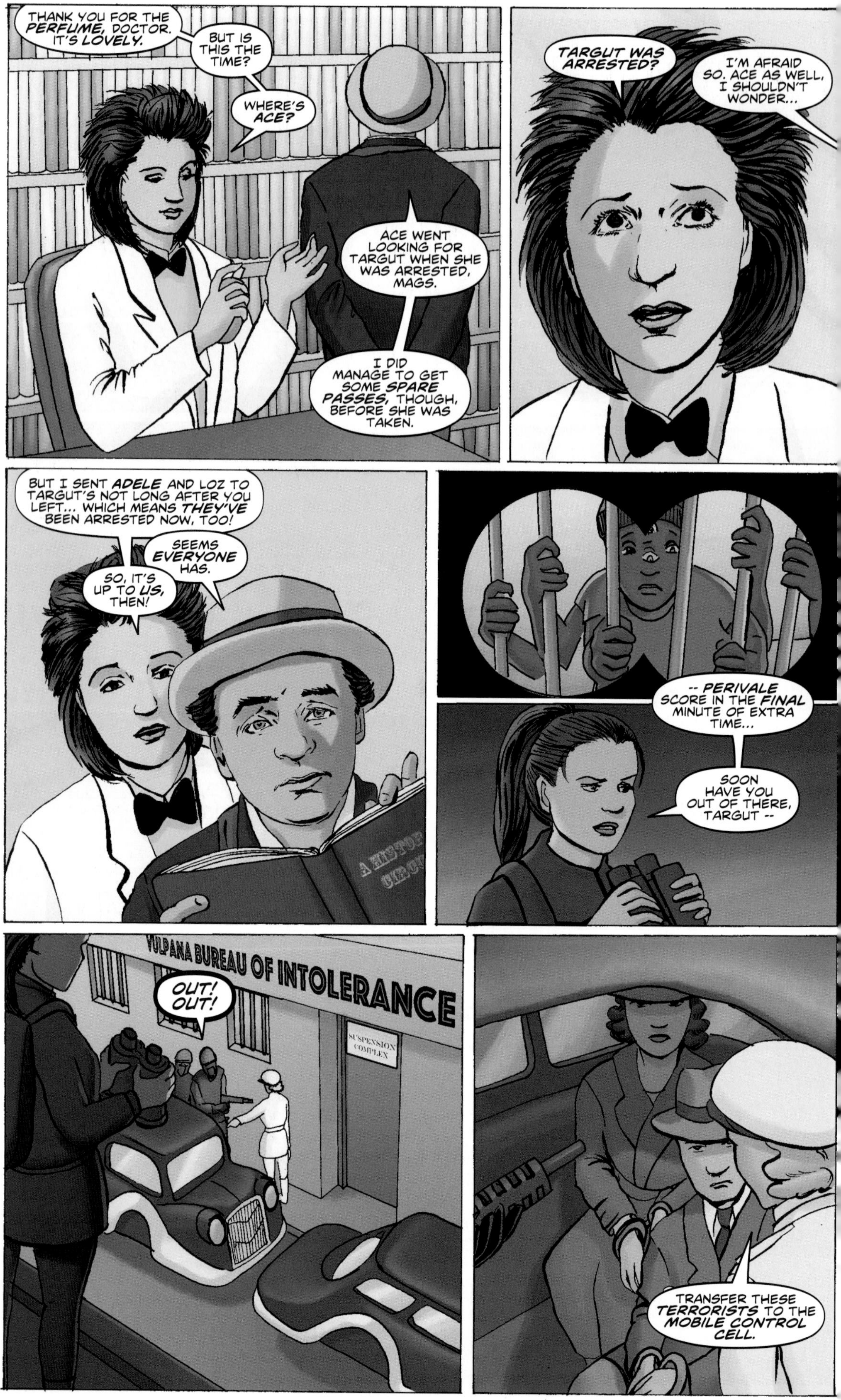

THANK YOU FOR THE PERFUME, DOCTOR. IT'S LOVELY.
BUT IS THIS THE TIME?
WHERE'S ACE?
ACE WENT LOOKING FOR TARGUT WHEN SHE WAS ARRESTED, MAGS.
I DID MANAGE TO GET SOME SPARE PASSES, THOUGH, BEFORE SHE WAS TAKEN.
TARGUT WAS ARRESTED?
I'M AFRAID SO. ACE AS WELL, I SHOULDN'T WONDER...
BUT I SENT ADELE AND LOZ TO TARGUT'S NOT LONG AFTER YOU LEFT... WHICH MEANS THEY'VE BEEN ARRESTED NOW, TOO!
SEEMS EVERYONE HAS.
SO, IT'S UP TO US, THEN!
-- PERIVALE SCORE IN THE FINAL MINUTE OF EXTRA TIME...
SOON HAVE YOU OUT OF THERE, TARGUT --
VULPANA BUREAU OF INTOLERANCE
OUT! OUT!
SUSPENSION COMPLEX
TRANSFER THESE TERRORISTS TO THE MOBILE CONTROL CELL.

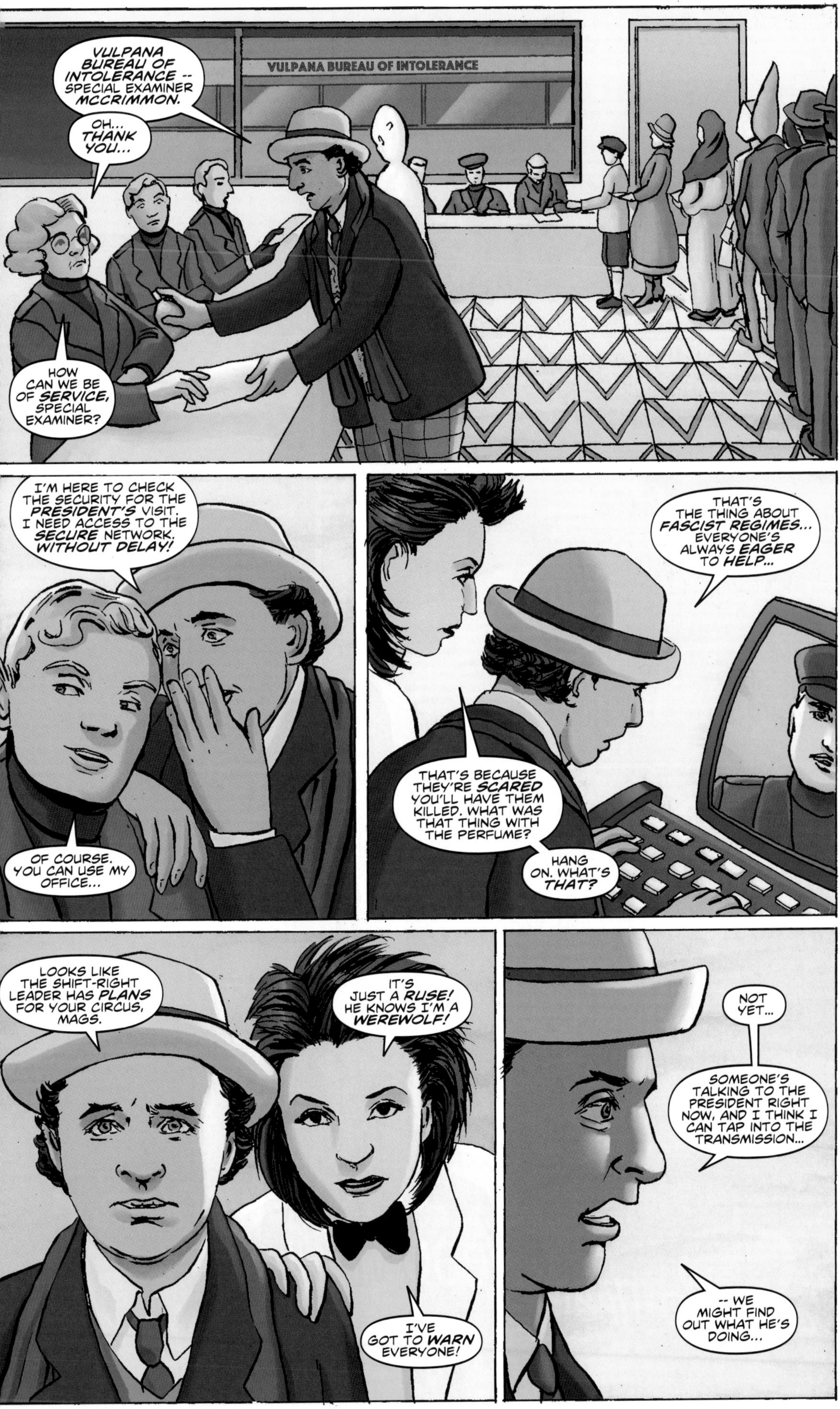
VULPANA BUREAU OF INTOLERANCE
VULPANA BUREAU OF INTOLERANCE -- SPECIAL EXAMINER MCCRIMMON.
OH... THANK YOU...
HOW CAN WE BE OF SERVICE, SPECIAL EXAMINER?
I'M HERE TO CHECK THE SECURITY FOR THE PRESIDENT'S VISIT. I NEED ACCESS TO THE SECURE NETWORK. WITHOUT DELAY!
OF COURSE. YOU CAN USE MY OFFICE...
THAT'S THE THING ABOUT FASCIST REGIMES... EVERYONE'S ALWAYS EAGER TO HELP...
THAT'S BECAUSE THEY'RE SCARED YOU'LL HAVE THEM KILLED. WHAT WAS THAT THING WITH THE PERFUME?
HANG ON. WHAT'S THAT?
LOOKS LIKE THE SHIFT-RIGHT LEADER HAS PLANS FOR YOUR CIRCUS, MAGS.
IT'S JUST A RUSE! HE KNOWS I'M A WEREWOLF!
I'VE GOT TO WARN EVERYONE!
NOT YET...
SOMEONE'S TALKING TO THE PRESIDENT RIGHT NOW, AND I THINK I CAN TAP INTO THE TRANSMISSION...
-- WE MIGHT FIND OUT WHAT HE'S DOING...

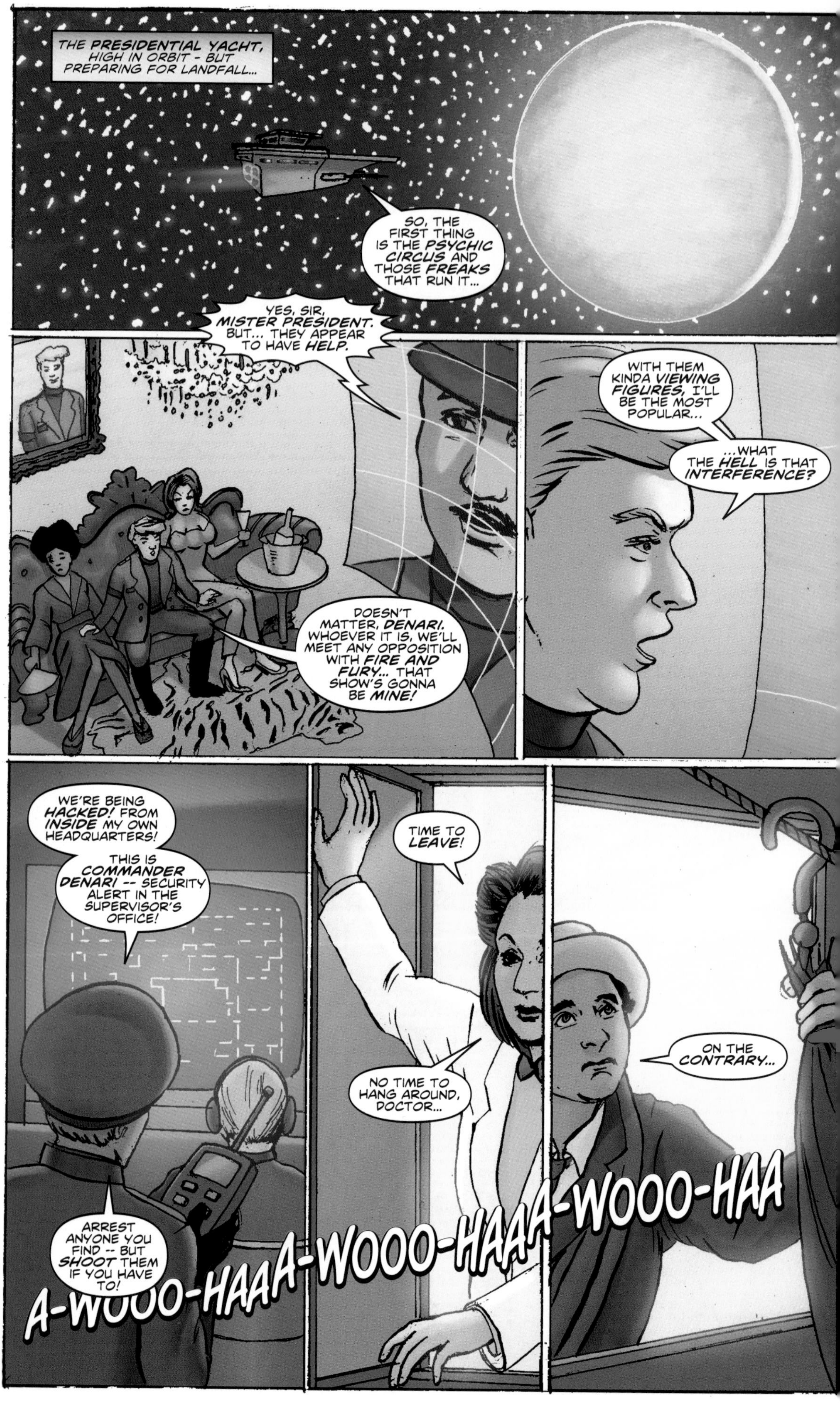

THE PRESIDENTIAL YACHT, HIGH IN ORBIT - BUT PREPARING FOR LANDFALL...
SO, THE FIRST THING IS THE PSYCHIC CIRCUS AND THOSE FREAKS THAT RUN IT...
YES, SIR, MISTER PRESIDENT. BUT... THEY APPEAR TO HAVE HELP.
DOESN'T MATTER, DENARI. WHOEVER IT IS, WE'LL MEET ANY OPPOSITION WITH FIRE AND FURY... THAT SHOW'S GONNA BE MINE!
WITH THEM KINDA VIEWING FIGURES, I'LL BE THE MOST POPULAR...
...WHAT THE HELL IS THAT INTERFERENCE?
WE'RE BEING HACKED! FROM INSIDE MY OWN HEADQUARTERS!
THIS IS COMMANDER DENARI -- SECURITY ALERT IN THE SUPERVISOR'S OFFICE!
ARREST ANYONE YOU FIND -- BUT SHOOT THEM IF YOU HAVE TO!
TIME TO LEAVE!
NO TIME TO HANG AROUND, DOCTOR...
ON THE CONTRARY...
A-WOOO-HAAA-WOOO-HAAA-WOOO-HAA

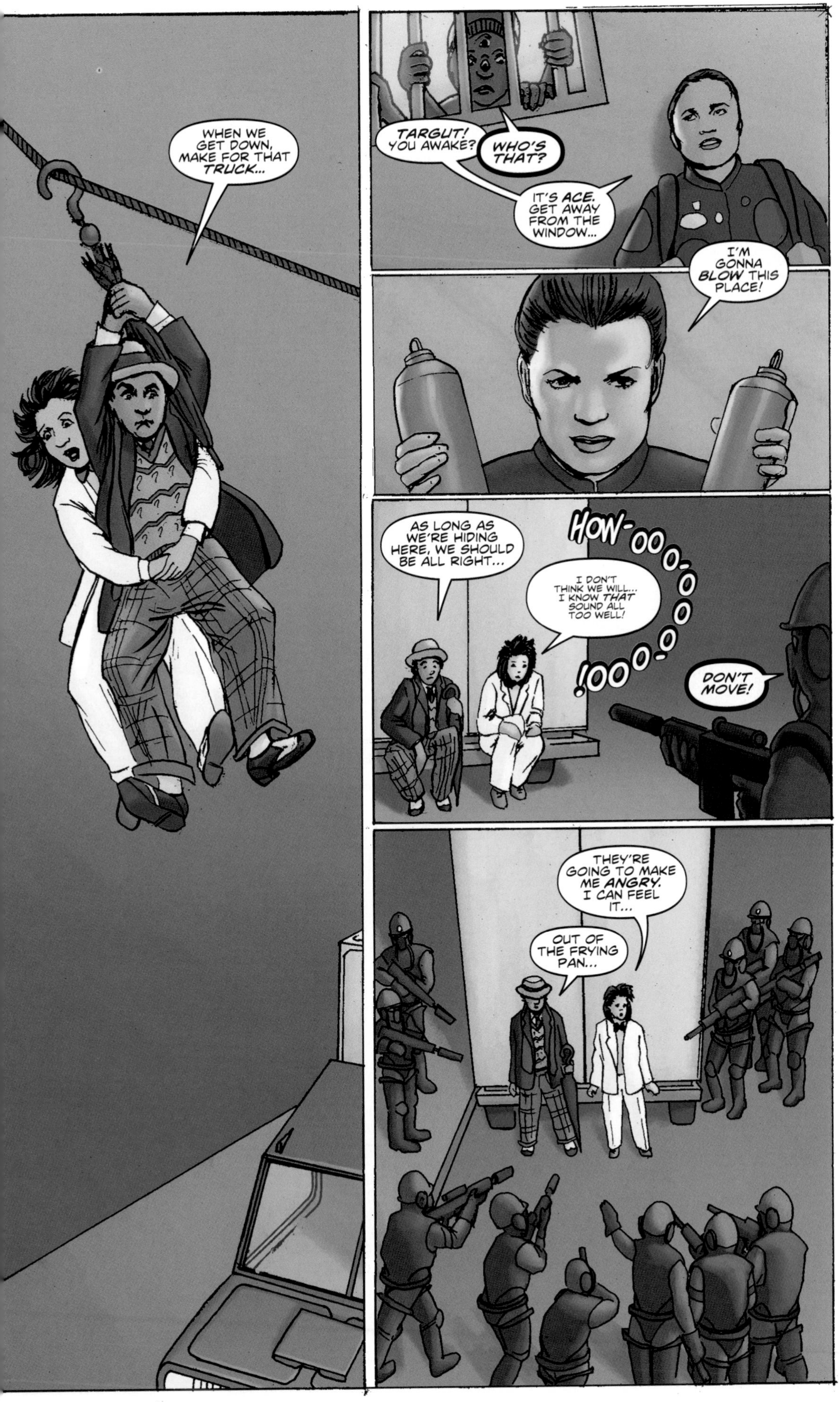
WHEN WE GET DOWN, MAKE FOR THAT TRUCK...
TARGUT! YOU AWAKE?
WHO'S THAT?
IT'S ACE. GET AWAY FROM THE WINDOW...
I'M GONNA BLOW THIS PLACE!
AS LONG AS WE'RE HIDING HERE, WE SHOULD BE ALL RIGHT...
HOW-OOO-OOO-OOO!
I DON'T THINK WE WILL... I KNOW THAT SOUND ALL TOO WELL!
DON'T MOVE!
THEY'RE GOING TO MAKE ME ANGRY. I CAN FEEL IT...
OUT OF THE FRYING PAN...

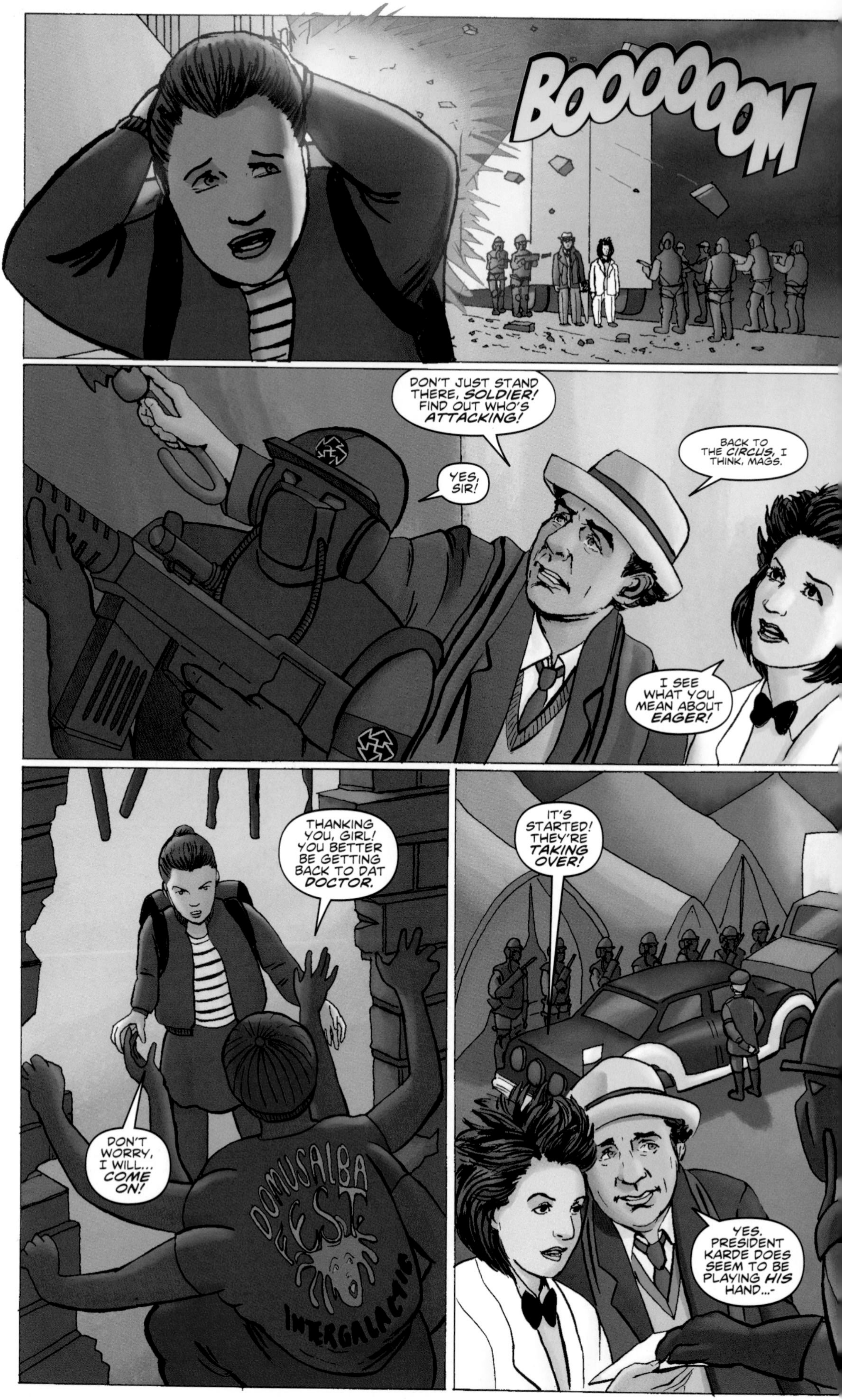
BOOOOOOM
DON'T JUST STAND THERE, SOLDIER! FIND OUT WHO'S ATTACKING!
YES, SIR!
BACK TO THE CIRCUS, I THINK, MAGS.
I SEE WHAT YOU MEAN ABOUT EAGER!
THANKING YOU, GIRL! YOU BETTER BE GETTING BACK TO DAT DOCTOR.
DON'T WORRY, I WILL... COME ON!
DOMUSALBA
FEST
INTERGALACTIC
IT'S STARTED! THEY'RE TAKING OVER!
YES. PRESIDENT KARDE DOES SEEM TO BE PLAYING HIS HAND...-

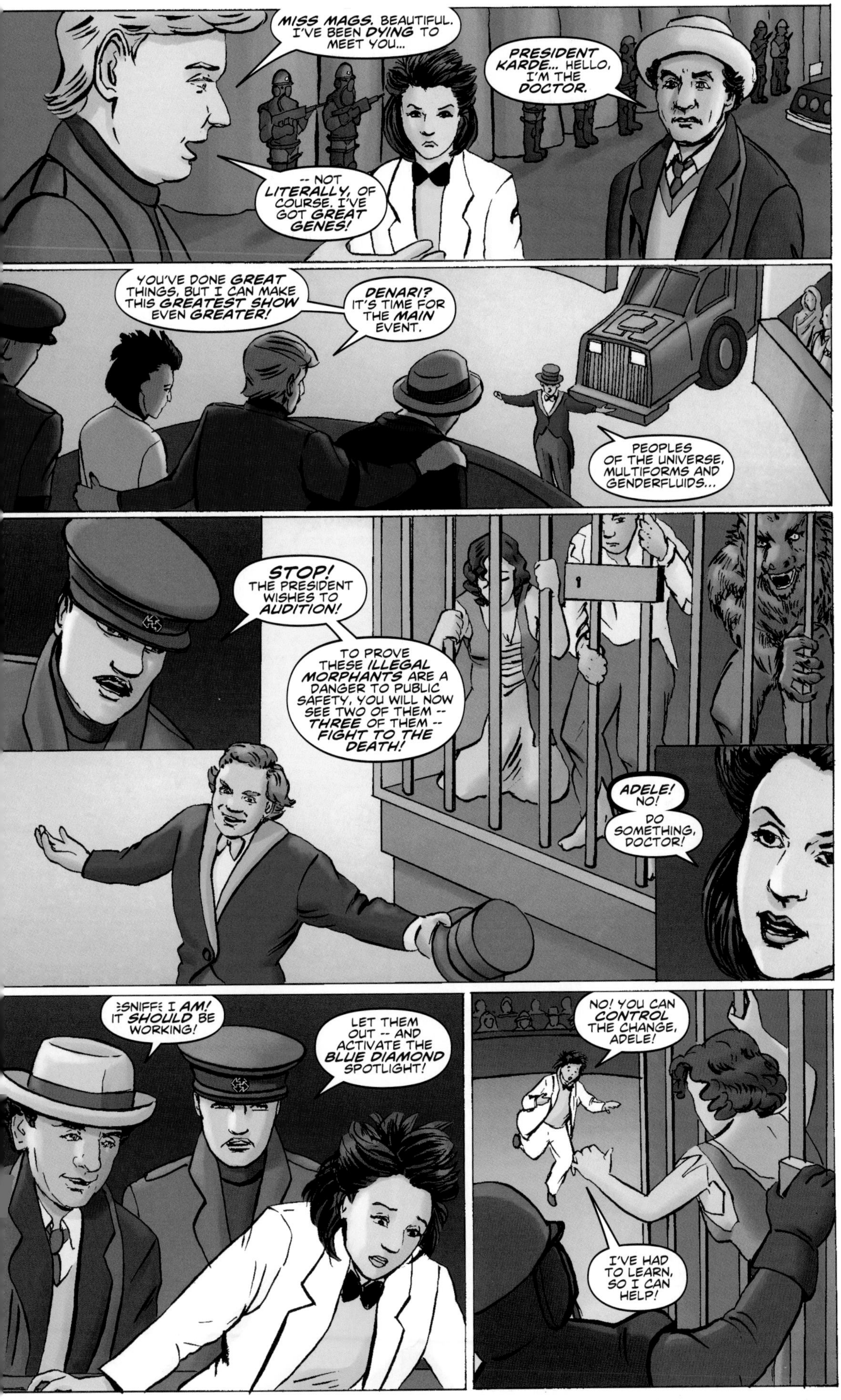
MISS MAGS. BEAUTIFUL. I'VE BEEN DYING TO MEET YOU...
-- NOT LITERALLY, OF COURSE. I'VE GOT GREAT GENES!
PRESIDENT KARDE... HELLO, I'M THE DOCTOR.
YOU'VE DONE GREAT THINGS, BUT I CAN MAKE THIS GREATEST SHOW EVEN GREATER!
DENARI? IT'S TIME FOR THE MAIN EVENT.
PEOPLES OF THE UNIVERSE, MULTIFORMS AND GENDERFLUIDS...
STOP! THE PRESIDENT WISHES TO AUDITION!
TO PROVE THESE ILLEGAL MORPHANTS ARE A DANGER TO PUBLIC SAFETY, YOU WILL NOW SEE TWO OF THEM -- THREE OF THEM -- FIGHT TO THE DEATH!
ADELE! NO!
DO SOMETHING, DOCTOR!
ƸSNIFFƷ I AM! IT SHOULD BE WORKING!
LET THEM OUT -- AND ACTIVATE THE BLUE DIAMOND SPOTLIGHT!
NO! YOU CAN CONTROL THE CHANGE, ADELE!
I'VE HAD TO LEARN, SO I CAN HELP!

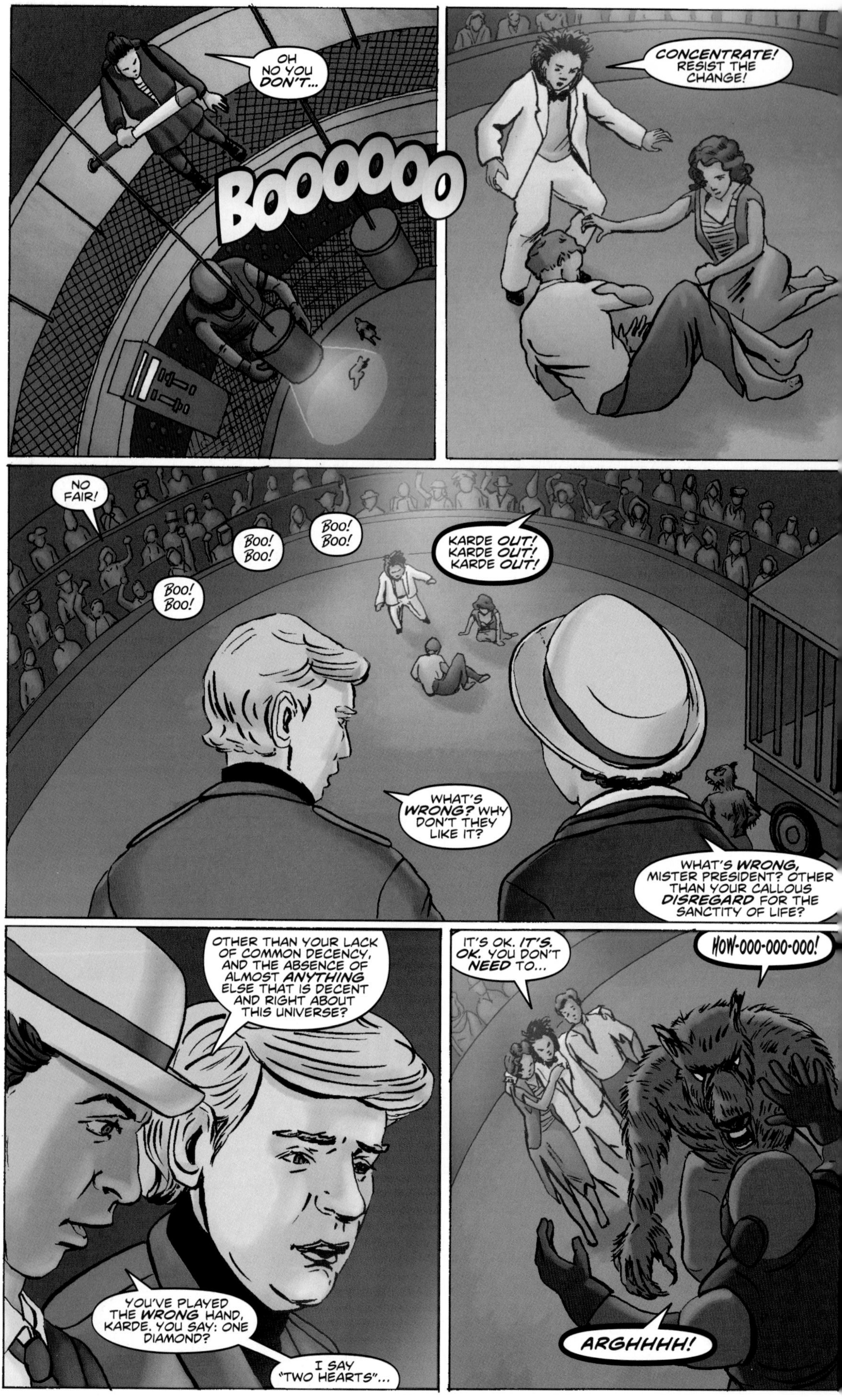
OH NO YOU DON'T...
BOOOOOO
CONCENTRATE! RESIST THE CHANGE!
NO FAIR!
BOO! BOO!
BOO! BOO!
BOO! BOO!
KARDE OUT! KARDE OUT! KARDE OUT!
WHAT'S WRONG? WHY DON'T THEY LIKE IT?
WHAT'S WRONG, MISTER PRESIDENT? OTHER THAN YOUR CALLOUS DISREGARD FOR THE SANCTITY OF LIFE?
OTHER THAN YOUR LACK OF COMMON DECENCY, AND THE ABSENCE OF ALMOST ANYTHING ELSE THAT IS DECENT AND RIGHT ABOUT THIS UNIVERSE?
YOU'VE PLAYED THE WRONG HAND, KARDE. YOU SAY: ONE DIAMOND?
I SAY "TWO HEARTS"...
IT'S OK. IT'S. OK. YOU DON'T NEED TO...
HOW-OOO-OOO-OOO!
ARGHHHH!

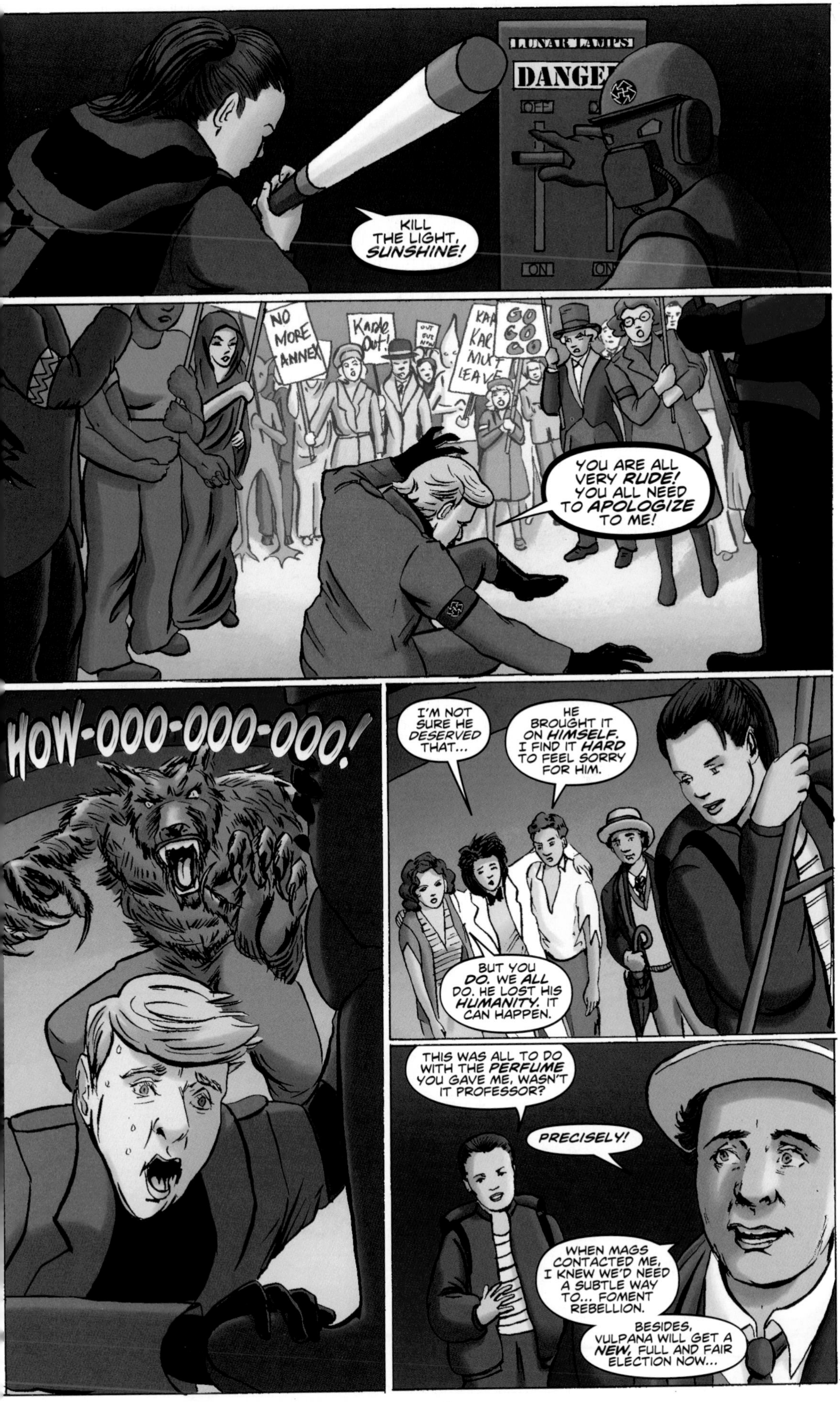
LUNAR LAMPS
DANGER
OFF
ON
ON
KILL THE LIGHT, SUNSHINE!
NO MORE ANNEX
Karde Out!
OUT OUT NOW
KARDE KARDE MUST LEAVE
GO GO GO GO
YOU ARE ALL VERY RUDE! YOU ALL NEED TO APOLOGIZE TO ME!
HOW-OOO-OOO-OOO!
I'M NOT SURE HE DESERVED THAT...
HE BROUGHT IT ON HIMSELF. I FIND IT HARD TO FEEL SORRY FOR HIM.
BUT YOU DO. WE ALL DO. HE LOST HIS HUMANITY. IT CAN HAPPEN.
THIS WAS ALL TO DO WITH THE PERFUME YOU GAVE ME, WASN'T IT PROFESSOR?
PRECISELY!
WHEN MAGS CONTACTED ME, I KNEW WE'D NEED A SUBTLE WAY TO... FOMENT REBELLION.
BESIDES, VULPANA WILL GET A NEW, FULL AND FAIR ELECTION NOW...

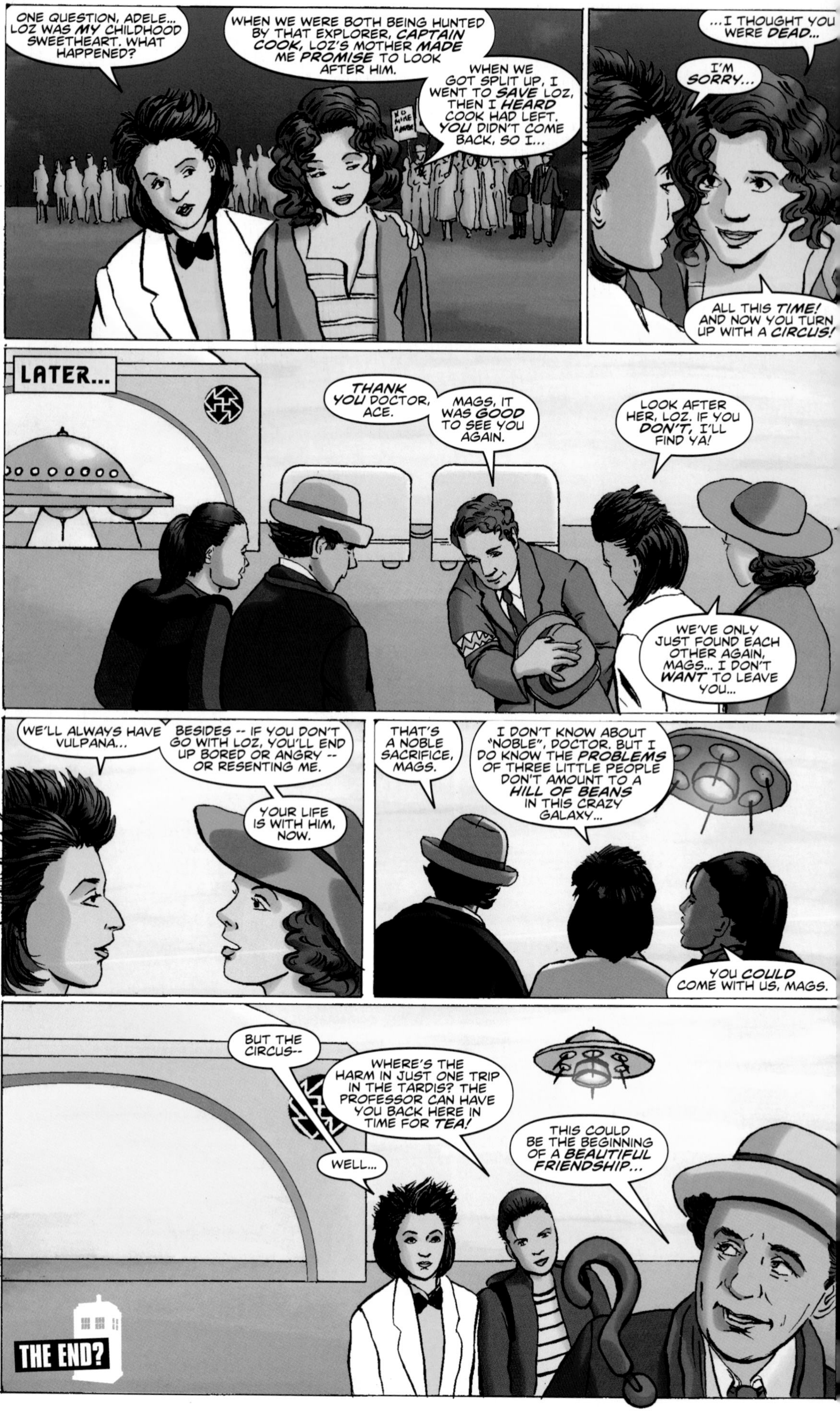

ONE QUESTION, ADELE... LOZ WAS MY CHILDHOOD SWEETHEART. WHAT HAPPENED?
WHEN WE WERE BOTH BEING HUNTED BY THAT EXPLORER, CAPTAIN COOK, LOZ'S MOTHER MADE ME PROMISE TO LOOK AFTER HIM.
WHEN WE GOT SPLIT UP, I WENT TO SAVE LOZ, THEN I HEARD COOK HAD LEFT. YOU DIDN'T COME BACK, SO I...
...I THOUGHT YOU WERE DEAD...
I'M SORRY...
ALL THIS TIME! AND NOW YOU TURN UP WITH A CIRCUS!
LATER...
THANK YOU DOCTOR, ACE.
MAGS, IT WAS GOOD TO SEE YOU AGAIN.
LOOK AFTER HER, LOZ. IF YOU DON'T, I'LL FIND YA!
WE'VE ONLY JUST FOUND EACH OTHER AGAIN, MAGS... I DON'T WANT TO LEAVE YOU...
WE'LL ALWAYS HAVE VULPANA...
BESIDES -- IF YOU DON'T GO WITH LOZ, YOU'LL END UP BORED OR ANGRY -- OR RESENTING ME.
YOUR LIFE IS WITH HIM, NOW.
THAT'S A NOBLE SACRIFICE, MAGS.
I DON'T KNOW ABOUT "NOBLE", DOCTOR. BUT I DO KNOW THE PROBLEMS OF THREE LITTLE PEOPLE DON'T AMOUNT TO A HILL OF BEANS IN THIS CRAZY GALAXY...
YOU COULD COME WITH US, MAGS.
BUT THE CIRCUS--
WHERE'S THE HARM IN JUST ONE TRIP IN THE TARDIS? THE PROFESSOR CAN HAVE YOU BACK HERE IN TIME FOR TEA!
WELL...
THIS COULD BE THE BEGINNING OF A BEAUTIFUL FRIENDSHIP...
THE END?

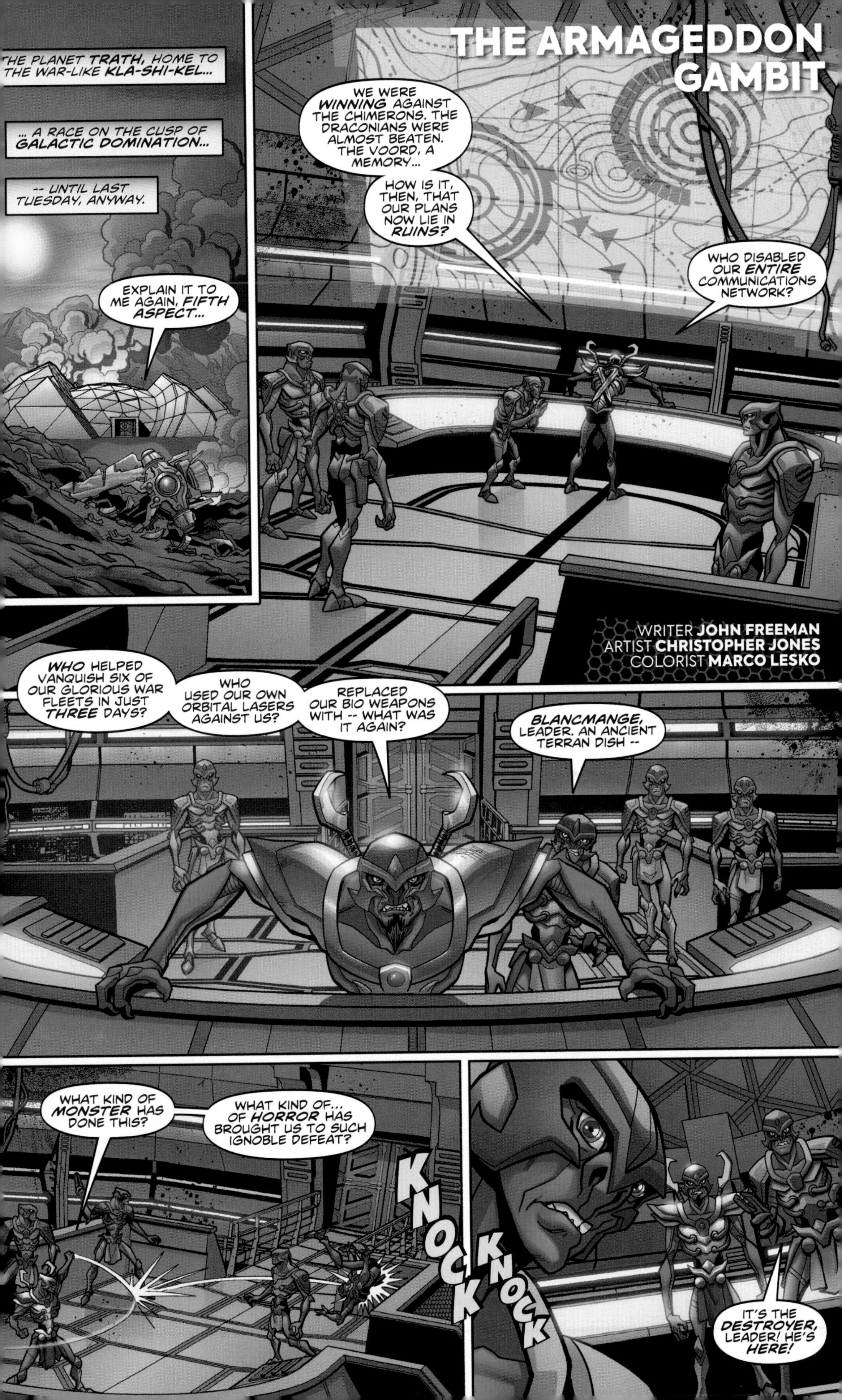
THE ARMAGEDDON GAMBIT
THE PLANET TRATH, HOME TO THE WAR-LIKE KLA-SHI-KEL...
... A RACE ON THE CUSP OF GALACTIC DOMINATION...
-- UNTIL LAST TUESDAY, ANYWAY.
EXPLAIN IT TO ME AGAIN, FIFTH ASPECT...
WE WERE WINNING AGAINST THE CHIMERONS. THE DRACONIANS WERE ALMOST BEATEN. THE VOORD, A MEMORY...
HOW IS IT, THEN, THAT OUR PLANS NOW LIE IN RUINS?
WHO DISABLED OUR ENTIRE COMMUNICATIONS NETWORK?
WRITER JOHN FREEMAN
ARTIST CHRISTOPHER JONES
COLORIST MARCO LESKO
WHO HELPED VANQUISH SIX OF OUR GLORIOUS WAR FLEETS IN JUST THREE DAYS?
WHO USED OUR OWN ORBITAL LASERS AGAINST US?
REPLACED OUR BIO WEAPONS WITH -- WHAT WAS IT AGAIN?
BLANCMANGE, LEADER. AN ANCIENT TERRAN DISH --
WHAT KIND OF MONSTER HAS DONE THIS?
WHAT KIND OF... OF HORROR HAS BROUGHT US TO SUCH IGNOBLE DEFEAT?
KNOCK
KNOCK
IT'S THE DESTROYER, LEADER! HE'S HERE!

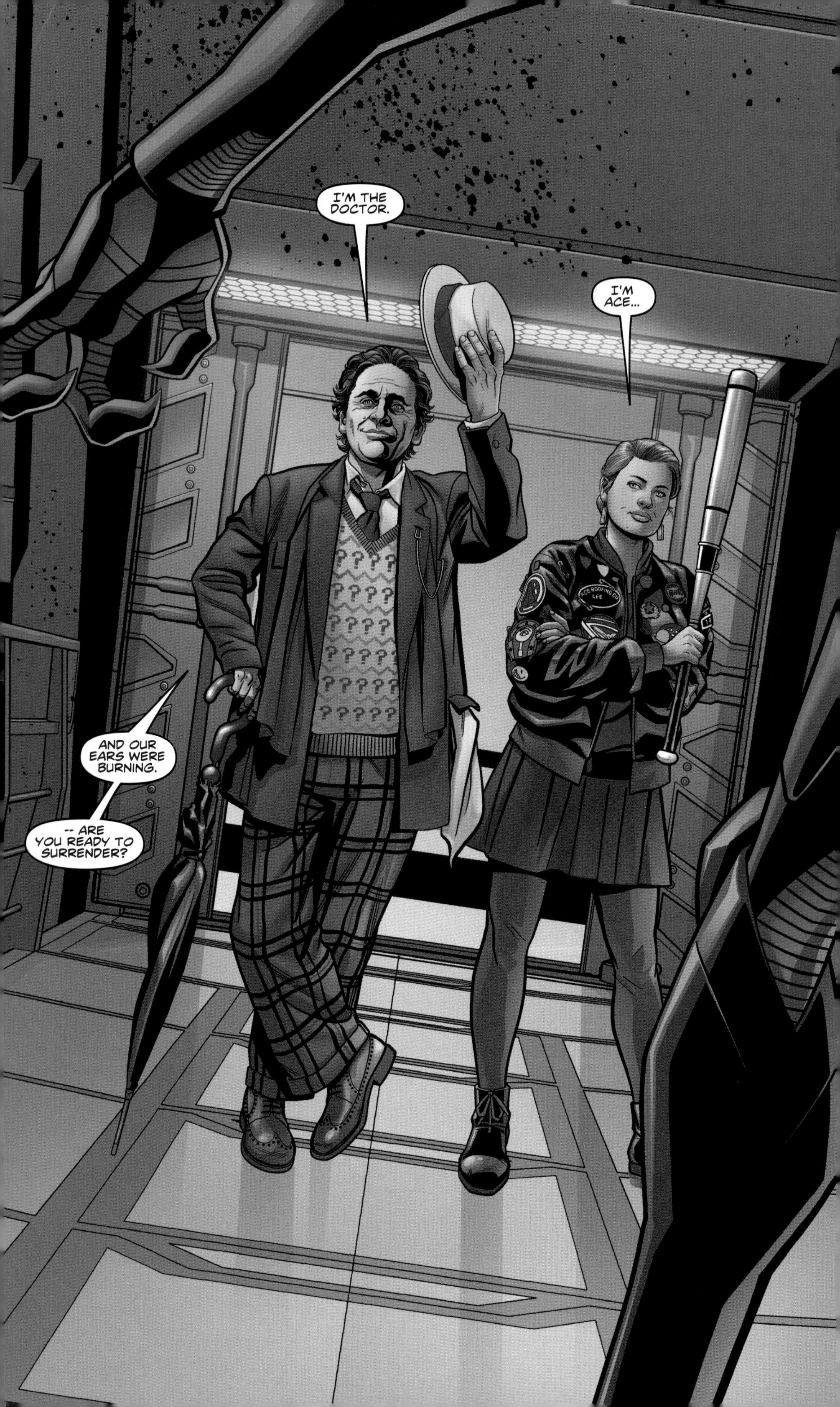
I'M THE DOCTOR.
I'M ACE...
AND OUR EARS WERE BURNING.
-- ARE YOU READY TO SURRENDER?

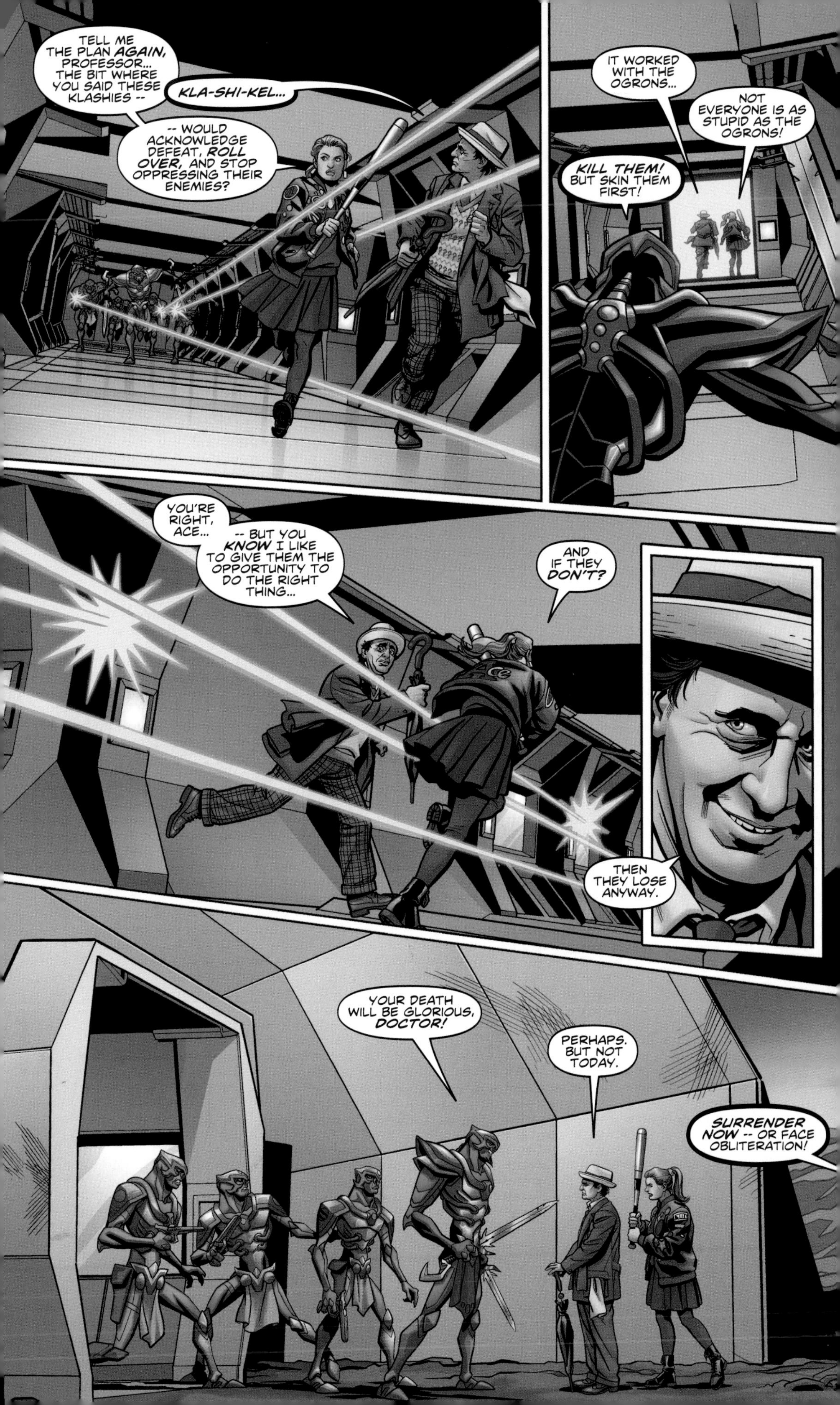

TELL ME THE PLAN **AGAIN,** PROFESSOR... THE BIT WHERE YOU SAID THESE KLASHIES --
KLA-SHI-KEL...
-- WOULD ACKNOWLEDGE DEFEAT, **ROLL OVER,** AND STOP OPPRESSING THEIR ENEMIES?
IT WORKED WITH THE OGRONS...
NOT EVERYONE IS AS STUPID AS THE OGRONS!
KILL THEM! BUT SKIN THEM FIRST!
YOU'RE RIGHT, ACE...
-- BUT YOU **KNOW** I LIKE TO GIVE THEM THE OPPORTUNITY TO DO THE RIGHT THING...
AND IF THEY **DON'T?**
THEN THEY LOSE ANYWAY.
YOUR DEATH WILL BE GLORIOUS, **DOCTOR!**
PERHAPS. BUT NOT TODAY.
SURRENDER NOW -- OR FACE OBLITERATION!

IT'S *OVER*, TRATH. WE JUST NEEDED YOU OUT OF THE BUNKER.

BUT... *WHY?* YOU COULD HAVE DESTROYED US --

BECAUSE *EVERYONE* DESERVES A SECOND CHANCE.

I WOULDN'T WASTE IT, IF I WERE YOU.

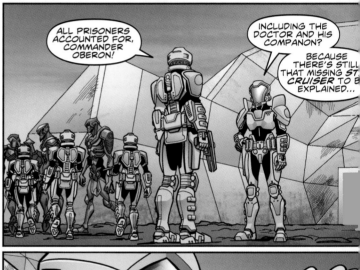

ALL PRISONERS ACCOUNTED FOR, COMMANDER OBERON!

INCLUDING THE DOCTOR AND HIS COMPANON?

BECAUSE THERE'S STILL THAT MISSING ST CRUISER TO B EXPLAINED...

AH. ANOTHER TIME, THEN, DOCTOR...

VWOORRRP

NOT A BAD DAY, PROFESSOR...

DOCTOR.

WHERE TO NOW...?

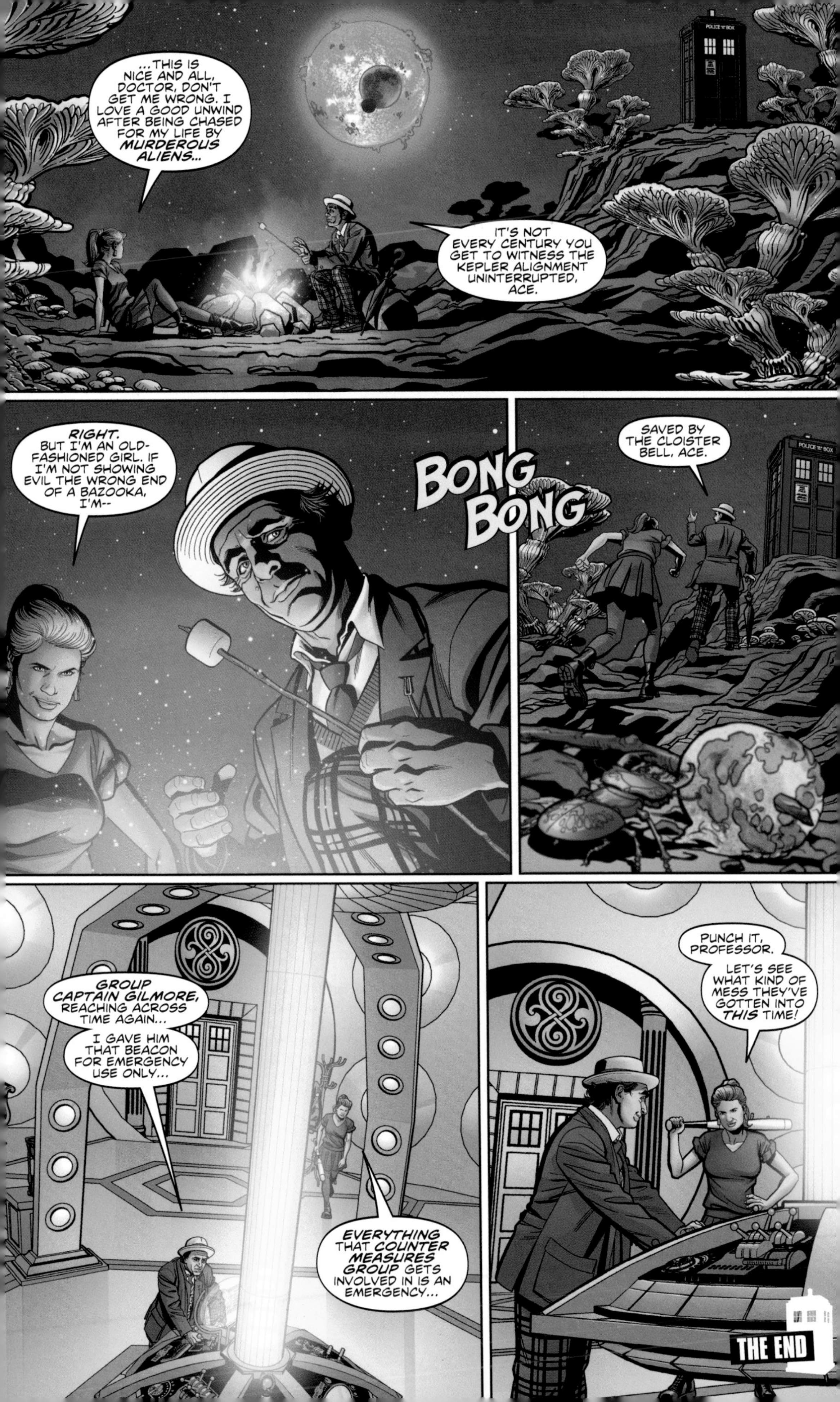
...THIS IS NICE AND ALL, DOCTOR, DON'T GET ME WRONG. I LOVE A GOOD UNWIND AFTER BEING CHASED FOR MY LIFE BY MURDEROUS ALIENS...
IT'S NOT EVERY CENTURY YOU GET TO WITNESS THE KEPLER ALIGNMENT UNINTERRUPTED, ACE.
RIGHT. BUT I'M AN OLD-FASHIONED GIRL. IF I'M NOT SHOWING EVIL THE WRONG END OF A BAZOOKA, I'M--
BONG BONG
SAVED BY THE CLOISTER BELL, ACE.
GROUP CAPTAIN GILMORE, REACHING ACROSS TIME AGAIN...
I GAVE HIM THAT BEACON FOR EMERGENCY USE ONLY...
EVERYTHING THAT COUNTER MEASURES GROUP GETS INVOLVED IN IS AN EMERGENCY...
PUNCH IT, PROFESSOR.
LET'S SEE WHAT KIND OF MESS THEY'VE GOTTEN INTO THIS TIME!
THE END

BBC

DOCTOR WHO

THE FIRST DOCTOR

In-Between Times

WRITER
PAUL CORNELL

ARTIST
JOHN STOKES

When *Doctor Who* went off the air in 1989, the Seventh Doctor and Ace didn't just walk off into the sunset, they walked into a universe of all-new spin-off adventures, conjured in prose and comics by a multitude of talents — many of whom went on to bring the show back to life on television, when the show returned to our screens in 2005.

Paul Cornell was one of the authors keeping the flame of *Doctor Who* alive, with his contributions to the Virgin New Adventures series of novels.

Like Ben Aaronovitch and Andrew Cartmel, Paul's contributions to *Doctor Who* span multiple media and several decades.

In celebration of that spirit, Paul and his artistic collaborator John Stokes here present an **exclusive bonus comic strip,** returning to the black-and-white days of the very first Doctor, William Hartnell, and featuring his companions Ian, Barbara, and his granddaughter Susan — portrayed on-screen by William Russell, Jacqueline Hill, and Carole Ann Ford.

In the depths of TARDIS, in the middle of the night, Ian and Barbara go in search of urgent answers...

TITAN®
COMICS

BBC

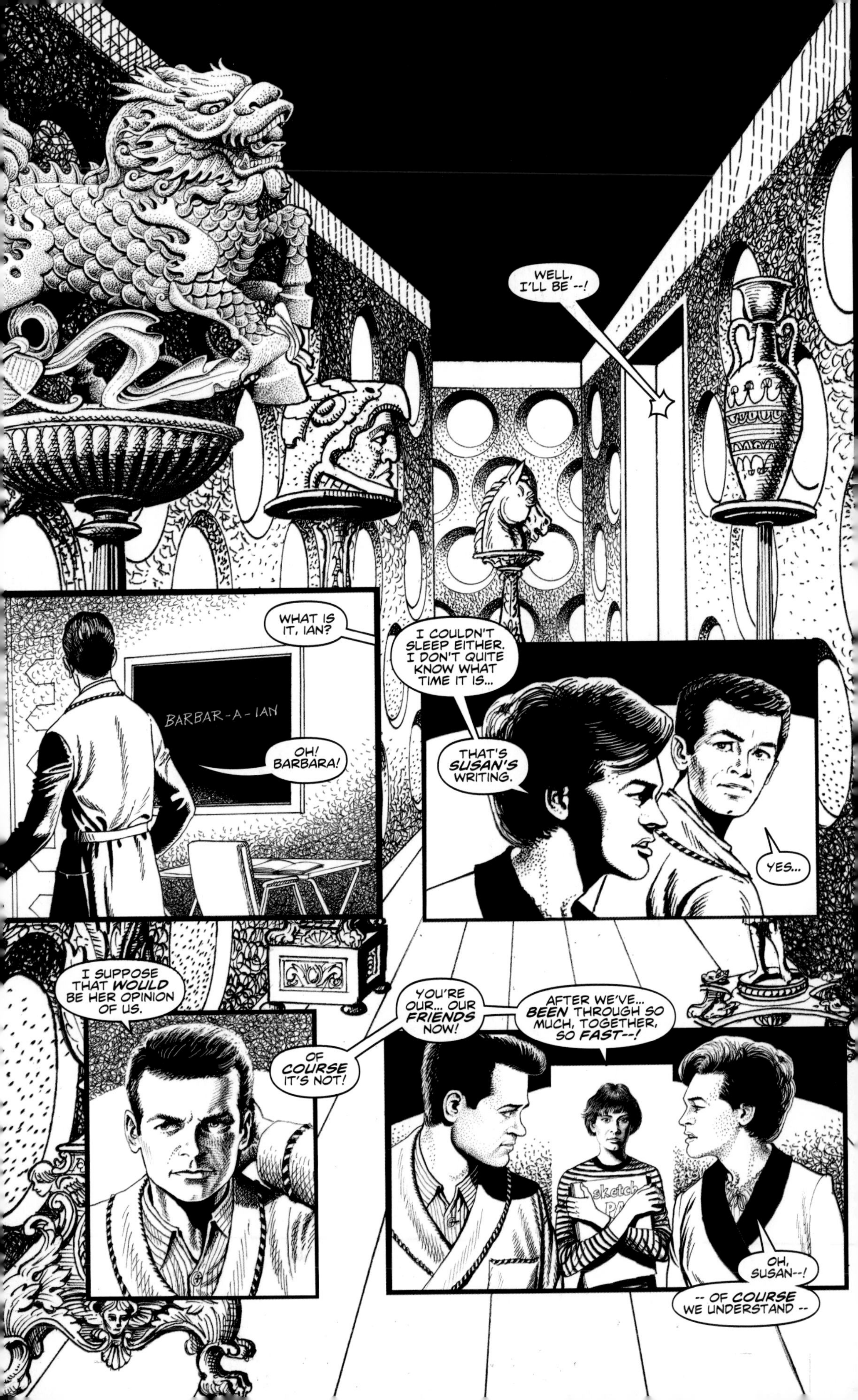
WELL, I'LL BE --!
WHAT IS IT, IAN?
BARBAR-A-IAN
OH! BARBARA!
I COULDN'T SLEEP EITHER. I DON'T QUITE KNOW WHAT TIME IT IS...
THAT'S SUSAN'S WRITING.
YES...
I SUPPOSE THAT WOULD BE HER OPINION OF US.
OF COURSE IT'S NOT!
YOU'RE OUR... OUR FRIENDS NOW!
AFTER WE'VE... BEEN THROUGH SO MUCH, TOGETHER, SO FAST--!
OH, SUSAN--!
-- OF COURSE WE UNDERSTAND --

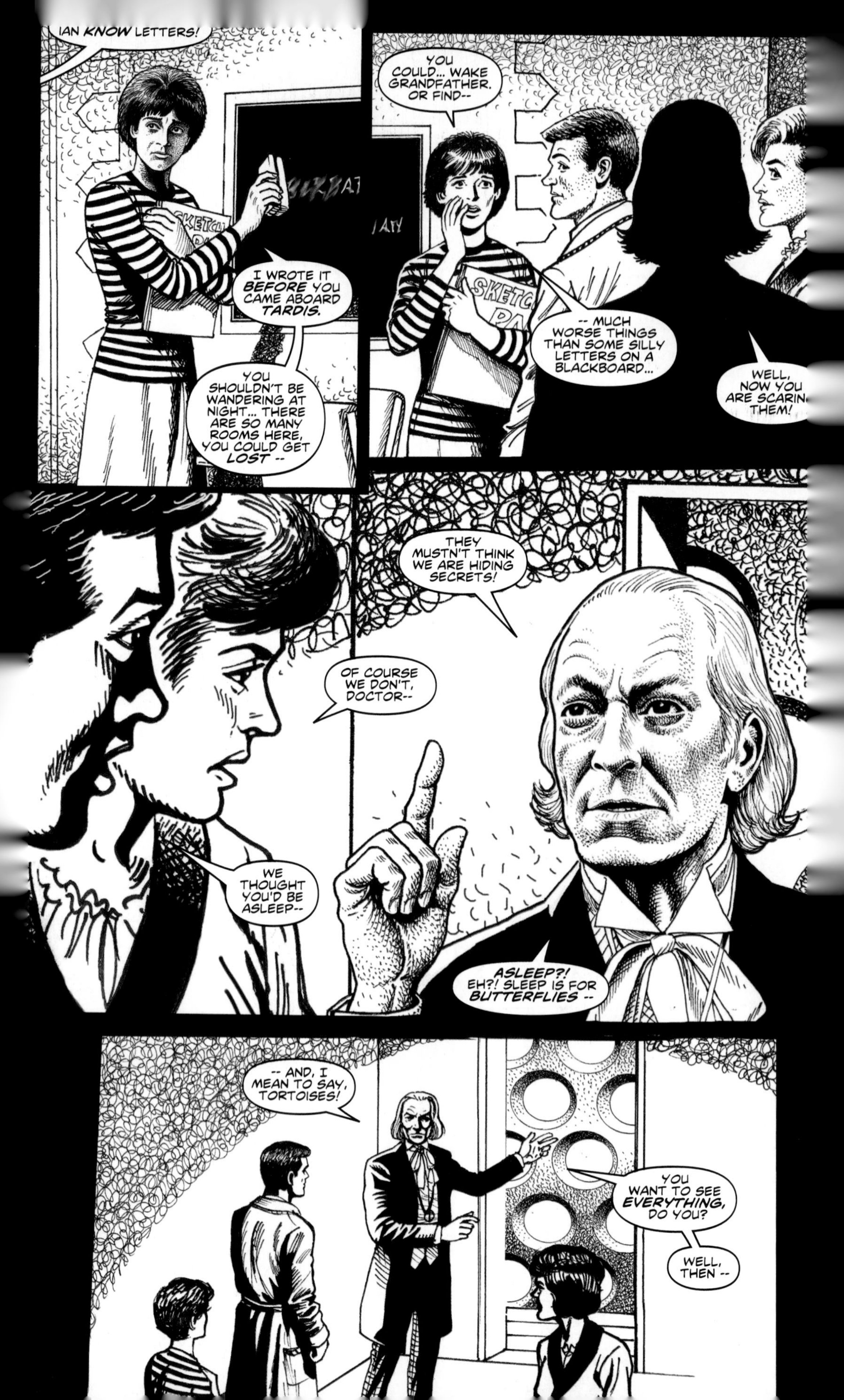

IAN KNOW LETTERS!
I WROTE IT BEFORE YOU CAME ABOARD TARDIS.
YOU SHOULDN'T BE WANDERING AT NIGHT... THERE ARE SO MANY ROOMS HERE, YOU COULD GET LOST --
YOU COULD... WAKE GRANDFATHER. OR FIND--
-- MUCH WORSE THINGS THAN SOME SILLY LETTERS ON A BLACKBOARD...
WELL, NOW YOU ARE SCARIN THEM!
THEY MUSTN'T THINK WE ARE HIDING SECRETS!
OF COURSE WE DON'T, DOCTOR--
WE THOUGHT YOU'D BE ASLEEP--
ASLEEP?! EH?! SLEEP IS FOR BUTTERFLIES --
-- AND, I MEAN TO SAY, TORTOISES!
YOU WANT TO SEE EVERYTHING, DO YOU?
WELL, THEN --

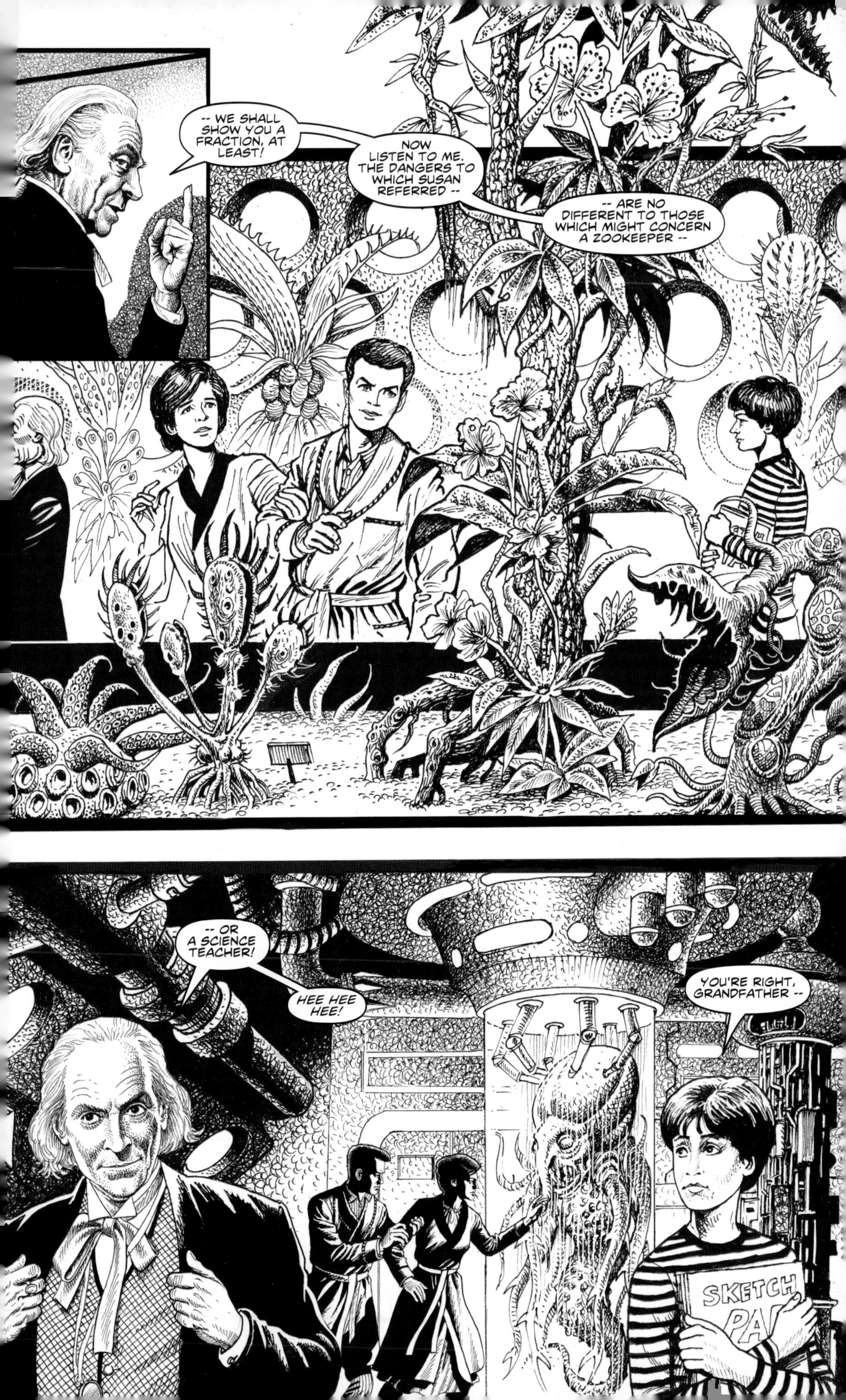
-- WE SHALL SHOW YOU A FRACTION, AT LEAST!
NOW LISTEN TO ME. THE DANGERS TO WHICH SUSAN REFERRED --
-- ARE NO DIFFERENT TO THOSE WHICH MIGHT CONCERN A ZOOKEEPER --
-- OR A SCIENCE TEACHER!
HEE HEE HEE!
YOU'RE RIGHT, GRANDFATHER --
SKETCH

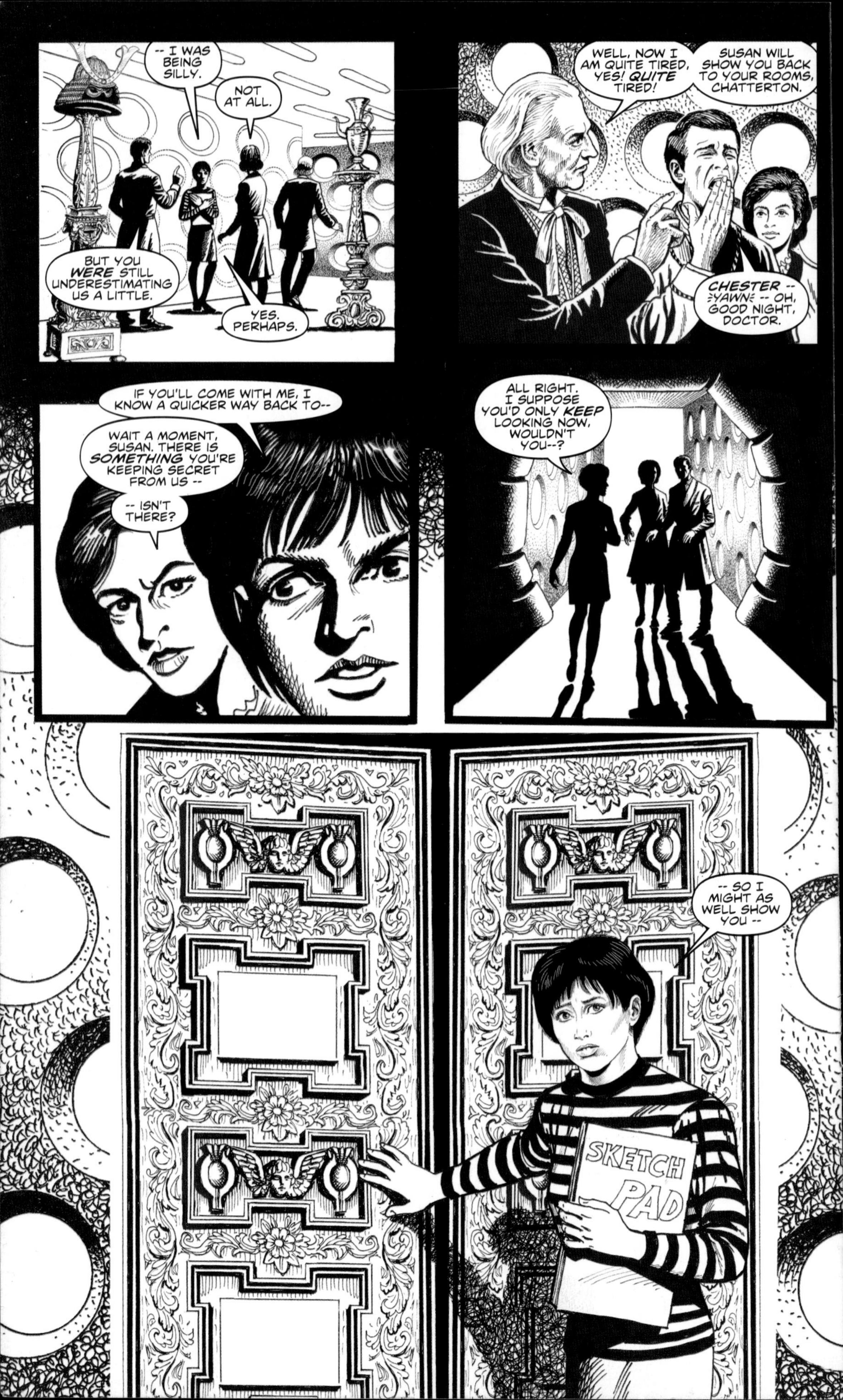
-- I WAS BEING SILLY.
NOT AT ALL.
BUT YOU WERE STILL UNDERESTIMATING US A LITTLE.
YES. PERHAPS.
WELL, NOW I AM QUITE TIRED, YES! QUITE TIRED!
SUSAN WILL SHOW YOU BACK TO YOUR ROOMS, CHATTERTON.
CHESTER -- YAWN -- OH, GOOD NIGHT, DOCTOR.
IF YOU'LL COME WITH ME, I KNOW A QUICKER WAY BACK TO--
WAIT A MOMENT, SUSAN. THERE IS SOMETHING YOU'RE KEEPING SECRET FROM US --
-- ISN'T THERE?
ALL RIGHT. I SUPPOSE YOU'D ONLY KEEP LOOKING NOW, WOULDN'T YOU--?
-- SO I MIGHT AS WELL SHOW YOU --
SKETCH PAD

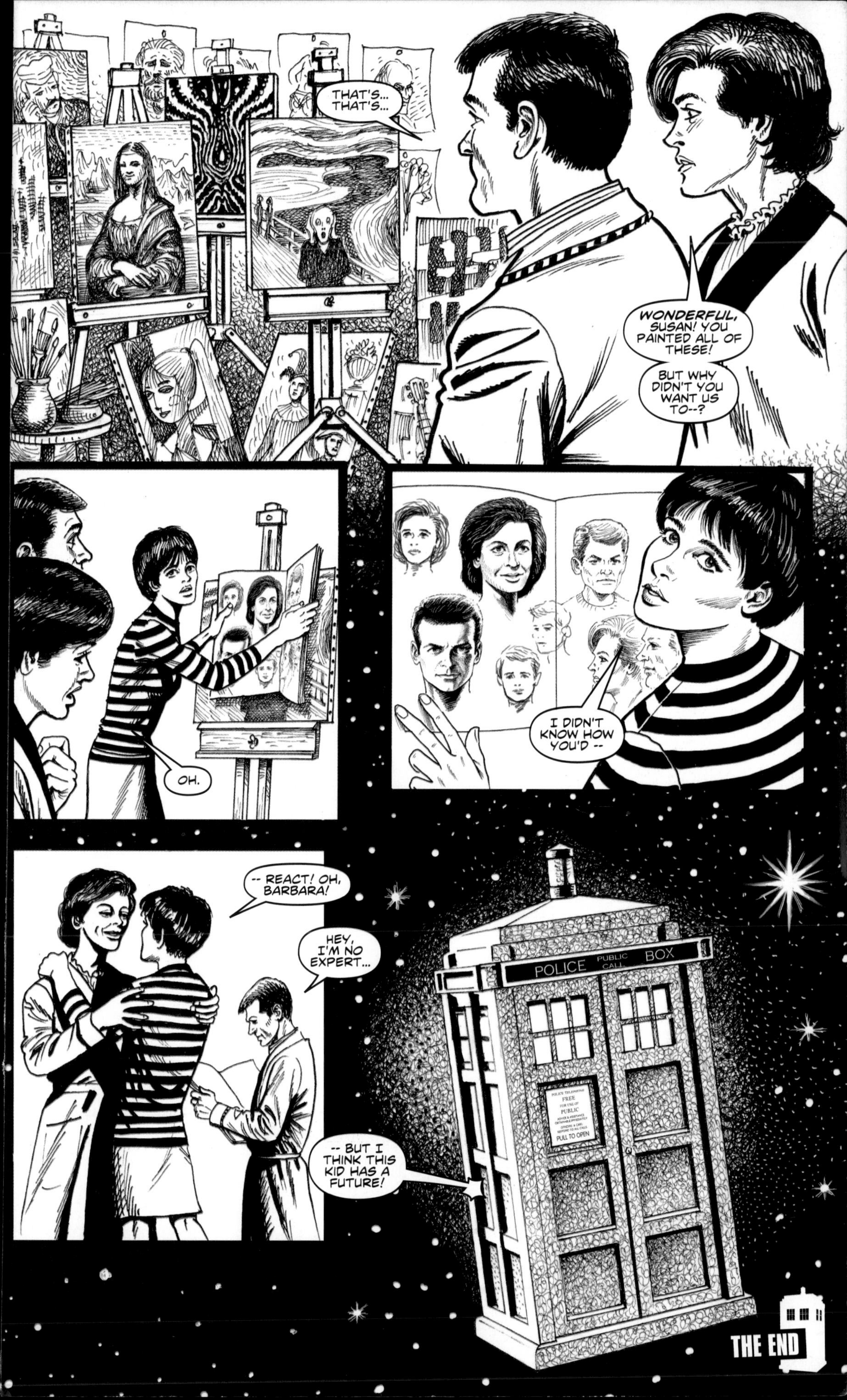
THAT'S... THAT'S...
WONDERFUL, SUSAN! YOU PAINTED ALL OF THESE!
BUT WHY DIDN'T YOU WANT US TO--?
OH.
I DIDN'T KNOW HOW YOU'D --
-- REACT! OH, BARBARA!
HEY, I'M NO EXPERT...
-- BUT I THINK THIS KID HAS A FUTURE!
POLICE PUBLIC CALL BOX
THE END

BBC DOCTOR WHO

READER'S GUIDE

With so many amazing *Doctor Who* collections on the shelves, it can be difficult to know where to start. That's where this handy guide comes in but don't be overwhelmed, every collection is designed to be welcomin

THE TWELFTH DOCTOR

DOCTOR WHO
TERRORFORMER
DOCTOR WHO
FRACTURES
DOCTOR WHO
HYPERION
DOCTOR WHO
THE SCHOOL OF DEATH
DOCTOR WHO
THE TWIST

VOL. 1: TERRORFORMER

VOL. 2: FRACTURES

VOL. 3: HYPERION

YEAR TWO BEGINS! VOL. 4: SCHOOL OF DEATH

VOL. 5: THE TWIST

THE ELEVENTH DOCTOR

DOCTOR WHO
AFTER LIFE
DOCTOR WHO
SERVE YOU
DOCTOR WHO
CONVERSION
DOCTOR WHO
THE THEN AND THE NOW
DOCTOR WHO
THE ONE

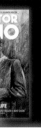

VOL. 1: AFTER LIFE

VOL. 2: SERVE YOU

VOL. 3: CONVERSION

YEAR TWO BEGINS! VOL. 4: THE THEN AND THE NOW

VOL. 5: THE ONE

THE TENTH DOCTOR

DOCTOR WHO
REVOLUTIONS OF TERROR
DOCTOR WHO
THE WEEPING ANGELS OF MONS
DOCTOR WHO
THE FOUNTAINS OF FOREVER
DOCTOR WHO
THE ENDLESS SONG
DOCTOR WHO
ARENA OF FEAR

VOL. 1: REVOLUTIONS OF TERROR

VOL. 2: THE WEEPING ANGELS OF MONS

VOL. 3: THE FOUNTAINS OF FOREVER

YEAR TWO BEGINS! VOL. 4: THE ENDLESS SONG

VOL. 5: ARENA OF FEAR

THE NINTH DOCTOR

DOCTOR WHO
WEAPONS OF PAST DESTRUCTION
DOCTOR WHO
DOCTORMANIA
DOCTOR WHO
OFFICIAL SECRETS
DOCTOR WHO
SIN EATERS

VOL. 1: WEAPONS OF PAST DESTRUCTION

VOL. 2: DOCTORMANIA

VOL. 3: OFFICIAL SECRETS

VOL. 4: SIN EATERS